Denali

a literary anthology

Denali

a literary anthology

edited by
Bill Sherwonit

THE
MOUNTAINEERS
BOOKS

TO THE HIGH ONE
and
TO ALL WHO'VE WORKED TO PRESERVE THE DENALI REGION'S WILDERNESS SPIRIT

 Published by
The Mountaineers Books
1001 SW Klickitat Way, Suite 201
Seattle, WA 98134

First edition, 2000

Published simultaneously in Great Britain by Cordee, 3a DeMontfort Street, Leicester, England, LE1 7HD

Manufactured in the United States of America

Project Editor: Christine Ummel Hosler
Editor: Karen Parkin
Maps: Moore Creative Design
Cover design, text design, and book layout: Ani Rucki

Cover photograph: *Denali National Park, Alaska, East Fork Toklat River, autumn, The Alaska Range* © Pat O'Hara
Frontispiece: *Denali National Park, Alaska, Mount McKinley, Reflection Lake, morning light* © Pat O'Hara

Library of Congress Cataloging-in-Publication Data
    Denali : a literary anthology / edited by Bill Sherwonit.— 1st ed.
      p. cm.
    ISBN 0-89886-710-X (pbk.)
    1. American literature—Alaska. 2. Denali National Park and Preserve (Alaska)—Literary collections. 3. Natural history—Alaska—Literary collections. 4. Alaska—Literary collections. 5. Nature—Literary collections. I. Sherwonit, Bill, 1950- II. Title.
PS571.A4 D46 2000
979.8'3—dc21   00-009433
                                                       CIP

Contents

PART V: Modern Adventures

Acknowledgments

First and foremost, I owe immense thanks to the writers and oral-tradition storytellers for their stories about Denali—both the mountain and the region. They have inspired this anthology and enlarged my own relationship with this place of wildness. I'm also deeply grateful to all those who permitted the stories in this collection to be reprinted.

Thanks to the many people who helped in my search for stories, photos, and permissions, particularly Danielle Arnold, Ann Doyle, Jim Fall, Dianne Gudgel-Holmes, Myna Jacobs, Willie Karidis, Charlie Loeb, Tom Meacham, Daryl Miller, Marty Mitchell, Richard Nelson, Ann Sheldon Osgood, Alison Osius, Sharon Palmisano, Mark Stasik, Anne Webster, Rodman Wilson, and Jennifer Wolk.

Special thanks to The Mountaineers for their support of this project. I'm especially indebted to assistant acquisitions editor Margaret Sullivan, project editor Christine Hosler, managing editor Kathleen Cubley, and editor Karen Parkin. Thanks also to mapmaker Tony Moore and designer Ani Rucki.

I'm continually grateful to all those who have inspired and encouraged my participation in the writing life. Thanks to Nels for being such a wonderful role model, and to members of my writing group, an immeasurable source of delight and discipline: Jim Adams, William Ashton, Ellen Bielawski, Nancy Deschu, Jon Nickles, and Andromeda Romano-Lax. Above all, I thank my wife and sweetheart, Dulcy Boehle, for her ongoing support, encouragement, and love.

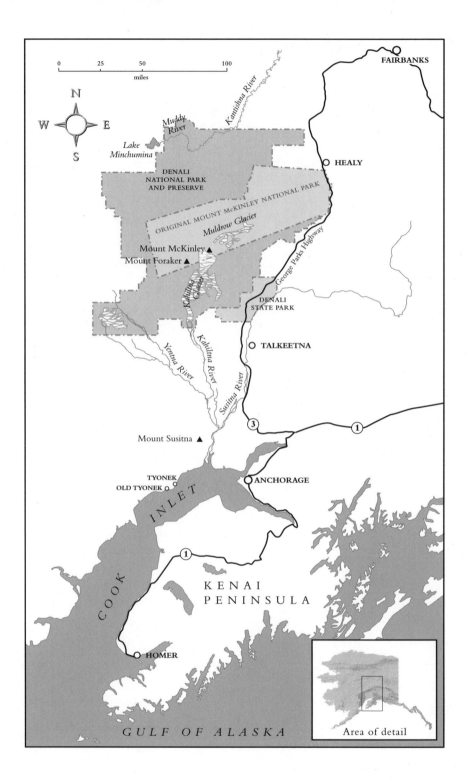

FAIRBANKS

0 25 50 100
miles

N
W   E
S

Muddy
River

Kantishna River

Lake
Minchumina

HEALY

DENALI
NATIONAL PARK
AND PRESERVE

ORIGINAL MOUNT McKINLEY NATIONAL PARK

Muldrow Glacier

Mount McKinley ▲
Mount Foraker ▲

Kahiltna Glacier

George Parks Highway

DENALI
STATE PARK

Yentna River

Kahiltna River

Susitna River

TALKEETNA

3

1

Mount Susitna ▲

TYONEK
OLD TYONEK

ANCHORAGE

COOK   INLET

1

KENAI
PENINSULA

HOMER

GULF OF ALASKA

Area of detail

Introduction

Near the end of the nineteenth century, a Princeton-educated entrepreneur named William Dickey abandoned his life in the Seattle area after a series of failed business ventures. Like so many other fortune-seekers then and now, Dickey turned his attention north to the promise of Alaska. In May 1896, he joined thousands of gold prospectors who stampeded to the territory's Cook Inlet region. After a summer in which he and some prospecting companions found traces of gold—but no fortune—Dickey returned south bearing news of a great ice mountain that, he felt certain, must be the continent's highest.

This mountain, which Dickey correctly guessed to be higher than 20,000 feet, already had many names. Early Russian explorers knew it as Bulshaia Gora ("great mountain") and an 1889 party of American prospectors called it Densmore's Mountain, after one of their own. Alaska's Athabascan tribes, too, had named the peak. Linguist James Kari of Fairbanks has identified eight name variations that translate into English as either "Big Mountain" or "The High One." Among them are Dghelay Ka'a, Denadhe, and Deenaalee—from which Denali is derived. Dickey, however, preferred Mount McKinley, after Ohio Republican presidential candidate William McKinley.

Back in the states, Dickey spread word of The Mountain, and his name for it, in a story published by a New York newspaper, *The Sun*. Titled "Discoveries in Alaska (1896)," the January 24, 1897, article reached a large audience and, in doing so, legitimized Dickey's appellation: Mount McKinley has remained the official title for North America's tallest mountain, despite numerous attempts to change it back to the more poetically descriptive and locally relevant name, Denali.

Dickey left a second and less controversial legacy: His newspaper article was the first published and widely read story in what has become an impressive literature of place. During the past century, dozens of books and hundreds—if not thousands—of newspaper and magazine stories have been written about 20,320-foot Denali and the region that it dominates. In Alaskan literature, as in most people's image of the forty-ninth state, Denali dominates all.

This is the first collection of original stories from that large and rapidly growing body of Denali literature. Divided thematically into five sections, its

9

twenty-three selections span 101 years of published writings, from Dickey's "Discoveries in Alaska" to the recent works of essayist Sherry Simpson; "trapline twins" Miki and Julie Collins; and several wolf researchers, led by L. David Mech.

Some of the works represented here are "northern classics"; for example, Adolph Murie's *A Naturalist in Alaska,* Hudson Stuck's *The Ascent of Denali,* or Art Davidson's *Minus 148°.* Others are well known in Alaska, but largely unknown outside the state. And a few will be recognized by only the most avid Denaliphiles.

From another perspective, this collection reaches back untold centuries. The English translations of three Alaska Native stories, originally published during the 1900s and reprinted here, are derived from the much older oral traditions of Athabascan storytelling. Two of the three selections in part I are creation stories that include accounts of Denali's origins: "The Second Making of Man"

Shem Pete at Eklutna in the summer of 1980 (Photo by James Kari. #1380-1-49, The Anchorage Museum of History and Art)

was translated by missionary and linguist Julius Jetté, who lived with Alaska's Ten'a (pronounced Dee-nay) people at the start of the twentieth century; the other legend was told by Koonah, a blind shaman living in the lowlands northeast of Denali, and recorded through an interpreter by Judge James Wickersham during his 1903 expedition to the peak. The story later was published as "The Sage of Kantishna—Legends of Denali" in Wickersham's book, *Old Yukon— Tales, Trails, and Trials.*

The third tale is a "distant time" story about humans and the "marmot people," told by Dena'ina Athabascan elder Shem Pete to anthropologist Jim Fall in 1978 and later published in both Dena'ina and English. Similar to many stories from traditional Athabascan culture, "The 'Whistler' Story" is intended in part to present guidelines for human behavior.

Though our modern western culture tends to characterize traditional Native stories as "myths" or "tales," it would be more accurate—and respectful—to call them "sacred stories," which present an indigenous world view. What's more, Athabascan stories, according to Jim Fall, "are set in the past, but just how far in the past is usually not specified. Some take place at a relatively distant time when the world was still being shaped. Others evidently occurred later. In the world in which these stories take place, animals and people speak the same language and transformations between human form and animal form are possible. Indeed, the separation between the 'natural' world of animals, plants, and other entities and the 'cultural' world of human beings is very narrow, if not nonexistent."

The book's other four sections present a past-to-present glimpse of western, non-Native attitudes towards Denali and its wild surroundings. The voices and perspectives are those of prospectors, explorers, government topographers, mountaineers, naturalists, biologists, park rangers, trappers, hunters, conservationists, modern homesteaders, and wilderness activists.

In part II, "Early Explorations," pioneers describe the Denali region while the landscape is still largely *terra incognita.* William Dickey's "Discoveries in Alaska" naturally begins the section, although, for all his influence, Dickey barely touched the southernmost edges of what Alaskans today call the "Denali region." But his travel narrative clearly shows the obstacles that explorers faced when trying to find an overland route from Cook Inlet north to the Alaska Range. And his description of The Mountain certainly piqued the interest of adventurers, who suddenly had a new highest peak to conquer.

Gold fever lured Dickey north again in 1898, this time into Canada. That same year, the prospects of more Alaskan gold strikes prompted the federal government to launch a series of trailblazing expeditions into the territory.

During the next four years, several mapping parties would pass near or through the Denali region, including one led by geologist Alfred Brooks. In August 1902, Brooks became the first person in recorded history to walk upon Denali's slopes. Brooks reached only 7500 feet before retreating, but he later proposed a "Plan for Climbing Mount McKinley" in *National Geographic*. The best account of Brooks's own approach to Denali appeared in *The Journal of Geography*; it is included here.

The summer after Brooks published his climbing plan, explorer Dr. Frederick Cook led an expedition to the Alaska Range, determined to reach Denali's top. The team failed in that regard, but during their travels team members circumnavigated both Denali and neighboring 17,400-foot Mount Foraker—an epic ninety-four-day journey that is still considered one of the most remarkable Alaska wilderness trips ever accomplished. Journalist Robert Dunn's chronicle of that 1903 expedition, *The Shameless Diary of an Explorer,* is considered a classic example of exploration exposé writing.

The final entry in this section is taken from Charles Sheldon's book *The Wilderness of Denali*. A passionate naturalist and hunter, Sheldon came to the Denali region in 1906 and 1907, drawn not by mountains but by a desire to study and hunt Dall sheep. During his stay, he also learned about the region's other wildlife, landscape, weather, and seasonal cycles. Upon returning east, Sheldon began a decade-long campaign that led, in 1917, to the formation of Mount McKinley National Park. Excerpts in this anthology are taken from his initial pursuit of Dall sheep rams.

Part III, "Mountaineering," includes a small sampling of the many climbing books published about Denali and its Alaska Range neighbors. I have opted to emphasize early milestone expeditions.

Until Dickey's report of a mountain "over 20,000 feet high"—confirmed in 1898 by government surveyors—European and American explorers and climbers had assumed 18,008-foot Mount St. Elias, along Alaska's southern coast, to be the continent's highest. Climbing teams came in the late 1800s to claim that prize, and only in the early 1900s did mountaineers turn their attention to the Alaska Range.

Climbers launched the first two attempts on Denali in 1903, one led by Judge James Wickersham, the other by explorer Frederick Cook. Neither team ascended higher than 11,000 feet or so. Cook returned in 1906 to try again—and once more it appeared his expedition had been thwarted. But just as his party was breaking up, Cook decided to make one "last desperate attempt," accompanied only by horsepacker Ed Barrill. A few weeks later, Cook reappeared, claiming success. His claim, now widely discredited, led to one of the

Charles Sheldon   (PCA 01-3394, Early Prints of Alaska, Alaska State Library)

great controversies in North American mountaineering, still ongoing in some quarters. Accounts from Cook's 1903 and 1906 expeditions are included here, excerpted from his book *To the Top of the Continent.*

An experienced outdoorsman and member of Frederick Cook's 1906 expedition, Belmore Browne almost immediately questioned Cook's supposed conquest. Four years after Cook's 1906 expedition, Browne and Herschel Parker would lead another party into the Alaska Range and find evidence to disprove Cook's claim. In 1912, Browne and Parker returned to the range a third time. On June 29, Browne, Parker, and teammate Merl La Voy came within a few hundred yards of Denali's top, only to be halted by a ferocious storm. Browne's account of that heartbreaking denial is reprinted from his book *The Conquest of Mount McKinley.*

No discussion of Denali mountaineering would be complete without some mention of the remarkable Sourdough Expedition. In 1910, a team of four gold miners with no technical climbing experience challenged North America's highest peak using only the most rudimentary equipment, to disprove

Frederick Cook's 1906 claim to success. They succeeded in a brazen style; but instead of ascending Denali's 20,320-foot south peak, they chose the 19,470-foot north peak. Bradford Washburn's account of the Sourdough Expedition is taken from *Mount McKinley: The Conquest of Denali.* Now in his nineties, Washburn is the world's leading authority on Denali; he has devoted much of his life to its study and has acted as its climbing "visionary." In a second *Mount McKinley* excerpt, Washburn considers some of the challenges still awaiting mountaineers.

By 1912, eight parties had attempted to climb Denali, but none had reached its absolute top. Enter Hudson Stuck, a missionary and self-professed amateur climber who had come north to work with Alaska's Natives. Long enamored of Denali, Stuck organized a 1913 expedition to the peak and with three other men, none of them experienced mountaineers, he reached the roof of the continent. His account is reprinted from a mountaineering classic, *The Ascent of Denali.*

We jump now to the late 1960s, when Denali was no longer a mysterious place—except in winter. In January 1967, an eight-man expedition flew into the Alaska Range to attempt the first winter ascent. Three team members—

Several members of the 1913 Stuck Expedition (Denali National Park and Preserve Archive)

Art Davidson, Dave Johnston, and Ray Genet—reached the summit, then survived a severe winter storm on their descent. Davidson recounted the climb and survival story in *Minus 148°: The Winter Ascent of Mt. McKinley,* from which a chapter has been taken.

Much has changed since Cook, Browne, and Stuck challenged Denali in the early 1900s. Improved access; the availability of guiding services; and advances in climbing gear, clothing, and food have opened the mountain to thousands of adventurers. One of the biggest changes has been air access: Today nearly all Denali climbers fly into the Alaska Range from Talkeetna, a small town appropriately nicknamed the "Gateway to Denali." The first and most famous of Talkeetna's "Denali Flyers" was Don Sheldon, a pioneering pilot who assisted mountaineers from the 1950s until his death in 1975. An account of one Sheldon air-rescue episode, taken from James Greiner's book *Wager with the Wind,* is the final mountaineering entry.

Many of the early accounts in parts II and III include place names and other words which have changed in spelling over the years. For example, the Bering Sea was once the Behring Sea, the Alaska Range was known as the Alaskan Range, and so on. These words have been kept as they appeared in the original writings, as they reflect the usage of the time.

Part IV, "Natural History," presents a look at Denali's wildlife and wild lands, through the experiences and musings of those who have closely studied the region's nonhuman inhabitants. The section might logically begin with the writings of hunter-naturalist Charles Sheldon, who painstakingly documented his encounters with the region's wildlife in *The Wilderness of Denali.* Because Sheldon's writings—for equally good reasons—have been placed in part II, "Early Explorations," the next logical choice to lead off part IV is an account by biologist Adolph Murie. Though best known for his groundbreaking study of wolf-sheep relationships during the late 1930s and early 1940s, Murie closely observed all of Denali's wildlife. Between the 1920s and 1970s, he wrote scores of reports and several popular books about the mammals, birds, and general ecology of then Mount McKinley National Park. The story featured in this collection is a chapter from his book *A Naturalist in Alaska.*

Nearly a half-century after Murie began his wolf-sheep studies, a group of biologists launched the most comprehensive investigation of Denali's wolves ever attempted. Led by renowned wolf researcher L. David Mech, team members followed wolf packs throughout 6-million-acre Denali National Park and Preserve from 1986 to 1994 and recorded all they could learn about the wolves' lives. The findings and interpretations have been published in *The Wolves of Denali.* The book's final chapter presents a narrative overview of Denali's wolf-prey relationships.

Grizzly bears, perhaps even more than wolves, have come to symbolize Denali National Park's rich wildness. Nearly everyone who enters the Denali wilderness comes away with a grizzly story, or so it seems. During the 1980s, naturalist Rick McIntyre closely observed grizzlies while working as a Denali park ranger. One bear, in particular, grabbed McIntyre's attention, and he tells the story of "Little Stony" in a chapter from his book *Grizzly Cub: Five Years in the Life of a Bear.*

Yet another of Denali's large mammals piqued the scientific curiosity of researcher Vic Van Ballenberghe. Since 1980, Van Ballenberghe has collared, tagged, and studied the lives of more than seventy moose inside Denali National Park. Each spring he watches cow moose give birth to calves, and every fall he studies the interactions of cows and bulls during the annual rut. Writer Sherry Simpson helps us to understand Van Ballenberghe's passion for moose in her essay "Strange Grace," while painting an intimate portrait of both the scientist and his subject of study.

The final natural history observations in part IV are shared by Tom Walker. A long-time resident of the Denali region, Walker is best known as a wildlife photographer, but he's also an accomplished writer. His *Denali Journal* is adapted from diary entries and documents memorable encounters with the region's wildlife from the early seventies through 1990.

Part V, "Modern Adventures," includes stories by those who today live in Denali's shadow or explore its wild lands. More than a century after William Dickey wandered up the valleys south of the Alaska Range, the Denali region remains a mostly wild place. Six million acres are protected within Denali National Park and Preserve, another 325,000 acres in neighboring Denali State Park; outside the parks is a patchwork mix of state, borough, local, and privately owned lands. Living within the region is a community of people who have carved out niches and found adventure as homesteaders, miners, trappers, guides, rangers, entrepreneurs, and writers.

One of four hundred people who live in Talkeetna, the southern "Gateway to Denali," Daryl Miller first attempted to climb the great peak in 1981. Now Denali National Park's chief mountaineering ranger, he has joined in more than a dozen Denali climbing expeditions and assisted in more than thirty mountain rescues. Miller also treks through the surrounding wilderness of rugged mountains, tundra-topped foothills, and expansive lowlands. In the mid-1990s, he and buddy Mark Stasik completed one of the most ambitious journeys of Denali's modern era: a winter circumnavigation of the Alaska Range's two highest peaks. Miller tells their story in "The Alaskan Mile."

Extended winter journeys are a seasonal way of life for Miki and Julie Collins, though these self-described "trapline twins" prefer sled dog teams to other modes of travel. The sisters were born and raised along the shores of Lake Minchumina, near the northwest corner of Denali National Park and Preserve. Now in their 40s, they continue to lead a subsistence lifestyle deep in the wilderness. One chapter of their lives is told here in an excerpt from *Riding the Wild Side of Denali.*

Richard Leo, by contrast, is a relative newcomer to the Denali region. In 1981 he left the corporate world of New York City and headed north to Alaska, where his search for a new life eventually led to the Upper Susitna Valley, on Denali's southern side. There, on a remote homestead, Leo has built an adventurous life with his wife, three boys, and kennel of dogs, in a neighborhood that includes the continent's tallest mountain, glacial rivers, lush forests, grizzlies, and wolves. In this excerpt from *Way Out Here,* he describes his life in Denali's wilds.

The south side of Denali where Richard Leo and Daryl Miller reside is also home to 325,000-acre Denali State Park, or "Little Denali" as some call

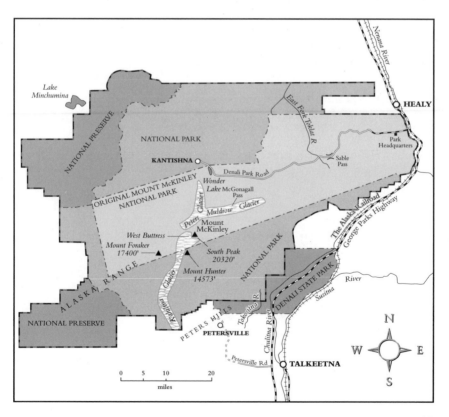

it. Among the most accessible of all Alaskan parklands—it is bisected by the George Parks Highway and bordered on its eastern edge by the Alaska Railroad—Denali State Park remains one of the least known. But that is changing, as tourism development builds along the park's boundaries and even within it, on private inholdings. I present a portrait of Little Denali in the essay "Denali State Park: In the Shadow of the High One," taken from the book *Alaska's Accessible Wilderness.*

The final selection is a series of short essays from Kim Heacox's book *In Denali.* A naturalist, photographer, and author, Heacox has worked to preserve Denali National Park's wildness since his one season as a Denali ranger in 1981. Now a resident of Southeast Alaska, Heacox lived near the national park's entrance from 1991 to 1995, and he has made dozens of trips into its remote backcountry. His book both celebrates Denali's wildness and mourns the gradual loss of its "wild essence" because of increased human demands.

From Athabascan distant-time legends to contemporary tales of modern-day adventurers, the storytellers in this anthology powerfully portray the wild nature of Denali, The High One, and the vast wilderness region that surrounds The Mountain. They tell us of the landscape's dangers, its obstacles, and its abundant wildlife; and they share its allures, whether gold or mountaintops, snow-white sheep or wilderness solitude. Here we discover why men and women who are drawn to this place find hope, challenge, inspiration—and sometimes sorrow—in Denali and the broad shadow that The Mountain casts. We learn, too, of the possibilities for personal discovery, both past and present, and the essence of the "wilderness spirit" that draws people here and sometimes will not let go. Finally, we learn of threats to the region's wildness that prompt writers and other storytellers to continue sharing the story of Denali and the ancient magic that must be protected.

Part I

Native Sacred Stories

1

The Second Making of Man

by Julius Jetté

A scholarly and spiritual man, Julius Jetté (1864–1927) was a Canadian-born Jesuit missionary who spent nearly half his life with Alaska's Athabascan Indians. Jetté came to Alaska in 1898 and settled in the Yukon River region northwest of Denali. Over the next twenty-nine years, he worked as a missionary, linguist, translator, and recorder of local stories. Though he studied all aspects of Native life, Jetté took a special interest in the Ten'a (pronounced Dee-nay) or Koyukon language. According to Jesuit priest and university professor Louis Renner, "He was to master this language as no white man before or after him ever mastered it." Historians, anthropologists, and linguists generally agree that Jetté's "undisputed masterpiece" was his seven-volume, 2344-page dictionary of the Ten'a language. A later anthropologist, Reverend Robert J. Sullivan, described this prodigious work as "much more than a mere compilation of Native terms, for Father Jetté has elaborated his work with minute descriptions of the customs and ways of life of this people."

A sharp observer, enthusiastic student, and prolific writer, Jetté carried notebooks wherever he went and wrote, in great detail, about the Ten'a culture. He documented the role of shamans, or medicine men, compiled some one thousand geographical names, described the Ten'a's sixteen-month calendar, and recorded their stories and riddles. Most of Jetté's voluminous writings remain unpublished, but several of his articles appeared in scholarly journals, such as *Anthropos* and the *Journal of the Royal Anthropological Institute of Great Britain and Ireland*. The *Journal's* 1908–1909 edition contains an eighty-five-page article by Jetté, "On Ten'a Folklore," which compiles many stories that Jetté heard and translated. Jetté loved to listen to Native storytellers; as he once commented, "Storytelling among the Ten'a is quite an enviable accomplishment, and those who can do it well are highly valued for it. At night, when all are in bed, the lights put out, heavy curtains fastened on the outside of the windows, everything perfectly dark, someone suggests *rorloih*—let us have a story. And then someone who does not feel too sleepy starts with one of those fantastical tales such as were told to us when we were very young children." Storytelling was especially anticipated in winter, to help pass the long nights, and was usually done spontaneously. Though we often call such traditional Native stories tales or myths, anthropologist Richard Nelson says that, more accurately, they were considered "sacred stories" to the Ten'a people.

This creation story, "The Second Making of Man," includes a reference to Dinale, or Denali. It is taken from Jetté's article "On Ten'a Folklore," published in the Royal Anthropological Institute's *Journal*, Vol. 38 (1908).

In a populous settlement there lived a rich youth and his four nephews. Far away, across the sea, there lived a very desirable young girl, but who did not care for men, and this girl he desired to marry. So, he undertook to cross over in his canoe, in order to propose to her. She was the daughter of a rich man, and many young men, rich ones only, had asked her hand, but she had rejected all their offers. To all proposals she invariably answered no. Now then, this young man began to think with himself, "If I were to go and propose, in my turn, perhaps she would accept me." And he started, his four nephews accompanying him in their own canoes. They arrived, and he said to her: "I have come across the water in order to take you to wife." But she answered: "I will not marry you."

And so, the next morning they made ready to start back. The young man was already in his boat, down on the beach; his nephews had packed all their things, and they were just ready to go. Many people had come out of their houses to see them going, and were standing in a crowd on top of the high bank. Among them there stood a woman carrying her young child on her arm, a baby, not yet weaned. This woman then, talking to her baby, said: "And what of this little girl? If they want a girl, why not take this little one of mine?" Of course, it was only baby talk. Still the young man, on hearing it, held out his paddle toward the woman, and said: "Put her upon this, the little one you speak of." And the woman did so. The young man placed the child behind him in the canoe, and off he paddled, his nephews following him.

Meanwhile the girl whom he had intended to marry came down to get water. But as she stepped on the soft mud at the water's edge, she began to sink down into it. "Oh! oh!" she cried, "here I am sinking up to my knees!" The young man retorted: "It is your own fault." And she sank still further, up to her waist, and exclaimed: "Oh! oh! now I am in up to my waist!" And he said again: "It is your own fault." By this time she had sunk up to her neck. "Oh! oh!" said she, "I am in up to my neck." Again he replied: "It is your own fault!" and she disappeared, being dragged down under the ground. Very probably the young man caused this, by his very powerful thought: "Let it be so," thought he.

But the girl's mother had some tame brown bears, and seeing what had happened, she took them down to the bank, to the water, and laying hold of their tails she said to them: "Raise a strong wind," hoping that the young man might get drowned. The bears began to dig the bottom in a fury, and made huge waves. At the same time the water rose exceedingly. But the young man pulled out a thin white stone which he was carrying with him and threw it ahead. Whereupon the water became perfectly smooth over a narrow space ahead of him, just where he was to pass, whilst on both sides the waves were enormous and raging. All his nephews were drowned, and all the inhabitants of that village also perished in the waves, except the mother of the baby and her husband. These were the only two who escaped.

During this frightful storm the young man was paddling, always on the smooth water. But he was exhausted. Nothing but water and big waves, all over. Then he took a harpoon and threw it. It hit the crest of a wave. But the effort he had made to concentrate his thought whilst throwing the harpoon overpowered him; he fainted. His head bent down in the fore-part of the canoe. Soon after, however, he recovered himself, and oh wonder! There he was, in his canoe, in a forest of spruce-trees. The land had been formed again. The wave he had hit with his harpoon had become a mountain, it is the one we call: Totson-to-kedatłkoihten, *i.e.*, The-one-whose-top-was-hit-by-the-Raven. The harpoon had glanced on the mountain top, as the wave hardened into rock and had struck again another huge wave, changing it into a mountain; this is the one we call Dinale, *i.e.*, The-high-one. Again the harpoon made a bound on the hard rock, but this time it went up and stuck into the sky. We cannot see it, ourselves, though it is still there; the medicine-men only see it and know where it is.

The young man then turned towards the child whom he had left sitting behind his back, but she was no more a child, she was a grown-up girl, who had just reached the age of puberty; she had to be put apart (having had her first menstruation). Hence she felt very much ashamed, and kept her eyes cast down. But she was quite beautiful, with a face as bright as the sun.

It is from this woman that men were made anew to re-people the earth, for she had children from the young man. But the two who had been saved from the waters, as we have seen, these were the ancestors of the people beyond the seas.

Editor's afterword: Besides the Ten'a stories, Jetté compiled more than 100 of their riddles in the journal *Anthropos*. Through riddles the Ten'a expressed their knowledge of the natural world and affection for it. Here is one recorded by Jetté:

Riddle me: the stars are rottening on my sides. Answer: Dinale, the high one.

To answer this riddle, Jetté wrote, the Ten'a explain that "the migratory birds, such as geese, ducks, cranes, etc., do not soar above [Dinale] in their flight, and when going southward, during September, they butt against it, in the dark, and die there. The truth is that bones and carcasses are found scattered over its gulches. In the question, these birds are metaphorically termed 'stars,' on account of their flying high in the sky."

2

The Sage of Kantishna—Legends of Denali

by James Wickersham

One of the most influential Alaskans of the early twentieth century, James Wickersham served the U.S. Territory as a federal district judge and, later, a Congressional delegate, in a public career that spanned more than three decades. Among his many accomplishments, Wickersham played a key political role in the push to establish Mount McKinley National Park (although, unlike Charles Sheldon, his vision had more to do with tourism and economic benefits to Alaska than wildlife preservation). In climbing circles, however, he is better known as the leader of the first mountaineering expedition to Denali.

In 1900 Wickersham was reassigned from Seattle to Alaska and given a judicial district that covered half the territory. Initially he worked out of Eagle, a small town along the Yukon River near the Alaska–Canada border. Two years after his arrival, a gold strike to the west began a new stampede and gave rise to a booming community: Fairbanks. Correctly guessing that Fairbanks would become Interior Alaska's commercial center, Wickersham moved his court to that mining camp in 1903. By spring, with everything in order and the next court session scheduled to begin in late July, Wickersham began looking for a challenge to occupy his time. He settled on a trip to "that monarch of North American mountains, Mount McKinley." Joined by four "young and vigorous" friends, plus two mules for packing, Wickersham attacked the peak's north side. Following the Peters Glacier, the team ascended to the base of "a tremendous precipice beyond which we cannot go." Frustrated by their blocked path and worried that warm weather was weakening the snowpack, thus making it more avalanche prone, the climbers turned back at about 8000 feet. The enormous rock face that stopped them would later be named the Wickersham Wall and would remain unclimbed until 1963.

Wickersham documented that first-ever attempt to climb Denali, along with many other events from his life, in *Old Yukon—Tales, Trails, and Trials* (published in 1938 by the Washington Law Book Co.). In that same book, he described a meeting with the Ten'a chief and "sage,"

Koonah, whose tribe had established a summer camp along the Kantishna River, northeast of Denali. A slightly shortened excerpt is included here. Besides his descriptions of Athabascan camp life, Wickersham recounts Koonah's story about Yako, an ancient shaman, who battled the wicked war chief Totson. Though the details are different, readers will note similarities between this Ten'a creation story and the one translated by Jesuit missionary Julius Jetté. Koonah's is among the few recorded Native stories that make reference to Denali or the surrounding region.

O'er evergreen valley and low Tena home,
The crest of Denali towers massive and lone;
By wintry clouds hidden from mortal sight,
It stands resplendent in summer light;
Its sunlit walls bared to azure sky
Promise lowland Tena their God is nigh.

'Tis the throne of Sâ, Master of Life,
Who comes each season in Godlike strife
To stay Dzadu, dread demon of snow,
To renew antlered herds for Tena below;
To bring sweet rains, budding trees,
Spawning fish, and golden bees.

We are gathered at Tuktawgana, in the land of Koonah, the blind sage of Kantishna. Here is wood and water and hunting. It is the spring-and-summer camp of Koonah's band. Our boat was hauled into the harbor of the shallow slough fronting the camp and our outfit quickly unloaded, our tent raised, and we began housekeeping near our Tena friends. We paid fifteen dollars and the old coat to Kudan, the guide, who quickly disappeared into the wilderness on his homeward journey.

May 23, 1903. From Koonah's camp there is a beautiful view of the snowy mountains to the south and east. The land rises by gentle gradations from our valley to the rounded foothills thence ascending to an elevated tableland upon which rests the mountain-mass, from which it leaps skyward to the massive dome of Denali. The valley of the Kantishna is wide, and forested with a light

25

growth of spruce and birch, while a denser growth of larger and better timber stretches along the sinuosities of the streams far up into the foothills. Here and there are wide open spaces in which lie lakes, large and small, fed by descending streams glistening in the sunlight. The rising summer heat has not yet dissolved the greater snowbanks which last winter's storms deposited in the gorges and sheltered places on the slopes of the lower mountains, though larger windswept areas are bare and brown. These extensive snowbanks, spotting the frontal slopes of the dark foothills, give a parti-colored aspect to the mountain view which is particularly pleasing. They add freshness and beauty to the landscape and conserve the moisture for the lower slopes and valleys during the heat of summer. In these hills, and rising above the small range which extends into the great valley and divides the Toclat watershed from the Kantishna, is a small but prominent mountain, which the Indians tell us they call Chitsia, or Heart Mountain, because its peak resembles the point of a moose heart. Far beyond Chitsia and above the frontal range which it over-lords, rise half-a-dozen snowy peaks, some of them reaching a height of ten or twelve thousand feet (judging by Mount McKinley), and covered with perpetual snow. But these great peaks are mere hills by the side of the gigantic mass and towering summit of Mount McKinley, which rises almost two miles above their tops, and more than nineteen thousand feet—nearly four miles—above our valley camp. From this place, Chitsia, which is about four thousand feet high, stands a little to the east of south, and Mount McKinley stands an equal distance west of south. The Indians tell us the small river which comes down from Chitsia and which we will see farther up, is called Chitsiana, or Moose Heart river.

Koonah's camp is a moving panorama of Indian life and color. It is situated on an open spot on the lower end of an island formed by the Kantishna on the west and a wide marshy slough on the east. Its view opens eastward and south, across the still, clear waters of the lakelike slough, and its background of dark spruce forest gives shelter from northern winds and supplies an abundance of fuel. On this high, dry ground, open to sunlight, stand the summer tents and rough bark houses of his people—the high drying racks for jerking caribou and moose steaks, and smoking salmon above the fangs of climbing curs. Next to the still waters of the slough on a sloping sandbar, is the Tena shipyard. Here birch-bark canoes are framed, sewed, and caulked before launching, and nearby are the lower racks where fishnets are stretched for drying and mending. A fleet of canoes and boats, including our transport, the *Mudlark*, are anchored in the quiet harbor abreast the village. Children at play and scampering dogs give movement and sound to the scene. One ancient dame, gray-haired and bent with the work of many years, is laboriously scraping a wet moose hide which is held across a horizontal pole, shoulder high. Her scraping implement is a thin stone, and with it she skillfully removes the hair and fat from the skin so it may be rubbed soft and dry for tanning. Another squaw, having cleaned both sides of a great hide, has tied both ends to a post and, having inserted a round stick in the loop of skin, is twisting it with all her strength to squeeze out the water and make it dry. Another, having stripped a skin of its hair and fat and wrung it dry, has stretched it over a pole frame underneath which she has built a smudge to give it a beautiful brown color on one side, leaving the other side white. Thus cleaned, tanned, and smoke-colored, the finished product is made up by the squaws into moccasins, leggings, and other articles.

Soon after we arrived at this camp yesterday afternoon we called at old Koonah's wigwam to pay our respects to the sachem of Tuktawgana. When we entered he rose and received us with a native modesty and simplicity that adorns and ennobles the primitive man. He is blind, slender, and rather tall, though well-proportioned, and about fifty years of age. He enjoys the blessings and labor of two wives; the youngest is an active bright-eyed Tena Hebe, who keeps the chieftain's home cheerful and neat and his moccasins dry; the elder tans mephitic moose hides and prepares odorous salmon for the drying rack, beneath which she keeps the fire asmudge that the fish may be dry and brittle for the well-worn teeth of her master, and keeps away fish-loving malamute dogs with a club and a raucous voice. In civilized lands, or in a Circle City court, the old lady would have had the law on the correspondent long ago, and possibly alimony of at least two of Koonah's best dogs and one moose hide per annum, but in Tenaland she snares rabbits for the household and sleeps by the blaze under the fish rack.

The Tena is a modest and peaceful gentleman. Born in the solitudes of the birch and spruce forests, he has never known the necessity for war, offensive or defensive. If he cannot retire when war or personal encounter threatens, he meekly turns the other cheek. Retaining the ancient hunting grounds of their forefathers, occupying their earliest camping places, living the simple life their common ancestors lived before the southern bands migrated to the Columbia Basin, to Oregon, Arizona, and Mexico, the Gens de Butte, the men of the mountains, the Tanana Tena, still exhibit the childlike character and peaceful disposition of Yako, the gentle magician, the Athabascan Adam.

The Tena is a storyteller—a transmitter of oral tales. Having no written annals to assist his memory or hamper his imagination, he passes tribal legends along by oral communication from father to son. His quiet and gentle nature is clearly disclosed in his timidity while thus engaged, for any exhibition of unusual interest, such as inquiry and preparations to write down his statements, will cause him to retire behind a barrier of silence from which he cannot be coaxed. He loves to relate them at the twilight hour, beside a low campfire in the great forest or, still better, under the darkness of night to his young native friends resting beneath adjoining sleeping robes or in the spruce bough beds. He shrinks from exposing his modest oratory or his tribal traditions to those who claim superiority of education, of position, or of race, or to those who smile as they are related.

It is always the midnight hour to old Koonah, but the loss of his sight has sharpened his other senses, and he will not relate the ancient tales until there is restful peace among his listeners, be they Tena or alien. Thus, in silence, we rested on fresh spruce boughs round his glowing campfire, while he talked to us softly and slowly about the divinities and demons of Tenaland; of those wicked men of former days whom Yako, the ancient shaman, changed into animals, birds, or bees, to be forever the servants of their Tena brothers; of other animals, birds, and bees given immortality through vernal reproduction, that they might have eternal life and happiness in the land of their fathers; of the supernal divinities of Denali, whose everlasting snows he can no longer see, but whose majestic heights and stupendous outlines are imprinted on his memory with photographic accuracy.

"Long ago," he began, "long before Denali, the high one, was raised to the sky, Yako dwelt in the land where the Tena live. He was young and strong and as straight and tall as a spruce tree growing by the river. He was as gentle as a young caribou, as strong as a bull moose, as wise as the beaver. He dwelt alone, for there was no woman in the land to be his wife; there were no villages, no people, no Tena. Yako was a mighty magician, as cunning as the fox, as quick as the weasel, as silent as the shadow. He possessed power to change the form of animals, the land, and the sea, but, withal, he had no wife, which he now greatly desired.

Ses, the great brown bear, told Yako that far to the westward lived a mighty hunter of bear and walrus, Totson, the Raven war chief, who killed both men and animals, in whose village there were beautiful females of the race of Yako. This information pleased the youthful magician, though he was distressed that female creatures of his race should be found in the tribe of Totson the warrior. And not until Ses further told him these beautiful creatures did not kill but were moved to pity and tears at the sight of bloodshed and death, would he permit his mind to dwell upon them with longing. Yako now determined to journey into the distant west, to Yunana, the sunset land, to the village of

Totson the war chief, the hunter of men and animals, that he might see these beautiful females and take one for his wife.

Yako went into the forest early in the spring after the winter's snows had melted from underneath the shade; cut large spruce trees with his stone axe, and rived, with moose horn wedge, long sinewy strips of the inner tough wood, without knot or blemish, for a canoe frame; he cut and carved strong birch for the ribs and bow and stern posts; and dug long spruce roots for sewing. When the warm spring sun was hurrying the sap of life from the bosom of Mother Earth up the outer bole of the tree, he stripped broad sheets of white birch bark for canoe covering and gathered spruce gum for caulking.

He chose a favorable and sandy spot on the bank of the great river, measured thereon the length and width of his magic canoe, drove strong birch stakes for stock, and wrought from day to day till the first birch bark canoe was finished. He sewed it with strong spruce roots, caulked it with gum from the forest, and painted the framework red, as the Tena have ever since done.

When the canoe was finished, Yako launched it on the waters of the Yukon and floated upon its swift current to the westward where the river flood entered the great salt water, and thence he paddled across the summer sea to the shores of Yunana, to sunset land, where dwelt the tribes of Totson, the Raven chief, on the seashore.

With slow and measured stroke he approached the village of the Raven tribe, and from his canoe rocking on the waves just off the village beach, sang a song, saying:

> *'Oh, mighty Totson, chief of the Raven tribe, hunter of men and animals, I am Yako, come from the eastern land from across the salt water, from the great river whose banks are lined with forests of spruce and cottonwood and waving birch, from the land of the moose, the caribou, the beaver, and the bear, to see the beautiful female creatures of men and ask you for one to be my wife. I am the friend of men and of animals. Ses, the brown bear, told me that in your village there are beautiful young women as straight as the spruce, as graceful as the birch, and as gentle as the white sheep ewe on my hills in the eastern land. Totson, chief of the Ravens, Yako asks to see those beautiful creatures, and begs that you give him one for a wife, that he may have children in the eastern land, in the great river valley.'*

Yako sang the song of his journey, of the rivers and the sea, of the forests and the animals of his homeland, and all the tribe of the Raven warrior gathered on the shore of the sea in front of the village to hear him. Now Totson, the Raven chief, was a warrior who delighted in killing both men and animals and in the sight of flowing blood. He was jealous of Yako, of his youth and manly beauty, of his strength and power as a shaman, and he hated him for the music and sweetness of his song. Totson refused to come to the sea bank with his people to hear Yako's song, or to welcome him to his village in Yunana, in the sunset land, but sat far back in the darkness of his underground house sharpening his magic war spear and preparing his throwing sticks and arrows with which to kill his friendly visitor.

All the young women of the village gathered on the high bank overlooking the sea beach to hear Yako's song, and when it was ended they were pleased but also expectant and frightened. A woman of good countenance and happy face, the wife of the second chief of Yunana, came down to the beach and spoke softly to Yako, saying:

> 'Yako, you may have my daughter, Tsukala, who is yet a child, but who will grow big and strong and good, for your wife. Take her and go quickly for Totson, the Raven chief, is now preparing his weapons to kill you.'

Upon hearing this a group of village girls, led by Totson's daughter, filled with a jealous rage that this handsome young man, though a stranger, was to have the child of the second chief for his wife, came shrieking and clawing at Tsukala's mother to prevent her from giving her daughter to the youth from the eastern land.

Yako extended his magic paddle to the beach and told the mother to put Tsukala on its broad surface, which she did just as the screaming crowd of envious creatures reached her. Yako drew back his paddle and tenderly placed Tsukala behind him beneath the deck covering of his canoe, in a warm, dry bed of white sheep's wool. As the village girls reached Tsukala's mother with clubs raised to strike her, a high wave filled with magic swept the beach and overwhelmed them, though it cast Tsukala's mother upon the bank in safety.

Totson now rushed from his underground home in warrior rage and began to cast war arrows and feathered spears at Yako, who turned the prow of his canoe seaward, toward the eastern land, and urged it forward across the waters with mighty strokes of his paddle. Totson, the magician, caused a storm to rise, the winds to blow, and great green waves to roll, hoping thereby to destroy Yako's light canoe and drown him. The Raven chief entered his skin war boat, armed with his mighty spear, with his war bow backed with the sinews of the walrus, and a quiver of arrows, with his throwing stick and a bundle of spears, and from Yunana, the sunset land, he pursued Yako over the wild sea waves, over the sea toward the home of Yako.

Totson was skilled in the management of his sea boat and wielded his paddle dexterously. He knew the ways of the green sea waves and rode them as fearlessly as the gull. By his magic he caused them to grow higher and stronger, hoping thereby to overcome the fleeing canoe. But Yako was a greater magician than Totson. He carried a wave-quelling stone fastened in the braid of his long black hair, which he now threw with great strength far ahead to its home in Tenaland. The magic stone leaped from wave to wave as flat stones do which children skip on quiet waters before their village homes, and where the stone passed the waves were leveled and the sea stilled. Yako sped swiftly across the sea in this path of quiet waters, though mountainous green waves rolled threateningly on each side and behind him, where Totson labored in the pursuing canoe.

The Raven chief came rapidly forward on the crests of the rolling waves; his arms were strong, he was skilled in the use of the paddle, and gained on the fleeing Yako, at whom he shot arrows until they were gone; at whom he threw spears with his powerful throwing board until they were gone, hoping with each arrow shot and each spear cast to strike Yako in the back and kill him. His efforts were in vain, for Yako plied his paddle lustily, keeping always in the straight trough of the sea stilled by his magic stone, and the arrows and the spears of the pursuer flew over his head. Totson now gained on Yako, and putting forth all his skill and strength, and guided by the flying black hair streaming back from Yako's head, he prepared to kill him with one mighty thrust of his never-failing great war spear. Rising in his canoe to gain strength and better aim in the cast, Totson threw his spear straight toward the back of his fleeing enemy, just as two great waves reached toward him, one on each side. Yako saw the glistening spear as it rose in the air over the green sea wave pursuing him, and instantly bringing his most powerful magic force to his aid, he changed the oncoming rear wave into a mountain of stone, upon whose crest the war spear struck with a crash of breaking rock, and from whose stony summit the weapon glanced upward, high over the still waters where Yako's canoe raced forward in safety. As the great spear rose higher in the air from the power of Totson's arm, and flew skyward and far over the still waters, it touched the crest of the greater wave coming from the opposite direction, which Yako's magic instantly turned into a greater mountain of stone. From the summit of this mighty mountain the spear again glanced upward and flew high into the southern sky, where Koonah, the blind shaman, the descendent of Yako and the possessor of his power and magic, can see it through his darkened orbs, though no man with mortal eyes may do so.

Disaster now overtook Totson, the Raven war chief, the bloody-handed warrior, the pursuer of Yako. When Yako's powerful magic changed the rear wave into a mountain of stone, Totson's canoe struck on its sharp, angular walls. Standing in his seat, he was thrown headlong upon the rocks where he instantly changed into a large black bird, the croaking Raven, which flapped dripping and weaponless to the mountain top.

Yako's exertions had been so constant, so powerful and exhausting, that he fell forward across the thwart of his canoe, where he lay long insensible and asleep. When finally he awoke he was transported with happiness to find his canoe in the midst of a beautiful forest of stately spruce and graceful birch trees at his home camp, on the banks of the Yukon, where Tsukala, now grown to young womanhood, stood by his side with a dish of berries and dried salmon which she had prepared for his supper. Gazing round the horizon Yako saw the mountains he had created from the threatening waves of the sea, the smaller one in the west, half way back to Yunana, the sunset land, while the greater one, the mighty dome from whose crest the spear of Totson glanced as it sped to its position amid the stars, was that which the Tena call 'Denali,' the 'high one.' Far above him, above the mountains and the forests of Tenaland, floating lazily on outstretched wing, he saw Totson, the croaking raven.

The path of stilled waters, between the two great waves which Yako turned into mountains, is now the wide and lovely valley of the Yukon and the Tanana, forested with spruce, cottonwood, and birch; the home of the moose, the caribou, and the furred animals; and also ever since the home of the Tena, the descendents of Yako, the magician, and Tsukala, their grandmother. Totson has killed neither man nor animal since that fatal day. He is obliged to preserve his life by eating carrion, which Ses may leave for him, and the fish refuse from Tena camps. He often sits on the fish rack near the Indian houses, talking in harsh notes to his relatives, the Tena, the children of Tsukala of the tribe of Totson, though none but Koonah can understand his speech. To Koonah he constantly repeats the story of the race across the sea, the casting of the great war spear and the disaster which immediately followed. He invariably ends with a petition to Yako to be transformed again into man and warrior, but no answer has ever come of his prayers.

These first parents built a village where their magic canoe rested in the forest on the north bank of the river, and peopled the land. Their children, the mild and gentle Tena, have gone far to the east and south, far from the old home, until Koonah does not know their limit of migration.

When Yako grew old, his bald head touched the sky. Tsukala grew strong and large like Yako and they were kind and gentle and beloved by their children, the Tena. Yako taught the Tena to make birch bark canoes, fish traps, and drying racks; to make the long sled and to work the dog in harness. Tsukala, our grandmother, taught her daughters to tan moose and caribou skins, to cut and make clothes to cover their bodies and to keep them warm; to clean and dry fish; to cook berries and make baskets of roots and of birch bark. And there was peace in the land and plenty in Tena caches.

Far to the south on the shores of the great water dwelt the Nahotetiyu, of the stature of Yako, but fierce and quarrelsome, slayers of men like Totson the Raven chief. These enemies prepared to invade Tenaland to kill Yako and make slaves of his children. Tetsen, the wild goose, pointed out the trail to them; Tebay, the white sheep chief, conducted them safely through the mountain pass to his lookout on Chitsia, and pointed out to them, far across the wide forested valley, the village where Yako dwelt on the bank of the great river.

These treacherous warriors from the southern sea crept cautiously through the forests to Yako's village and suddenly attacked him. He wrestled with them in combat for a long time, the very earth trembling with the fierceness of the conflict. The Nahotetiyu warriors sought to thrust their copper knives into his breast, and their great bear spears into his bowels, but he caught his enemies in his arms and held them powerless to do him injury.

The Klazzetena, one of the tribes of Yako's children, had secretly cultivated and possessed the warlike spirit which Yako had not, and while the gentle giant held his four enemies so they might not injure him, without injuring them, the Klazzetena cut the tendons above the heels of each struggling Nahotetiyu, and thus hamstrung they were no longer able to fight and were killed by the Klazzetena.

Yako was just as well as gentle. He caused the snows to gather on Denali and the glaciers to push down its slopes, so Tebay, the white sheep, cannot climb its sides to escape from warrior wolves; he painted it the color of the clouds that Tetsen, the wild goose, in his annual flight to and from his home in Tenaland, where he comes at nesting-time each year, may strike its sides and fall dead at its base where his body is eaten by Ses, the great brown bear, who makes his home amid the boulders nearby. This punishment, Tebay the white sheep, and the tribe of Tetsen, the wild goose, must endure forever, for it is the decree of Yako. Nor were the Klazzetena permitted to escape punishment for taking the lives of the Nahotetiyu. Knowing they had violated the law of Yako, they scattered and fled to the forests, but such of them as remained in Tenaland, were transformed into the tribe of yellow jackets. Sâ gives them immortality

33

by renewing their lives each summer, and permits them to inhabit the forests and camping grounds of their fathers, the children of Yako."

The campfire had long since burned out; Koonah's voice grew low and sleepy, and that of the interpreter finally ceased. We silently stole away to our tents and our midnight slumbers for the tales of Koonah, the sage of Kantishna, were ended.

3

Shq'uɫa Tsukdu: The "Whistler" (Hoary Marmot) Story

by Shem Pete, as told to Jim Fall

Dena'ina Athabascan Shem Pete witnessed enormous changes during his lifetime, which spanned nearly a century, from the 1890s through 1989 (no one knows exactly when he was born). A member of the Susitnuht'ana tribe, or "People of the Sand River," Pete was born and raised in Susitna River country, north of Cook Inlet and south of the Alaska Range (his Dena'ina name was K'etech'ayutiɫen, or "One Who Brings Gun Among Game"). He spent most of his days in the lowlands and coastal areas south of the Denali region, but occasionally hunted in the Alaska Range foothills and traveled up the Chulitna River valley toward Dghelay Ka'a, or "Big Mountain," as his people call North America's highest peak. The mountain, clearly, was part of Shem Pete's world.

Over the years, Pete watched Upper Cook Inlet become flooded by non-Natives. As his homeland evolved into Alaska's most populated, urban region, Pete's Dena'ina culture slipped away. Seeing the loss, he spent his later years working to preserve its stories, values, and traditions. Blessed with a sharp memory, Pete relished telling traditional stories in the Dena'ina language. When cultural anthropologist Jim Fall met Pete in the late 1970s, Shem was "generally acknowledged by his people as a singer, historian, and storyteller without peer." Pete had already begun collaborating with Jim Kari, a linguist with the Alaska Native Language Center, to preserve oral traditions. Along with son Billy, Shem "spent countless hours telling stories, reporting place names, and commenting on Dena'ina traditions from 1974 until just a few weeks before his death," says Fall, who now works for the State of Alaska's Division of Subsistence.

Fall met the Petes in 1978 while researching upper inlet Dena'ina traditions for his University of Wisconsin graduate studies. From September 1978 through July 1979, he visited them for months on end. "I had to earn the privilege of listening to Shem's stories, as had young Dena'ina people in former times," he recalls. "This meant working for him as a helper: splitting wood, carrying water, providing transportation."

35

Among Pete's offerings were *dghelay'a tsukdu* (mountain stories), reflecting his people's ties to the Alaska Range and other mountains.

In 1987, Kari and Fall produced *Shem Pete's Alaska: The Territory of the Upper Cook Inlet Dena'ina,* an anthology of oral histories and catalog of Dena'ina place names. Three years later, not long after Pete's death, Fall produced a report for the Alaska Humanities Forum, *Upper Cook Inlet Dena'ina Oral Traditions: An Introduction to the Narrative Art of an Alaskan Athabascan People.* Among the stories in that report are several by Shem Pete; his "Whistler Story" is included here, with an introduction by Jim Fall.

J im Fall: Shem Pete's *"Shq'uła Tsukdu,"* or "The Whistler Story," is an example of a category of Dena'ina narratives called *dghelay'a tsukdu* (mountain stories). The circumstances under which the "Whistler Story" was recorded illustrate many aspects of Dena'ina storytelling and as such are important background for understanding the story itself. Shem first mentioned this story to me on October 24, 1978. We had been reviewing the Dena'ina names for furbearers, and I asked about the name for the "whistler" (the hoary marmot), *shq'uła.* Shem then revealed that there is a "groundhog story," and that he might tell me this story in the next day or so because I had become his and Billy's friend. He then proceeded to tell most or all of the story to Billy in Dena'ina, standing the whole time. This was, in essence, a rehearsal. Shem instructed me not to record the story then, because he thought he might tell it again soon.

Later that day, I purchased a supply of firewood for Billy and Shem. I transported the wood back to their cabin and split some of it. They were not home at the time, but they used some of the wood later that day.

When I returned the next morning, Shem was ready to tell me a story. After some discussion (in Dena'ina) between Billy and Shem about which one to tell, I mentioned the "Whistler Story" that Shem had told to Billy the day before. Shem agreed to record this story. Except for a Raven story and one about the origin of the Nulchina (sky) Clan, this was the first *tsukdu* that Shem told me. [Hoary marmots are nicknamed whistlers because of their distinctive call.]

I have always believed that Shem's choice of this story to tell me so early in my work with him was deliberate. I know of few other Dena'ina *tsukdu* that express so vividly and concisely so many of the values and themes that are central to Dena'ina culture, such as the rule of "nothing to excess" balanced with the desire of every Dena'ina to "get rich" and accumulating and then distributing wealth, the nature of partnership and friendship, and the reciprocity that exists between the human and nonhuman world. For a young person (and today, any person) wishing to understand the Dena'ina world, there is no better introduction than the *"Shq'uła Tsukdu."*

The text of the "Whistler Story" is presented here in a transcription by linguist Jim Kari of the original Dena'ina as Shem Pete told it and an English version based on Billy Pete's original translation. The reader will notice that occasionally, Shem inserted English words, phrases, or whole lines (sometimes to emphasize what he'd just said in Dena'ina). These have been retained. Involuntary repetitions and false starts have been deleted. Line breaks follow Shem's delivery as much as possible. Additions and explanations in brackets have been added sparingly to clarify the narrative flow for a non-Dena'ina audience.

It must be remembered that the story takes place in a different time and a different culture, when seasonal movements between the river valleys and the mountains were the norm, and when communication between the human and nonhuman world was direct and filled with consequences.

The reader will note that at one point, Billy Pete insisted that an episode be added to the text to make it "complete." This section clarifies, especially for non-Dena'ina, the nature of one partner's violation of cultural rules. Although this is part of the story, it is unlikely that its omission would be all that critical to a Dena'ina audience, who would know from the earlier exchange between the partners just what the man had done wrong.

Billy's suggestion that this portion of the story be inserted is not at all inconsistent with Dena'ina storytelling conventions. Shem Pete himself on several occasions recalled an episode of a tale after he'd finished his narration. He'd instruct me to turn on the tape recorder again. Then, he'd add the section and direct me to "splice" the new part in its proper location in the story. In 1988, Billy described traditional Dena'ina storytelling events as follows:

> *[Telling stories] was just like radio to those guys [the Dena'ina]. When they got lonesome, they told stories. Each evening they all went to one house. Each old guy told stories. And they'd ask each other, 'Am I telling the story right?' And they'd answer, 'Yes.' And he'd keep going. If he [the storyteller] thought he made a mistake, he'd stop, and they'd correct him. If he forgot one part, he'd stop and ask and they'd correct him and he'd go on. So the younger generation will know that story just the way it was told from the beginning. . . . The story was just like a book, from one generation to another, down to my father.*

37

Finally, an explanation might be useful about why the text is presented in both Dena'ina and English even though very few people can read Dena'ina today. It is important to remind readers that this is a story from the Dena'ina *oral* tradition which was told in Dena'ina in a particular style by a master of the art. If the interlinear printing or the line by line format bothers you, try reading the English version of the story out loud!

Nił'ida'ina.
[There were] two friends.

Nił'ida'ina ghuna dghelaych' q'anqudił łu.
Those two friends used to go up to the mountains [every year].

Ts'iłt'an ghunen, qunsha ghini, one hundred.
One of those men [always caught] one hundred of those parka squirrels.

Ts'ełq'i qunsha qeyełnih Dena'ina ghuna.
Those Dena'ina call [that many] "*ts'iłq'i qunsha.*"

One hundred again *nulyish.*
He brought one hundred back [to their camp] again.

Bida ghunhdi ighi shq'uła, shq'uła eight *nulyish.*
His friend used to bring eight whistlers back to their camp.

Everyday *dghelay qedił dghu.*
Everyday they went higher up into the mountains [from their camp].

Yaqech' tqet'an hnq'u qeba htaydlan. Ch'u.
They kept doing that until it was becoming fall time. And,

daha q'iłdu qilan nichił ey'un.
[then] they went back to where they had their *nichił* [a multifamily dwelling occupied in the lowlands in winter].

Yet nuhyilyash.
They brought back [everything they had killed].

Yehch'u t'qet'an hnuq'u.
They kept on doing that.

Dahdi hey q'adałchina dina?
How many years did they keep doing that?

Yethdi,
And then,

dida ghun dach' yełni,
[one partner] asked his friend this,

"Ohhhhh! Shq'uła chinł'ish tgheshuni."
"Ohhhhh! Let me go to where you catch whistlers."

"Eyyyyy!" yełni. "K'itigi nghe tihniłt'a."
"Eyyyyy!" his friend replied. "You're too greedy."

"Dach'u shi k'i k'ghe dunu'elggesh shit'i," yełni.
"I go into the animals' den," he [continued].

"K'eghe dunu'eshdush.
"I go into the animals' den.

"Ch'u,
"And,

"du'eltlet gheli ch'u,
"I run right in, and,

"shq'uła ghu tuchishnk'nałk'et' t'en'it'a.
"those whistlers' [skin] coats are all hanging there with a string through their noses.

"Ts'ełq'i ełyał gheli, ch'u
"I grab one right away, and

"shtunuhudelt'eh.
"I run away.

39

"Yutsen ghu hech' des'et hnuq'u łtaqil'i shq'uła łah.
"When I get outside, I throw [the skin] down hard and it becomes eight whistler [skins].

"Elghel ch'u shtunu'elggesh.
"I make a pack and I go away.

"Shi dach'u shq'uła chi'eł'ish shit'i."
"That's how I kill whistlers."

"Aa. Shihti yutsi ghu dinłeni gga dinłen ghu.
"Yes," [the other partner said]. "I go down to a little creek.

"Nilt'u tihqeshchet three times.
"I make little dams, three times.

"Tudeh nilt'u tihqeshchet, ch'u
"I make three little dams, and

"k't'un delggeyi ghini heni ghu tudeltl'et.
"I toss those white leaves in the water upstream of the uppermost dam.

"Uyakah nisheldeshtesh ch'u,
"I run ahead of the leaves, and,

"etl' gga beł idesges.
"I tear the [first] little dam down.

"Beł idesges.
"I tear it down.

"Het'u dghu ghini nich'tuydeyish hnuq'u yet kiq'u desges.
"When all the leaves drift down to the middle dam, I tear that one down next.

"Ch'u three 'eł k'ilani ghini tuq'i k'ilani ghudi,
"And when they drift down to that third dam,

"yet benisheldeshtesh ch'u,
"I run down there [to the third dam] and,

40

"bigheshchet tiy ch'a'idełtl'it'.
"I lift up the leaves with my cupped hands and throw them up on the bank.

"K't'un delggeya ghu, ghu yungge hech' tel-tl'it' hnuq'u qunsha ka'a denlggeyi yan łah.
"When I throw those white leaves up above the water line, they all become big white parka squirrels.

"Qunsha ka'a gheli yan łah. One hundred.
"They all become one hundred really big parka squirrels.

"Ts'ełq'i gheli elgheł." Ch'u
"I make one pack." And,

gudih niłghedeh nundashchuq' niłghedeh.
he had three rope belts and he stuck the little heads one above the other.

Qeyeł deseydalyu qeyghesan'ił'u t'qisih.
[In those days, people wore] rope belts around their waists and they had a rope across each shoulder [in order to carry things].

Jit gheli qeyeł nudish, dek'isna ghuna. Kiłqay ghuna k'a.
Those women had a hard time making it home with [that many squirrels].
Those men [had a hard time] too.

"Yaqech'u qunsha chiteł'isht'i yaqech' tghilah da," yełni.
He said, "That's the way I kill those ground squirrels. Do that too."

"Yagheli," yełni.
"OK," his partner said, [but continued]

"Eyyyy! Qil!
"Eyyyy! It's no good!

K'itigi nghe tihniłt'a."
You're too greedy."

Ch'q'u
And, [he said]

"K'itigi nghe tihniłt'a, tihniłt'a q'u qil" yełni.
"You're too greedy. But you are going to go there [anyway] and that's bad,"
he said.

"Yagheli."
[His partner replied, "It will be] OK."

"Ch'adach' niłtidaghilał."
"But you will gather up a whole bunch of them."

"Yeqech' gheli q'u tgheshnił."
"I'm going to do whatever you tell me."

"Yagheli," yełni.
"Good," he said.

Q'u
And then,

[Later, while translating the story, Billy Pete added the following section, which
he said Shem had inadvertently left out, but should be part of the story:]

when that man who normally caught ground squirrels was in the den,
with all the whistler skins hanging from the ceiling,
he took his time inside there.
He looked at all the furs hanging from the ceiling.
He wanted to pick out the prettiest one he could find.
He heard the rocks falling down behind him by the door (den entrance),
but he paid no attention.
Then, he turned around and looked.
The place was all closed from a rock slide,
and he couldn't get back out.

Qunsha ghini tiy ch'ayiniłtl'it'.
[The other partner] took all those white leaves [which turned into ground
squirrels] and dumped them on the bank.

Nuyidghan.
He packed them back [to their camp].

Yeghuslash.
He was skinning them.

Dida ghin yen'ił'en.
He was waiting for his friend.

Yen'ił'en ch'u,
He waited and,

nch'uk'a benuyidul.
[his partner] didn't come back.

Nughiłghatl' kiq'u.
It got dark again.

"Eyyyy! Shida ghun nch'uk'a nu'idul." Yethdi chegh.
"Eyyyy! My friend didn't come back," he said. And then he cried.

Nayul.
He camped there.

Sukan q'u yeh tayu.
The next morning he went [to where his partner had gone].

Yeh ch'aniyu iłti,
When he was approaching that place,

hdakaq' ghu qałnigi q'edesan.
[his friend] was standing on a rock by the entrance of the den.

K'idełtl'ish.
He's whistling.

K'idełyish.
He's whistling.
[Shem whistles] [He made a] whistling cry.
He stood up there [on the rock] looking for his friend.

Gu yatayuh hnuq'u qałnigi yenutl'udghulnen.
When his friend approached close to him, he jumped down under the rock.

Ch'u yet niniyu binitsaynitsiy.
And when his friend came over there, he stuck his head out from behind the rock and looked at him.

"Ida biłni det q'u qil.
"My friend, I'm dying for lack of water.

"I'm dying for water," *yełni.*
"I'm dying for water," he said.

"Biłni shetuyiqush," yełni.
"Carry water for me," he said.

Biłni nu'itqun.
His friend got water for him.

"Shi tsa t'enłtl'it," yełni.
"Pour it in the crack of the rock," he told his friend.

Ch'u,
And,

biłni ghini tsa t'esq'e eyeghiłtl'it'.
he poured that water in the crack in the rock.

Yutnun.
He drank the water.

Q'u,
Then,

"Nushghilkit nch'u t'eshnil," yełni.
"You can't get me back [because something happened to me]," he said.

Yequdulniqi iłti beghu k'dilan.
When he stuck his hand out, it was covered with fur already [for he was turning into a marmot].
It had fur on it already.

"Ch'adach' ghilahni du?"
"What can you do?" [said rhetorically]

"Ugha nutidush," yełni.
"Now go home [back to camp]," he told him.

"Dach' q'u qunushił'ał.
"Do this: trap me in a rock deadfall trap.

"Yi ał ch'du'ideseni tq'it'a.
"It looks like the deadfall traps will bother me.

"My backbone *ghini k'itigi denłney.*
"[The vertebrae of] my backbone [are] too long."

Ghu,
So,

"Shdghilt'as.
"You will roast me over a fire.

"Shdghit'as ch'u
"You will roast me over a fire and,

"shinch'i, shinch'i gheli shatinaghilkeł."
"you will gnaw the bones off right up to my backbone."

Ch'u,
And, [he continued,]

45

"Sts'ena ghini, sts'ena ghini,
"My bones, my bones,

"yaghelich't'a, itidaghiłtl'eł, ch'u
"build a fire well, and

"łuq'u gheli yusdich' bataghiłcheł ts'en ghini.
"you will throw all my bones in the fire.

"Ch'u bech'adasgeditu'uł ch'u dach' ch'in'e gu.
"And my bones are going to start smoking and the smoke will go upstream.

"Dghelay ken ghu sdasgeda ghini k'tayggey htunił.
"The smoke is going to be in two layers like a stream of clouds alongside of the mountain.

"Yagheli tghełah da.
"Then be happy.

"Yet daq'u nuggugganutgheshdlah yet," yełni.
"If you see smoke go like that, then [you'll know that] I'm going to come back as an animal again," he said.

"Q'udi ghu sheł tsadaltl'it' hnuq'u ughasht'a gheli tsenaghiltlut da.
"[When the trap springs and] there is the noise of the rocks falling in the trap, run right over there.

"K'echan ghin tidaghides, ch'u
"Take the grass and roll it up and twist it, and

"shgeł yichik'dghiłyił.
"stuff it down my throat.

"Ughasht'a gheli shyich' ghini uqustlagh gheli," yełni.
"Soon I won't breathe anymore," he told him.

"Yetdahdi nushitaghidghał. Ch'u,
"Then you will pack me [back to the camp]. And,

"sdghilt'as ch'u łuq'u gheli shtghilqat.
"you will roast me over a fire and eat me all up.

"Sts'ena ghini,
"Those bones of mine [the vertebrae],

"sts'ena ghini qil gheli shyenghuga ghini.
"chew up all those bones of mine right up to my backbone.

"Satinaghilkeł.
"Gnaw them up.

"Q'u sts'ena ghinhti yusdich' batghiłcheł itidaghiłtl'eł.
"Take my bones and build a fire and put my bones in the fire.

"Sdasgeda ghini dghelaych' dghelay teł k'tayggey dahdi,
"When my smoke flows in a line like a stream around the mountains,

"neł yagheli nuqudlahda,
"you'll become happy,

"ninya quht'ana gheli nutgheshdlah."
"because I'm going to become an animal person again."

Nuyidghan. Ch'u,
[After trapping him,] he packed him back to camp. And,

ideyes ch'adingits'.
he pealed his hide off [like a rabbit skin].

Yeh q'u shq'uła iydlan, his friend ghunen.
That friend of his had really become a whistler.

Ch'u,
And,

ideyes ich'aydingits' yus hnik'eyeghiłyel.
he pealed the skin off him and put him at the end of a stick and put him by the fire.

Idalt'a.
He roasted him.

Idalt'a ch'q'u łuq'u suyult'eq'.
He roasted him and he ate him all up.

Its'ena ghini, nułtu idiłq'un yudeh dghelay q'e.
He packed his bones back up the mountain.

Inułtu nuydiłq'un ch'u deseydghilu.
He built a fire and put his bones in the fire.

Hnuq'u łet,
When his bones started burning,

bedasgeda ghini dghelayte beł k'tayggey.
that smoke of his drifted alongside the mountains in two layers.

Yet'u beł idghinich' t'ejuq.
It happened just as [his partner had] told him it would.

Beł yagheli.
He became happy.

"Ida, quht'ana nusdlan niyen," ch'u yagheli jitshlaq'u nugisdlan.
"My friend has become a person again," [he said] and he got a little happy again.

Yet yudeh hnuq'u,
Then, he just stayed up there by himself,
I don't know [for how long].

Q'u nuhtedeł hqugh nihdalnen.
It was becoming time for them to come home [to their *nichił* or winter dwelling].

Yenu'iju ch'u "q'u" yełni.
He went back to that rock and he told his friend, "Goodbye."

Ch'u
And [he said]

"Yutsen. Down the hill *nutgheshjuł, łitl'en qech'u."*
"I'm going to go home now down the hill, until spring."
[Long pause]

Niłnuqutnak ch'u,
They talked to each other and,

nu'iju deyan q'u.
he went home [to the camp] by himself.
"I'm lonesome," [he thought].

Beł qil qilan.
He didn't feel happy at all.

Hghu'u hu tets didaghiset ch'u itułqun hech' q'a qahałdeltles, qahałdeltles.
All night long and at dawn, there were the sounds of big bunches of packs dropping outside [of his shelter].

Q'u,
And then,

qahałdetnesh q'u.
there was the noise of packs dropping down.

[Billy Pete explains here that the marmot people *(shq'uła dnay)* are paying the man back with gifts for the service he had performed for his partner.]

"T'qidaghiłkegh."
"There's lots of room out there," [he said].

Ch'u,
And, [he said]

"Yeh qugh ni'ełdeł hech' ba'echet."
"Just keep putting the stuff out there."

49

Q'ut'en gga'ilnigi ełti ghu'uh gheli ghu nuchunhday'u gheli tq'ijuq.
When he got up in the morning, there was a big pile of all kinds of goods out there.

Tał ghinhdi yada ghudehdi shq'uła ghudehdi.
Lots of caribou skins and lots of whistler skins.

Shq'uła ch'da ghudehi shq'uła dghak.
Whistler blankets, and whistler coats.
Caribou skins and caribou meat.

Ch'u,
And,

nudebu t'yił'an nudebu łuq'u deqtuyinilu.
there was a big pile of goods and he kept relaying and relaying things down to the timberline.

Ch'u,
And,

ghun ghu yeh nuyilyash, nuyilyash ch'u qeynunastun shit'a.
that man kept packing and packing the stuff back [to the *nichił*], and [the people of his village] helped him.

Ch'u heyi gheli idałt'ay hqugh k'tsen.
It was enough meat for the whole winter.

Niniłkit.
He put up enough.

Dach' łu juq łu.
That's the way it was.
Billy: I believe he made a potlatch [a memorial feast] for him.
Shem: I think so. He potlatched all winter, I think.

All right. *Udakaq' qak'ninłggat.*
All right. Shut off the tape recorder.
Billy: He says that's good enough.

50

Part II

Early Explorations

4

Discoveries in Alaska

by William A. Dickey

The earliest people to bestow an English name upon the continent's tallest peak and estimate its height were not surveyors, map makers, geologists, or government-sponsored explorers, but prospectors. In 1889, the story goes, a party of gold seekers led by Frank Densmore enjoyed spectacular views of Denali from Lake Minchumina, to the north. Densmore so fervently praised the mountain's majesty that others began calling it "Densmore's Mountain." Densmore's connection to the great peak would prove to be a short-lived, local phenomenon, overshadowed eight years later by the exuberance and reporting skills of a New Hampshire-born, Princeton-educated prospector, William A. Dickey.

After graduation from college in 1885, Dickey migrated west to Seattle, where he dabbled in real estate, played baseball, opened an ill-fated grocery business, and worked in banking. In 1896, having failed to make his fortune in those endeavors, he went in search of Alaskan gold. Reaching the Cook Inlet region ("Cooks Inlet" to Dickey) in May, Dickey's party spent several months exploring the lands and waters south of the Alaska Range. Returning to the Lower 48, he wrote an account of his adventures that ran in a New York newspaper, *The Sun*. Besides (re)naming Mount McKinley, he also confidently proclaimed it the highest peak in North America and guessed it to be "over 20,000 feet high." Though mountaineering historians now laud Dickey for his remarkably accurate estimate, the prospector himself admitted that several other groups he encountered also believed the mountain to be more than 20,000 feet high.

By most accounts, Dickey's choice of names was a highly political one. During his Alaska travels, he apparently met prospectors who zealously promoted Democratic presidential candidate William Jennings Bryan's idea of free silver. He retaliated by naming the mountain after Republican candidate William McKinley of Ohio, champion of the gold

Previous page: Denali National Park, Moose Creek area, clearing storm   (© Pat O'Hara)

standard. Whatever his reasons, Dickey's chosen name, popularized by *The Sun*, has stuck despite numerous attempts to change it.

Besides naming the mountain and estimating its height, Dickey gives a strong sense of the landscape and physical hardships—from voracious mosquitoes to nearly impenetrable brush and dangerous river travel—that early explorers and Athabascan residents of the region had to endure. He also provides some revealing glimpses into the lives of Native Alaskans. It may be noted that several place names in Dickey's story have been officially renamed or are now spelled differently—Mount McKinley being a notable exception.

William Dickey's article, "Discoveries in Alaska (1896)," first appeared in the New York newspaper, *The Sun,* on Jan. 24, 1897, and was later reprinted in its entirety in the 1951 *American Alpine Journal.*

■

The largest unexplored region in the United States is the district north of Cooks Inlet, Alaska. The Kuskokwim and Nushagak flowing into Behring Sea, the Tanana into the Yukon, the Sushitna into Cooks Inlet, and the Copper River into the Gulf of Alaska drain this "terra incognita." They are all large, muddy rivers, draining great glaciers, and are at flood height throughout the short summer season. The difficulty of making headway against such swift streams, the clouds of gnats and mosquitoes, the reputed fierceness of the interior Indians (the Apaches of the north) have all served to keep out both the explorer and that most venturesome of all investigators, the prospector.

The discovery of paying placer mines on Cooks Inlet in the fall of 1895 brought about 2,000 prospectors to its shores last summer. They swarmed over Kenai Peninsula, staking out claims in the deep snow, and the surplus ventured into the Kiuk and Sushitna valleys, both unexplored districts. Over one hundred parties entered the Sushitna River, but only five attained any great distance up the river. One party provisioned for two years proclaimed that they were prepared to ascend the Sushitna to its source, and if they found nothing there they would go on to the Tanana; if still unsuccessful, they would keep on northward to the Arctic Ocean. In five days they were on their way back, saying they thought there must be some easier way to the North Pole. Another party gave up the attempt after nearly losing their lives, their boat, driven by the swift current, jerking them off the bank from which they were towing. One young man from Boston turned back after he and his mate had been about a week on the river without reaching the station, giving as a reason his unwillingness to prospect a country where he was obliged to tie up his head in a gunny sack every night in order to escape the mosquitoes.

We landed at Tyonick, near the head of Cooks Inlet, the first week in May 1896, in about two feet of snow, thick blocks of ice lining the shores, and awaited the opening of the Sushitna. Our object in prospecting the Sushitna was the hope of finding placer mines on its upper waters. There were several reasons leading to this conclusion. One of the most important was that anywhere on the shores of Cooks Inlet a few colors of fine gold could be found. Probably this gold came from the largest stream entering the inlet; then the Copper River, rising in the same district, was reputed to be rich in gold and copper.

Cooks Inlet is like the Bay of Fundy. It is shallow, with high, swift tides, the extreme being about sixty-five feet. It is often visited by violent storms, so violent that the natives pack many miles along its beach rather than venture out in boats.

Starting in an open dory, with the incoming tide, we reached the broad mud flats extending some fifteen miles from the mouth of the Sushitna. All night and a greater portion of the next day we spent on the flats hunting for the entrance to the river, for the Sushitna, like many Arctic rivers, has quite an extensive delta, which, with its network of channels, is eight or ten miles wide. Inside the entrance, the swift current, low, muddy, and caving banks, covered with thick brush and cottonwood trees, render progress very difficult. On all sides are the traces of great floods, the entire country for miles being subject to overflow. Many unable with oars to stem the mighty flood have given up the struggle before reaching the trading post thirty miles above tidewater on the river.

The river at the station has two channels: the eastern as measured on the ice is 855 yards wide, and flows swift and deep from shore to shore; the other channel is nearly as large, but not so swift and deep. Just above are the first high banks, perpendicular promontories of rock on each side, against which the stream rushes with great force. Whirlpools in the current seemed to threaten to engulf our boat, but as suddenly as they form they disappear, and we crossed in safety. Finding our sea dory too heavy to handle, we stopped at the station long enough to whipsaw lumber and make two river boats, such as are used on the Yukon, twenty-five feet in length over all, eighteen inches wide on the bottom, and forty inches at the top. Not having any tar, we pitched the seams with spruce gum and grease. Our equipment consisted of paddles, poles, and tow lines.

While building the boats we witnessed the annual run of candle fish, a species of smelt so fat that when dried they will burn like a candle. The natives stand on the bank with rude dips made of willow roots and catch quantities of them, which are dried on long racks in the sun. Indeed, the river was so full of the fish that it was impossible to dip a bucket of water without catching some of the little beauties. The lean Eskimo dogs put on a layer of fat during candle fish season. They stand on the bank and expertly paw the fish out of the water.

A short distance above the station a great branch comes in from the west. The Indians say that this branch runs around the head of Cooks Inlet and rises in a high range of mountains which we had seen from Tyonick. Above this fork the river again spreads out into many channels, so that it is difficult to tell where to go, the low banks affording no clue as to the probable main course of the river. Twenty miles farther along another large branch comes in from the west, the main river bearing almost due north. For two weeks we travelled amid islands and sloughs, the river at times several miles wide across its many channels.

On the east were the mountains that form the watershed between the Knik and Sushitna valleys, a low but rugged range from 3,000 to 6,000 feet in altitude. From these mountains several small rivers flow into the Sushitna, but they did not prospect as well as the main stream, which gave us from six to 200 colors per pan, it being almost impossible to get a pan which did not have some colors.

Several days of heavy rain, which carried off the snow still reaching almost to the river's banks, raised the stream to flood height, and further progress was for the time being impossible. The driftwood ran in a continuous stream, and the river rose until we had to move our camp. It seemed as though the whole country was to be submerged, when, as suddenly as the rise, the river commenced to fall, and after a week's delay we resumed our trip on the swollen stream. The first day we made only two miles, though we worked desperately hard, a part of the time in the icy water up to our waists, crossing and recrossing the channels. We were even obliged to unload our boats, take them out of the water, and carry them overland across islands to avoid places where great jams of driftwood, acting as wing dams, rendered the channels we were in impassable. The river here was full of cottonwood snags, around which the current rushes in great swirls, very dangerous to a boat. Where we could, we waded and towed our boats, relying on our quickness to cross safely the treacherous quicksands into which we frequently sank to our knees; at one place we actually lost one of our long poles, which was held so firmly in the quicksand that we could not pull it out.

The mosquitoes hung in clouds above us, compelling the constant use of veils and gloves. Even the Indians on this river wear cheese cloth veils over their faces. At night we pitched our tents low, sewed the entrance up tight, pulling the sides and ends under a canvas flooring on which we made our beds. Each of us taking a corner of the tent, we could kill off the mosquitoes that had come in with us as we crawled under the flap, and then sleep in peace. Luckily in June the days are so long that it is never too dark to see to kill mosquitoes.

On the clearing up of the weather we obtained our first good view of the great mountain, occasional glimpses of which we had had before, the first from near Tyonick, where we saw its cloud-like summit over Sushitna Mountain. This mountain is far in the interior from Cooks Inlet, and almost due north of Tyonick. All the Indians of Cooks Inlet call it the "Bulshoe" Mountain, which is their word for anything very large. As it now appeared to us, its huge peak towering far above the high, rugged range encircling its base, it compelled our unbounded admiration. On Cooks Inlet we had seen Iliamna's still smoking summit, 12,066 feet above us, rising precipitously from the salt water. Inland is a continuation of the same range, and even higher, probably 14,000 to 15,000 feet in altitude. On Puget Sound for years we had been admirers of Mount Rainier, over 14,000 feet high, but never before had we seen anything to compare with this mountain. My companion in the boat, Mr. Monks, was one of the few who made the ascent of Rainier the previous summer. In his opinion Rainier was about the same altitude as the range this side of the huge peak, which towered at least at least 6,000 feet above its neighbors. For days we had glorious views of this mountain range, many of whose glaciers emptied apparently into our river.

July 4 was ushered in with a heavy rain. While we were encamped waiting for the storm to pass over, a great rumbling proclaimed the approach of an earthquake, which was very violent and of considerable duration. This, the second violent earthquake since our arrival in this country, the high volcanoes still active, the great tides, the huge mountains covered with glaciers, impressed us that here man must indeed battle with nature. In fact, this whole country seems new, unfinished, unfit for the habitation of man. Few and scattered are the Indians who have the hardihood to withstand the severe winters and the many pests that make the short summer almost unbearable.

According to our journal, 100 miles above the trading station, the river again forked, this time into three branches. The branch from the northwest apparently drains the southern slope of the great range, and like a flowing sea of mud spreads out in many channels about two miles wide. The branch from the northeast is as white as milk, while the middle stream, which we concluded was the main river, was nearly clear. This last river had good towing banks, and but few channels, and we soon entered a narrow valley almost a canyon, between the mountains, which now enclosed us on both sides. As-cending one of the highest of these that stood out into the valley, we had a splendid view of the river valley below, and solved a question which had previous given us much study, namely, why such large branches came in from the west, where the Government chart of Alaska shows a great range of mountains.

The fact is, there is no range there, but a broad, flat valley extended west-ward as far as the eye could reach, heavily timbered with spruce and birch. It is apparently a continuation of the flat country that surrounds the upper por-tion of Cooks Inlet. I should estimate the dimensions of this valley as being nearly 100 miles each way. In the south, Mount Sushitna, some 5,000 or 6,000 feet high, marked the mouth of the river. In the east was the rugged but low range that separated us from the Kiuk Valley. In the northeast was an apparent gap in the range, through which our river ran, and whose course we could trace for thirty or forty miles. In the northwest was the greatest range of moun-tains we had ever seen, of which the great mountain previously mentioned was the culminating point.

We were amazed at the fine growth of grass, which in the short time since the snow had been gone, had attained a height of nearly four feet. In any open glade one could make most excellent hay. It is hard to understand why, with such fine feed in a country so sparsely inhabited, there are no more moose or reindeer. Perhaps it is due to the rigorous climate and the abundance of fierce timber wolves and a large brown bear as large and dangerous as the Rocky Mountain grizzly.

The river now had many boulders and rapids. On one side we passed a high bank in which were seams of coal of fair quality, eight or ten feet thick, to which a steamer could extend its gangplank and get a load with pick and wheelbarrow. After passing this coal formation the river entered a long series of canyons with slate walls. Back of these, some seven or eight miles, were low granite mountains. Some of this granite is a rich green, the most beautiful I have ever seen. About seventy miles from the great forks we came to a small village of the Kuilchau, or Copper River Indians, tall and fine looking, and great hunters. Throughout the long and arduous winter they camp on the trail of the caribou. They build huge fires of logs, then erect a reflector of skins back from the fire, between which reflector and the fire they sleep, practically out of doors, although the temperature reaches 50° below zero. We were sur-prised to find them outfitted with cooking stoves, planes, saws, axes, knives,

57

sleds sixteen feet in length, 1894 model rifles, etc. They were encamped near a fish trap which they had constructed across a small side stream, and were catching and drying red salmon. They had no permanent houses, living in Russian tents, with the entrance arranged like our own to keep out the gnats and mosquitoes. They informed us that we could go no farther with our boats, as the Sushitna now entered an impassable canon, whose upper end was blocked by a high waterfall. "Bulshoe!" they exclaimed, raising both hands high above their heads.

As the small side river on which they had their traps prospected well, we followed it for some distance, until it ran into a canon, where further progress was impossible without a long and hard detour over a mountainside.

One of the Indians undertook to show us the portage around the falls on the main river, but finding the path very steep and difficult, dangerous even to carry our packs, we gave up the attempt without seeing the falls, which must be very high, from the appearance of the canon and surrounding country.

The river at the highest point we reached was about 200 yards across, deep from shore to shore, with a millrace current. From the maps which the Indians made for us of the continuation of the river above the falls, we inferred that it ran a long distance to the northeast, probably from 150 to 200 miles, though none of the natives had been to its source. The Kuilchaus, who trade at the Kiuk station of the Alaska Commercial Company, say that some of the tribes live on a lake that empties into the headwaters of Copper River, and the balance on a lake not far distant, in which the Sushitna rises, and that it is only a short portage from either lake into the Tanana.

At all events, from the size of the Sushitna at the falls and from its direction it must flow nearly from the Copper River. Other prospectors who ascended the muddy western branch informed us that about forty miles from the great forks it branched, one stream flowing northward around the base of the great range from whose many glaciers it receives several tributaries: the other, flowing west, drains the southern side of the great range, finally turning back into the flat valley that runs a long way to the west. From a mountain top they could trace its course in the flat country for many miles. To the north they could see a stream apparently flowing west, which they thought was the Kuskokwim. One glacier at the forks came down almost to the river's bank and was the source of a large stream. They could trace the glacier far back toward the great mountain.

Unable to pass the falls on the main river we turned down the stream to the great forks. It was very exciting and dangerous running the rapids among the big boulders, the race-horse speed at which we travelled giving us no time to examine the river ahead. The boiling waves several times entered our boats, and we were constantly on the jump to keep them from swamping. We could make a greater distance down the stream in an hour than we could up in a day.

We ascended the western branch nearly to the canon, where we met a party of prospectors coming down. Their boat, which they were towing, had been dragged by the swift current under a snag and upset, and they lost all their outfit. They reported the canon ahead impassable, owing to the high water in the river. Two weeks of almost continual rain raised all the river to flood height. Our provisions being low, and one of the party being sick, we reluctantly turned back to the station, which we reached in two days. We ascended Mount Sushitna near the mouth of the river and confirmed our previous observations on the upper river, namely, the extent of the broad, flat country, and the total absence of the great Alaska range as marked on the Government charts of Alaska.

We named our great peak Mount McKinley, after William McKinley of Ohio, who had been nominated for the Presidency, and that fact was the first news we received on our way out of that wonderful wilderness. We have no doubt that this peak is the highest in North America, and estimate that it is over 20,000 feet high. We have talked with seven different parties who saw the mountain this summer, and they estimate its height at over 20,000 feet. Most of them think it is nearly 25,000 feet in altitude. Our last view of its towering summit was from one of the tideland islands at the mouth of the Sushitna. Here on a glorious evening we had a fine view of Iliamna, 100 miles south, and Mount McKinley, to the north. Field glasses brought out the details on Iliamna, but made no change in the appearance of Mount McKinley, which was nearly twice the distance away. Notwithstanding its greater distance, Mount McKinley looked much the higher of the two peaks.

Much interested in the geography of this country, and finding the Government charts so unreliable, we gathered all the information possible from the Indians and the few whites who had, during the summer, prospected on the upper river. The Kuilchaus drew for me a map of the river, holding the pencil by the extreme end, and much amused with their first experience with pencils and paper. When they reached as far in the drawing as they had ever been on the river, they drew their pencil around back and shook their heads, and we could not get them to venture any further opinion as to the river beyond. Their only way of estimating distances was by sleeps, as they had no conception of what a mile was; in fact, they did not know what the words Indian or white signified.

One of the Kiuk tribe, an intelligent and prosperous Indian who trades with the interior Indians and who travels every winter in the interior country, drew a map showing the relation of the upper Copper, Sushitna and Tanana rivers. He makes, as do all the interior Indians, the three rivers in close proximity at their headwaters.

We found colors of fine gold in nearly every pan, and on the upper river platinum. The formation for the last forty miles below the falls was slate porphyry and granite, many veins of white quartz running through the slate. One specimen assaying well in silver, copper and gold would be very valuable were it nearer means of transportation or in a less rigorous climate.

The natives on Cooks Inlet are devout Greek Catholics. Every village has its church and even the Copper River Indians fear the priests. Last winter some of the Copper River Indians who came down to trade at the Kiuk station had several wives. This the Greek priest said was wrong, and ordered them to put away all but the woman they had married first. Too superstitious to refuse, the Indians sent their extra wives away, but on the departure of the priest for other parishes the banished wives, who had only retired a short distance, promptly returned to their former lords.

Many Indians were killed or seriously wounded by the great brown bear, which they hold in great respect. They never bring in the head or claws, although they would bring higher prices at the store with them left on the skin. At Kuskutan last spring a hunter did not return to the village after his daily trips of inspection to his traps. The next morning another brave, axe in hand, went to search for him. He also failed to return, and the next day the whole village went in search of the missing. They found nothing except the axe and huge bear tracks. A few days later an enormous bear chased some of the natives to their very doors, notwithstanding the many wounds inflicted by the rifles of the pursued. After that he hung about the village, and although shot many times he would soon return. Just after dark one evening, he suddenly appeared at a window at one of the cabins, smashed in the glass, and gave the lamp standing inside a knock that sent it across the room. Without further ceremony the monster proceeded to climb into the room. Luckily all escaped through the door, and the men finally drove the bear away with no further damage than the wrecking of the furniture. All were now afraid, for surely this must be an evil spirit or shaman and not an ordinary bear, as bullets seemed to have no effect on him. As a last resort they took some bullets to the church, had special prayers recited and holy water sprinkled over them; then they marched three times around the church, carrying the sacred candles and praying for deliverance from the shaman. The next time the bear appeared one of the holy bullets found a mortal spot, and the huge bear came crashing to the earth. "God killed the bear and not our bullets," cried the old chief who told us the story, as he reverently stood with hands uplifted. I counted thirty-two holes in the hide he showed us; one hole in the head undoubtedly did the work.

Some idea of the remoteness of Cooks Inlet can be gained by the fact that it was more than seven weeks from the time we commenced our homeward voyage before we finally reached Seattle, much benefited by our summer's outing in unexplored Alaska.

5

An Exploration to Mount McKinley, America's Highest Mountain

by Alfred H. Brooks

Not long after he had graduated from Harvard College, Alfred Brooks was living in Paris and studying at the Sorbonne when officials of the U.S. Geological Survey (USGS) invited him on the adventure of a lifetime: Come to Alaska, they urged, and help us map that vast and still largely unknown territory. Brooks joined the USGS for the 1898 field season and spent his next four summers in Alaska's eastern regions. In 1902, now a veteran of subarctic wilderness travel, Brooks was selected to lead a geological mapping and survey crew from Cook Inlet, across the Alaska Range, to the Yukon River. With six other men and twenty pack horses, Brooks launched his 800-mile journey on June 2 from the Athabascan village of Tyonek—then spelled Tyonok—located on the inlet's western shores, across from present-day Anchorage. (In 1902, Anchorage's birth as a railroad tent city was still more than a decade away.)

Despite a variety of hardships—mosquitoes and river-crossings proved especially troublesome—the team kept to its schedule and reached the Yukon in mid-September, just in time to catch the season's last steamship to the coast. Along the way, Brooks became the first person in recorded history to set foot on Denali.

Later named the survey's chief Alaskan geologist, Brooks wrote several stories about his 1902 expedition, including a detailed USGS professional paper, published in 1911, and a January 1903 article for *National Geographic,* titled "Plans for Climbing Mt. McKinley." In that five-page story, Brooks outlined three possible approaches to the mountain. He preferred the northern route, using supplies cached near the mountain's base during the preceding winter and spring. From firsthand experience, he knew that any attempt from Cook Inlet would require too much time and effort during the trek to Denali's base. Brooks's vision proved correct. Of nine Denali expeditions staged over the next decade, those approaching from the south exhausted themselves, their time, or supplies before making any serious summit try. But teams attacking from the north side would pioneer a route that eventually led to the mountain's first ascent.

"An Exploration to Mount McKinley, America's Highest Mountain" is the best account of the daily challenges that the 1902 expedition faced; it is also here that Brooks describes in detail his own historic hike onto Denali's lower slopes. The article, presented here in shortened form, originally appeared in the November 1903 edition of *The Journal of Geography* (Volume II, No. 9).

A laska's southern shoreline makes a broad, crescentic sweep embracing that part of the northern Pacific known as the Gulf of Alaska. Of the many indentations which give this coast its jagged outline the largest is Cook Inlet, a deep embayment in the western arm of the crescent, which stretches northward for 150 miles from the headlands marking its entrance. There it receives the turbid waters of the Sushitna River, laden with the silt of glaciers which have their source in the great Alaskan Range lying northwest of the valley.

This Alaskan Range curves in a rugged mass around the headwaters of the Sushitna, forming the divide between the Cook Inlet drainage on the south and the waters flowing into Bering Sea through the Kuskokwim and Yukon rivers on the north. The southern end of the range lies in an unexplored region to the west of Cook Inlet, but probably does not include any peaks over 7,000 or 8,000 feet high. Towards the north its relief increases, culminating in Mt. McKinley, over 20,000 feet in altitude, and the highest mountain on the North American continent.

Strange as it may seem, though this mountain has been known to white men for upwards of a century—it is plainly visible from tidewater at Cook Inlet and from many points in the Yukon Basin—yet until very recent years it did not appear on any map and was barely referred to in literature. When the famous navigator, Captain Cook, in 1778 spent a few weeks exploring the inlet which now bears his name, the clouds hung low, or the mountain would not have escaped his attention. Vancouver, fifteen years later, while extending Cook's surveys in the Inlet, probably also had no view of it, though he distinctly mentions the range. [In his journal, Vancouver did, however, mention "distant stupendous mountains covered with snow, and apparently detached from one another." Historians now generally believe he referred to Denali and its companion peak, 17,400-foot Mount Foraker.] The Russians, who carried on their fur trade on this coast for over half a century, knew the

mountain and called it "Bulshaia," which like the native name "Trolika," signified "high mountain"; but Russian literature on Alaska, so far as we know,
contains no reference to this important geographical feature. Lieutenant Henry
T. Allen, too, who in 1885 made his hazardous exploration of the lower Tanana,
saw this peak, but at so great a distance that he was not specially impressed
with its altitude.

Thus it was that explorers and traders did not seem to be aware that they had
sighted the highest peak on the continent. When, in 1895, scores of prospectors
were attracted to Cook Inlet by the discovery of gold, they too saw the mountain, but apparently gave it no thought until the following year, when one of
them (a man named Dickey) recognized its importance and upon his return
published a description of it and proposed the name Mt. McKinley. Though the
mountain had been known to white men for over a century, and though scores
of others had been as near it as this prospector, or nearer, he was termed the
discoverer of Mt. McKinley. All honor to him for calling attention to it, but let
us not make the absurd blunder of crediting him with its discovery.

Two years after the naming of the mountain, George H. Eldridge and Robert Muldrow, of the U.S. Geological Survey, in the course of their exploration
of the Sushitna River, located it accurately and determined its altitude at over
20,000 feet. Its height and position were thus known, and something of the
character of the southern flank of the range above which it towers. The northern face of the range and the base of the mountain remained to be explored, and
this was the task assigned to me as part of the general system of exploratory
surveys undertaken by the Geological Survey in Alaska. I was fortunate in
having as associates in this enterprise Messrs. D.L. Reaburn and L.M. Prindle,
as well as four able and enthusiastic camp men.

On May 27th, 1902, the vessel bearing our party slowly steamed up Cook
Inlet. Hardly a ripple stirred the water, and through the hazy atmosphere we
could barely discern the outline of the low coast, beyond which, in a bank of
clouds, lay the high mountain range which we were to explore. At noon we
dropped anchor at Tyonok, a small native settlement on the west shore of the
Inlet with one trading post and a white population of half-a-dozen men.

We were forced to wait until the evening tide floated a large scow destined
to convey our horses to the shore. These, in spite of much struggling and kicking
on their part, were then unceremoniously hoisted out of the hold and dropped
over the side into the scow.

The important question was which route should be chosen to the base of
the mountains, for the crossing of the swampy and heavily timbered lowland
area which intervened presented the most serious difficulties. The agent of

the trading company, who was first interrogated, was rather skeptical of the proposed plans; and well he might be, for he had seen more than one exploring expedition start out with high hopes only to return disappointed a few months later. Should we go westward directly toward the mountains, our northeasterly course along the base of the range would be blocked by glaciers; should we take a more northerly course we would become lost in a maze of swamps and encounter a number of turbulent rivers. Such were the stories told by the white men, and the Indians, who were assembled in solemn conclave, were equally discouraging.

Our observations finally prompted us to choose the northwesterly route, as the shortest; other conditions being about equal, or at least equally impossible to foresee. To facilitate the crossing of the large rivers which were known to lie athwart our route to the mountains, a boat was sent ahead in charge of George Eberhardt and Louis Anderson, both experienced in frontier life and, as the event proved, eminently reliable men. We decided not to use Indian guides, in spite of the advice of the Tyonok sages, both because of the Indian's ignorance of horses and for the reason that his insatiable appetite for white men's stores makes him an undesirable addition to a party when the transportation of supplies is the difficult problem.

The adequate provisioning of a party like ours is the most important feature of the preparation. If the allowance of food is insufficient, the journey has to be curtailed, or risk of starvation encountered. On the other hand, if a greater quantity is taken than necessary, it may hamper the transportation facilities and result in failure to the expedition. A proper variety of food is also imperative, for on this will depend the health and strength of the party. The accumulated experience of five years of Alaskan travel enabled us to judge the proportions to a nicety. Practically nothing but dried foods were chosen: the staples, flour, bacon, beans, sugar, and evaporated fruit, were supplemented by farinaceous foods, cheese, evaporated eggs and potatoes, condensed soups, together with tea, coffee and a few pounds of delicacies such as macaroni and jelly. Our ration provided three pounds of food per man each day, an ample allowance if no canned goods are taken.

The provisions, sufficient to feed seven men for 105 days, were packed in fifty-pound waterproof bags. As for the rest of the equipment, everything was chosen with a view to lightness, the tents weighing only a few pounds and carbines being carried instead of rifles. Sleeping bags were substituted for blankets because they give a maximum of warmth for a minimum of weight. The entire equipment weighed about 3,500 pounds, of which 1,000 pounds were sent by boat and the rest distributed among the twenty horses.

As all our preparations were now completed and the grass was sufficiently advanced to insure an ample supply of feed for the horses, we set out from Tyonok on June 2nd.

At the outset our experience was a hard one. The horses were fresh and some of them objected seriously to the heavy burdens. Again and again they bucked their packs off and stampeded the entire herd. Our baggage was scattered to the four winds of heaven, and pieces had to be sought for carefully in the long grass which covered the upper part of the beach.

The task before us was to find a route across the swampy lowland, traverse the mountains, and following their northern front, approach from the inland slope as near the base of this culminating peak of the continent as conditions and means would permit; we must map the country and incidentally explore a route which some time could be used by that mountaineer to whom should fall the honor of first setting foot on the summit of Mt. McKinley.

At the Beluga River the course ran inland, and by good fortune an Indian trail lightened the labor of the axemen to a great extent. But it was designed for use in the fall and winter, when the ground was frozen; and its many bogs, which then only served to facilitate traveling, now caused our horses one long struggle to wallow through it with their heavy burdens. Almost continuously one or more of the animals became mired, and often the entire strength of the seven members of the party was required to drag them out.

A week after leaving tidewater, we emerged from the lowlands into a belt of foothills covered for the most part with tall grass, interspersed with symmetrical spruces and open groves of poplar. The landscape had a park-like appearance not unlike some of the farming regions of the East. The many familiar wild flowers added to the delusion, and it was hard to realize that we were in one of the unexplored parts of the world, for it seemed as if every rise of ground must bring us to the sight of a farm house with its fields and orchards.

As we climbed higher we left all timber behind us except the omnipresent willow and alder thickets. The horses revelled in an abundance of grass, while the camp larder was improved by the ptarmigan which were shot along our line of march. Another glimpse of Mt. McKinley enabled Reaburn, our topographer, to determine our location accurately.

The daily routine was now well established. All hands were called at five in the morning, and while the packers drove in the horses the others took down the tents. When the horses had been saddled and breakfast had been eaten, we all took a hand in the packing. It was no easy task to lift the 200-pound packs to the backs of the horses and adjust them. Nearly all of the men were now fairly expert at lashing them in place—"throwing the diamond hitch," as it is called. After two hours of hard work spent in this operation, the march began. In a timbered region two or three axemen preceded the train, but in the open country this was not necessary. Camp was made between three and four, and after an early supper the geologist and topographer usually made an excursion to some neighboring peak or valley.

In this foothill region we came in contact with our first bear. Fred, while forging ahead of the party in search of a trail, came upon a she-bear and cub. The old one at once charged. Hemmed in by alder thickets, with an axe as his only weapon, he faced his assailant with what seemed, even to an old hunter like himself, hardly a fighting chance for life. Fortunately, however, the Kodiak grizzly, though larger, is not so ferocious as his Rocky Mountain brother, and Fred made his escape, though the animal approached within a few feet of him.

The good traveling came to an end all too soon, and we plunged into the thick growth of timber covering the floor of the Yentna Valley. When on June 18th we reached the banks of that river, the turbulent silt-bearing waters, coursing through a score of channels, did not look inviting, and we had grave doubts whether a crossing could be made. It must be attempted, however, as it would save a week's time. Mounted on two of the stronger horses, from which the saddles had been stripped, Fred and I managed to ford some of the streams, though the horses barely kept their footing in the rushing waters which reached their shoulders. There still remained several of the widest channels. The unwilling animals were urged into the first of these and in a moment were swept off their feet by the muddy torrent, which for an instant engulfed both riders and horses and bore them down stream at a terrific rate. By an almost instinctive movement, we threw ourselves from the struggling brutes, seized them by their manes and swam alongside, thus at length guiding them back to the bank. We dragged ourselves out, both we and the horses shivering from our ducking in the icy waters. The plunge was but one of many similar incidents of the journey before us, but it was more significant, in that it showed the impossibility of making a crossing at this point without taking serious risks.

So perforce we headed down stream and spent weary days cutting a trail through the dense growth on the riverbank; until on the fourth day a welcome rifle shot told us that we were near the rendezvous with the men and boat. With the aid of these we at last succeeded in crossing the river. As it was, the passage occupied an entire day, and was not without its dangers to the horses, who had to be towed across behind the boat, in imminent risk of drowning in the eight-mile current, which at times carried them under water.

After agreeing upon a third rendezvous, the land party continued its trail-chopping and corduroy-building. This was the most disheartening part of the whole journey. The mid-days were sultry, and the endless chopping, harassed as we were by clouds of mosquitoes, was almost maddening. With our best efforts, we could make barely three miles a day, and though nearly a third of our provisions were consumed, we had completed hardly an eighth of our 800-mile journey. Day after day we toiled on, fighting mosquitoes, dragging horses out of mudholes, cutting our way through dense growths of alder. Occasionally we would determine our position by compass sights from the top of some tall cottonwood, and then we would lay a new course. At last, having reason to believe ourselves near the Keechatna, we halted for a day to reconnoitre and rest the tired horses and men.

The Keechatna was a less turbulent stream than the Yentna, and with the aid of the boat a crossing was effected without difficulty.

We now parted with Eberhardt and Anderson, who returned to Tyonok, taking the last letters we should be able to send out. Thenceforth until we reached the Yukon, about three months later, we were to be entirely cut off from the rest of the world.

The outlook was not encouraging, for we had nearly 700 miles of practically unknown territory to traverse, and the incessant labor of toiling through the swamp, added to the continuous annoyance from mosquitoes and horse-flies, was having a serious effect upon the strength of our horses. Night after night we would hear the tinkle of the bell-horse as he led the band of horses, maddened by the insects, back and forth. Though we blanketed them and built large fires as smudges, they seldom got relief for more than two or three hours of the twenty-four. It was terrible to see their suffering and be powerless to help them. They would frequently crowd into camp as if to implore us to relieve them from their misery.

The men, too, were becoming worn out by the mosquito pest, which harassed them continually during the day, though they found relief at night in the mosquito-proof tents. The soft blanket of moss, usually saturated with moisture, which nearly everywhere covers the face of the country, offers a breeding-ground for myriad insects. They are ever active, both day and night; on the mountaintops far above timber as well as in the lowlands. Five years of Alaskan travel have convinced me that there is no hardship so difficult to bear as this insect pest. I have seen horses, fairly maddened by the torment, blindly charge through the forest, oblivious to the trees and branches encountered, until they wore themselves out; then, in utter hopelessness, drop their heads and patiently endure the suffering. I have seen strong men, after days and nights of almost incessant torment, when they were too weary to offer further resistance to their relentless foes, weep with vexation. No part of an Alaskan traveler's outfit is more important than his mosquito-proof headdress and gloves. The former is made to fit closely around the rim of his hat and to his shoulders, for the mosquitoes will find the smallest opening. Unfortunately, the headdress has only too often to be discarded. When pushing through the undergrowth, using a surveying instrument, sighting a rifle or chopping a trail, the traveler is at the mercy of the mosquitoes, which follow him in clouds. While every other hardship of Alaskan travel is often grossly exaggerated, it is hardly possible to do this one justice.

[After a week of difficult travel along the Keechatna River], we entered the foothills of the range, and the conditions improved. The horses being now thoroughly broken in, and in fact almost devoid of spirit, three men could easily manage them while the others explored the adjacent hills. Grass was plentiful, and as the mosquitoes became less annoying after the timbered region was left behind, most of the horses began to recover strength.

The jaded horses now needed a day's rest, and while they enjoyed the abundant grass, Reaburn and I climbed a neighboring mountain. We found that we were well within a rugged range whose jagged peaks arose on every hand, and whose higher valleys were filled with glacial ice. There were still no indications of the pass we sought, so we again took up our march.

It was the middle of July when we threaded the narrow gap which led us from waters flowing into the Pacific Ocean to those tributary to the Bering Sea. The fair weather we had encountered almost from the beginning now gave place to storms, naturally suggesting the name "Rainy Pass" for the newly discovered gap. We were now in high spirits, for we all felt that whatever the summer might bring forth, we had at least located a route through this high mountain barrier.

With this thought to encourage us, we hastened to press on.

[After descending into lowland] spruce forest, we were startled by the discovery of a blazed trail, which was plainly not the work of natives. No one accustomed to the frontier can ever mistake the scars of an Alaskan Indian's axe, for he has never learned to cut a clean, sharp blow. No, this chopping had been done by white men, in winter, several years before. We followed the trail for some miles until it turned off out of our course. Who were these lonely travelers of this wild region? Whence had they come and whither did they go? These are questions that may never be answered. That they belonged to that class of Alaskan prospectors who have traversed the territory from the almost tropical jungles of its southern coast to the barren grounds which skirt the frozen sea on the north seems not unlikely. Often these pioneers make journeys that would put to shame the widely advertised explorations of many a well-equipped government expedition. Were the results of their efforts commensurate with the toil, danger and suffering involved, geographical science would be much enriched thereby. Unfortunately their ideas of where they have been are often almost as vague as of where they are going. Many a life has been lost on these hazardous journeys, and only too often are bleaching bones the sole record of unproclaimed and unrewarded heroism. These adventurers have no high ideals, often no thought beyond the desire of finding gold; but in the last three decades they have been carrying civilization northward and converted an unknown land into a populated territory which is now yielding millions of gold.

From the forest we now entered a belt of foothills, which formed a northern spur of the main range, and once more obtained a clear view of Mt. McKinley, still almost as far distant as when we first saw it from Mt. Sushitna six weeks before. This was no cause for depression, however, for then we were separated from our goal by an apparently impenetrable swamp and a great, snow-covered range; whereas now there seemed no serious obstacles to our achieving our purpose.

Among these foothills, averaging a height of 3,000 or 4,000 feet, dwelt large numbers of mountain sheep; their pure white color, which in this region remains unchanged throughout the year, making them conspicuous objects on the bare rocks or moss-covered slopes. In the course of one morning's roaming over the hills I counted more than 100 of these mountain dwellers. In fact, the abundance of sheep, bear, moose, and caribou found along the north slope of the Alaskan Range rank it as one of the finest hunting grounds in North America.

Our descent from the foothills brought us to a gravel-floored plateau which abutted directly upon the base of the range. Its smooth, moss-covered surface afforded such excellent footing and so few obstacles to progress that for days we hardly varied our direction a degree, heading straight for Mt. McKinley. That mountain and its twin peak, Mt. Foraker, now only fifty miles away, seemed to us to rise almost sheer from the gravel plain. We passed many large glaciers which debouched from the mountain valleys upon the plateau and discharged roaring, turbulent, boulder-filled rivers, which were our most serious impediment.

The other members of the party seemed to have no dread of these dangerous crossings; but for my part, I crossed every one we sighted a dozen times before we reached it. Late in the day, after the glaciers had felt the full influence of the sun's rays, the streams would often be so high as to be practically impassable, but morning would generally find the water fallen one or two feet. The large rivers were always reconnoitered on a horse stripped to the halter; then, if a crossing proved feasible, each man would mount on the back of his favorite horse and essay the perilous passage, guiding the unmanageable steed as best he could. The feat was ever exciting, with the animal plunging shoulder-high in the muddy, surging water, swaying from side to side and occasionally slipping on some hidden boulder. More than once a horse was carried off his feet, and sometimes rolled quite over. Nor was the ludicrous aspect entirely wanting, for often when the farther bank was reached the horses would make a sudden leap for it and a careless rider would be unceremoniously dumped over the animal's tail into the glacial river.

Since leaving the pass, we had subsisted largely upon moose and mountain sheep. Not a day was spent in hunting, but when the supply of meat ran low an animal was shot near camp or on the march. Not only was game plentiful, but so little did it know of man that it regarded us rather with curiosity than mistrust. During our journey across the piedmont plateau, for days and weeks together we were hardly out of sight of caribou. . . . There was no sport in hunting such innocently tame creatures, and we never molested them except when we needed meat.

These were the happiest days of the summer. Cheered by the thought that every day's march was bringing us visibly nearer to our goal, we lent ourselves readily to the influence of the clear, invigorating air and the inspiration of that majestic peak ever looming before us, the highest mountain of North America, which we were to be the first to explore.

[On August 3] we made our nearest camp to Mt. McKinley, in a broad, shallow valley incised in the piedmont plateau and drained by a stream which found its source in the ice-clad slopes of the high mountain. We had reached the base of the peak, and a part of our mission was accomplished, with a margin of six weeks left for its completion. This bade us make haste, for we must still traverse some 400 miles of unexplored region before we could hope to reach even the outskirts of civilization. Notwithstanding all of this, we decided to allow ourselves one day's delay so that we might actually set foot on the slopes of the mountain. The ascent of Mt. McKinley had never been part of our plan, for our mission was exploration and surveying, not mountaineering; but it seemed very hard to us that we had neither the time nor equipment to attempt the mastery of this highest peak of the continent.

The next morning dawned clear and bright. Climbing the bluff above our camp, I overlooked the upper part of the valley, spread before me like a broad amphitheater, its sides formed by the slopes of the mountain and its spurs. Here and there glistened in the sun the white surfaces of glaciers which found their way down from the peaks above. The great mountain rose 17,000 feet above our camp, apparently almost sheer from the flat valley floor. Its dome-shaped summit and upper slopes were white with snow, relieved here and there by black areas that marked cliffs too steep for the snow to lie upon.

A two hours' walk across the valley, through several deep glacial streams, brought me to the very base of the mountain. As I approached the top was soon lost to view; the slopes were so steep and I had to scramble as best I could. Soon all vegetation was left behind me, and my way zigzagged across smooth, bare rocks and talus slopes of broken fragments. My objective point was a shoulder of the mountain about 10,000 feet high, but at three in the afternoon I found my route blocked by a smooth expanse of ice. With the aid of my geologic pick I managed to cut steps in the slippery surface, and thus climbed a hundred feet higher; then the angle of slope became steeper, and as the ridge on which the glacier lay fell off at the sides in sheer cliffs, a slip would have been fatal. Convinced at length that it would be utterly foolhardy, alone as I was, to attempt to reach the shoulder for which I was headed, at 7,500 feet I turned and cautiously retraced my steps, finding the descent to bare ground more perilous than the ascent.

I had now consumed all the time that could be spared to explore this mountain which had been reached at the expense of so much preparation and hard toil; but at least I must leave a record to mark our highest point. On a prominent cliff near the base of the glacier, which had turned me back, I built a cairn in which I buried a cartridge-shell from my pistol, containing a brief account of the journey together with a roster of the party.

By this time I was forcibly reminded of the fact that I had forgotten to eat my lunch. As I sat resting from my labors, I surveyed a striking scene. Around me were bare rock, ice and snow; not a sign of life—the silence broken now and then by the roar of an avalanche loosed by the midday sun, tumbling like a waterfall over some cliff to find a resting-place thousands of feet below. I gazed along the precipitous slopes of the mountain and tried to realize again its great altitude, with a thrill of satisfaction at being the first man to approach the summit, which was only nine miles from where I smoked my pipe. No white man had ever before reached the base, and I was far beyond, where the moccasined foot of the roving Indian had never trod.

Editor's afterword: To complete its overland journey, Brooks's party traveled northeastward along the Alaska Range to the Cantwell River (since renamed the Nenana), which they followed north to a village on the Tanana River, arriving September 1. Still 100 miles from the Yukon River, expedition leaders decided to take their remaining packhorses cross-country across terrain Athabascan residents considered impassable. Along this final stretch, "the poor horses, even under the lightened loads, began to fail." In the final miles, "a horse was shot nearly every day." The team finally reached the village of Rampart and Brooks concludes his expedition account with the following:

Thus ended the longest cross-country exploration ever attempted in Alaska. Our plans had been carried out from start to finish: we had traversed 800 miles of the roughest part of Alaska in 105 days. While cooking our breakfast the next morning, a river steamer whistled, the last to make the journey down the Yukon before it was locked in the winter ice. Leaving our breakfast cooking on the fire, we hastily gathered up our more precious belongings, chiefly notes and specimens, and scrambled on board; the boat swung out in midstream, and with a farewell salute to the crowd of Indians and prospectors on the bank we rapidly steamed away, once more headed for civilization and home.

6

The Shameless Diary of an Explorer
by Robert Dunn

The summer after geologist Alfred Brooks published his "Plan for Climb-ing Mt. McKinley" in the January 1903 *National Geographic*, two expe-ditions launched the first-ever mountaineering assaults on the peak. One was organized by Alaska federal judge James Wickersham, the other by explorer Frederick Cook. Neither party came close to reaching Denali's summit. While both leaders later published stories about their adven-tures, Cook's expedition was also chronicled by Robert Dunn. A young reporter employed by the New York *Commercial Advertiser,* Dunn was second-in-command of a group that Bradford Washburn has called "one of the most motley teams in the history of exploration." It was, strangely enough, also a team without any experienced climbers. Other mem-bers included botanist Ralph Shainwald, a friend of Cook's and the son of a wealthy New Yorker; photographer Walter Miller; prospector Jack Carroll; and veteran Montana horsepacker Fred Printz, who had been on the 1902 Brooks expedition.

Though a journalist by training, the 26-year-old Dunn was chosen to be the expedition's geologist because, as he explained, "I have that fervor for geology, backed by small book knowledge, which blesses all habitual wanderers in the chaotic north." He had first been drawn north in 1898 by the Klondike gold strikes; two years later, he explored Alaska's Wrangell Mountains. Though he considered the team's chances for success to be small, any misgivings about the team's abilities or personalities were over-ridden by his longing to return to Alaska "at any cost."

According to author and Mount McKinley historian Terris Moore, Dunn was instructed by editor Lincoln Steffens to "write exactly what happens. Whether you reach the top or not, be the first to tell the whole truth about exploring. The rows, the bickering . . . " Dunn did not dis-appoint. His expedition account is a no-holds-barred story replete with sarcastic wit and biting criticisms of his teammates. Dunn is especially tough on Cook, whom he calls the Professor, and Shainwald, named

Simon in the story. Introducing his account, Dunn comments, "How each of us helped or hindered the day's work is all my story. . . . I hope that in reporting any inherent vanity in my fellows, I have hit off hardest my own insufferable egotism."

On returning East, Dunn wrote a series of five articles that appeared in *Outing* magazine from January to May 1904. Those were followed by his book *The Shameless Diary of an Explorer*, published in 1907 by The Outing Publishing Company. I have excerpted highlights of three chapters.

A final note: I have grouped Dunn's account with explorers (part II) rather than mountaineers (part III) because, more than anything, it documented a pioneering expedition across the Alaskan landscape.

FROM CHAPTER II, "GEOGRAPHICAL"

Our aim was to reach the top of Mt. McKinley, the highest point of North America, which lifts 20,300 feet of ice over the wastes of west Alaska. This was really a double task. With the means at hand, we knew that to gain the base of the mountain might be hardly easier than to climb it.

We planned to travel by pack-train from Tyonek, on Cook Inlet, up the western tributaries of the Sushitna, across the Alaskan range to the head of the south fork of the Kuskokwim, and follow along its face northeast to the mountain foot; *i.e.,* to follow the sides of a right angle pointed west, in order to reach a point almost due north of Cook Inlet. This was, in the main, [geologist Alfred] Brooks's route, and [Army Lt. Joseph] Herron had followed it in part, although we knew that most traces of their trails would be obliterated. The distance was about 450 miles, and Brooks had covered it with horses in seven weeks from Tyonek. The first half was to be over the tundras of the Sushitna Valley, the remainder across higher ground on the west side of the Alaskan range.

I dreaded that first half, the Sushitna tundra. Tundra, strictly speaking, is the coastal marshland of Siberia, yet any vast, low, and ill-drained country in the North, forested or no, is called tundra. [If true in Dunn's time, that definition no longer applies; tundra is the vegetation zone beyond treeline.] It was considered almost madness to venture into the interior overland from Tyonek. Stories were told of men who had set out from there to be driven back crazed by mosquitoes. I had traveled over tundra in Alaska, and knew its hateful yellow moss bordered by white skeleton spruces, its treacherous ponds sprinkled with white flowers, its willow thickets concealing abysses of red muck. The buzz of bull-dog flies, the hot anger and desperation of burdened cayuses kicking helplessly in a mire, were familiar enough. But I believed that to reach our mountain was just the old, old act of hitting the trail, hitting very, very hard, and staying with it.

The ascent seemed to be more doubtful. Ours must be a dash to the top, taking long chances, I thought, on success. Our time for reconnoitering in uncertain weather was too short. McKinley was a very large mountain, quite unexplored, deeply bedded in a great range. [18,008-foot Mount] St. Elias was not conquered until the fifth try, and then by trained alpine men, at a cost of $50,000. Ours was to be a first [actually second] attempt, by men of no alpine experience, who had hardly $5,000.

FROM CHAPTER IX, "I BREAK LOOSE TWICE"

July 20. My first brush with the Professor. I was tactless and hasty. Sorry.

We started, with no inkling of how long the skinny beasts [packhorses] must plug on. Through ghastly birches, grass which met over the tops of the packs, willow swamps, at last we met a box canyon of the foothills in three hours. It was pitiful, driving the beasts sheer down through the brush. Poor Miller gave up beating Bridget, I pelting mud from above. Somehow we did get him across the creek at the bottom. Then he spread his legs—played out again.

I was angry, ran ahead, and seeing the Professor, burst out about his having "sense knocked into him some time," knowing "nothing about horses, and not wanting to know." The torrent came too easily. "Dunn, it doesn't do any good to talk like that," he said quietly.

I went back with Simon, and we did bat Bridget along. Simon likes beating horses—when the Professor's around—but he left Miller and me to haul the beast up the opposite scarp of the canyon, on which Bridget rolled into a mudhole. Miller and I unpacked him, back-packed his load to the top, and dragged him up to the Professor. "I'm sorry if I put my feelings too strongly sometimes," I said to him. He only answered, "Dunn, you talk too much and too loud all the time." Now, on the way back to Bridget, I had cursed the Professor's leadership to Simon, who probably told him, or he had overheard—hence the "loud." Next, the Light Buckskin rolled off his pack, and we camped. Just three hours' travel again.

Yet, I'm happy tonight—if that can interest any one but the carelessly absent gnats. A strong wind blows. Over our swamp, sharp snow peaks, blue with the vague, questioning azure of the North, fuse whited spires into a burnished heaven. Evening casts queer shadows from the alder clumps, into the rank grass and snow patches of our hillsides.

July 21. We hit down good trailing through alder to the dozen silty channels of the Keechatna. All the beasts are better. The Brown mare didn't lie down once. I drive the train's rear still, with the six worst invalids to bat on; Roan, Whiteface, Bridget, Moth-eaten Bay, Big Buck. Fred says they've had "distemper," which means any old disease; the Professor that they were poisoned by the yellow-bellied flies, since they played out so suddenly. I remember that at Tyonek Light Buck and Little Gray had foul breath and ran at their noses; so others did at the Skwentna. The Moth-eaten and Dark Buck still have hardly a hair on their bodies, and couldn't live a minute among flies. Now the sickest are the Brown B horse and P. R. Sorrel, who carries and is always shipping that box of Simon's with his botany presses in—which Jack and I are planning to "lose"—so you can't blame the P. R. Light Buck and Little Gray haven't shown a sign of failing, so may not they all have only been suffering in getting acclimated, these two recovering from their dose first?

July 22. In four hours we have made ten miles, hitting the tangled river channels, which we "took across," as King [Fred Printz] says, fording incessantly from bar to bar. Simon, who seems to care for nothing but his own comfort, hates to wet his feet. At one fording, he jumped behind one of his bunch's pack, dashed among the rest, scattering them till they were swimming about and wetting the grub. The horses made it back to shore, and from the other side he refused to recross and corral them, which Miller and I had to do. At the next channel, he cut into the middle of my bunch on a narrow spit, and drove the P. R. back a quarter mile. He fetched her, and caught us at the next ford. All his beasts had plunged in ahead, so he sprang to ride one of mine, but I batted them all on furiously, and though I slumped in to my armpits, Simon had to wade. We others, except the Professor, who has only L. C. to manage, always wade. It's the only way to safeguard dry crossings for the grub. Every one is sore on Simon for these tricks, especially Fred and Jack, for besides wetting the grub, he soaks their favorite blankets. He hasn't yet any control over a horse, nor seems to want it.

July 23. Simon keeps up his fording stunts. Though the days are all too alike, the dazing tension of travel never relaxes; herding horses one by one over miles of muck; boiling beans, mixing bread, burning callous fingers on the hot, collapsing reflector: never an hour to rest, to dry off from the tortures of rheumatism, mend tattered boots and clothes, forget the roar of icy water about your waist, the crazing cloud of 'skeets.

July 24. Jack is sick with a pain in his chest. The Professor says it's neuralgia, and gives him white tablets. King says that Jack nearly caved in yesterday, and threatened to "lay down" on the trail, letting us go on without knowing. Though ill several days, he has confided in no one but King up to today, when, after crossing a large clear stream coming in from the north, he was weak enough to fall twice and be carried down with the current.

Today the Professor had his first practical idea: that we'd make better time always traveling the mile-wide riverbed, endlessly fording the twisty channels which get narrower and swifter; which we've done. And though King wanted to keep to the hills, because Brooks had hugged them, and swore that the glacial wash skinned hoofs, we've come near sixteen miles to camp by this slew.

This morning we opened the lone can of glucose syrup, long yearned for by Simon. "G———, it's ambrosia!" gasped he at breakfast, wallowing with it on his pancake. Carefully he hid the can in the empty coffee-bag on Bridget's right-side alforgus. Now, I hate sweet-tooth gluttony on the trail, so when we unpacked Bridget tonight—no syrup can. Yes, that right pack had slipped coming down the scarp to camp; Miller and I had noticed it; even the coffee-bag hanging out! Nobly Simon quelled his tears, and all but started can hunting on the back-trail. We got him to spoil his ambrosial appetite by eating a whole flapjack under plebeian sugar, before fondly we produced the syrup from the grass where Fred had slung it. Isn't it a shame to horse the boy so? This is Alaskan humor, in a crowd like this.

The Professor rears his conical tent on the gravel bar, to dodge the 'skeets, he says, though I notice he's built a baby smudge, which he reaches in a rubber-shoe ferry. Miller's picking currants; I've shaved, and am mending my pants and drawers with dunnage-bag canvas, where the whole shebang had worn through to the skin kneeling before cookpots. I have to do nearly as much cooking as ever. Simon never gets up in time to help mornings, but crawls out of his blankets just before Miller hollers, "Brek-faast!" and without washing, sneaks the first pancake off the pile. Just now, King and I are enlarging on how thick the 'skeets are in the tent—we've not been pestered with one for two nights—just to keep the kid from sleeping there. So, as he did last night, he's rigged a wicker hood over his bed with willows—near the grub as usual, I observe.

Jack sleeps. I wonder what would be done if any one were really laid up? The Professor hasn't a shadow of a notion, I'm sure. All day I had a bad pain over my appendix, so he said. It doesn't worry me. How could it? I can't imagine a man stranded on a rock in mid-ocean without grub or water *worrying*: can you?

July 25. Simon caught it today, and I'm ashamed again. Stubborn and vital he is, though maddeningly lazy, and slow as old women; yet compared to what might have been, and generally is, with such as we in Alaska, our hopeless and unending life is Arcadian.

He [Simon] kept up his tactics, leaping behind a packed horse at each ford, dashing across and scattering the train to swim in circles out of depth, soaking the precious grub. We swam a-thousand-and-one channels, pounded a-thousand-and-one gravel bars. Miller and I, getting angrier and angrier, stoned him through swift water, so he thumbed his nose at us. What do you think of a man who'll let an expedition go to keep his feet dry and then glory in it?

At last I got him. The icy water, hurtling boulders along bottom, roared under our armpits; we made a blind island, and drove the beasts right back again. Simon mounted the Roan, as I chased, beating the horse with a stick. The kid lost his temper, and lunged at me in midstream, saying he'd "do" me if I hit his horse again. I did, of course. When we landed, he made a dive for me. We clinched, and in ten seconds he was lying on his face, chewing silt and gravel, making suppressed, backhanded lunges. His spectacles and hat were lost. I didn't want to hurt him, so he began taking it out of me in talk. The worst he called me was a cad and a bully. He was foaming at the mouth and weepy, making foxy struggles to get up if I relaxed, till I landed him in six inches of slough water, and said he could freeze there or promise not to ride channels. Miller added insult by coming along laughing and taking a photograph of us— as Simon promised. "You act as if you ran this whole outfit," he whimpered. "Whatever you do is right, but if any one else makes a break, you come down hard on them." I grieve that can't be denied.

Ahead, the Professor had stopped the train, and asked Miller what the trouble was. "Oh, only Dunn and Simon," he answered, "settling a small difficulty." The Professor said nothing, and won't. Soon, every one was being carried off his feet in the next channel, soaked and pounded on the white granite bowlders. Miller went down with a look on his face as if he saw the Angel Gabriel, and the Professor flopped about with his paddle like a giant Dungeness crab. Twice I slipped into holes over my head, and though never carried away, lost my hat, as my horse bunch hit back for shore. And Simon, deprived of packhorses, was all but shipped to Cook Inlet! I pulled him out with a pole. Talk about coals of fire!

Now we are discussing how Herron and Brooks crossed the mountains. Brooks missed Herron's way—Simpson Pass—and found another, more circuitous, leading him first back to Skwentna headwaters. King remembers little about it all. We're hardly a day's travel now from whatever glaciers the Keechatna heads in. "We must get to work on a reconnaissance of Simpson's Pass tomorrow," says the Professor, pompously. Everything we guess and prophesy about it would drive you mad. Only higher and sharper tower these sudden mountains, the To-toy-lon subrange. Spruces cling only down along the river, which is a single, mad, chocolate thread. Today we passed the first bunches of glaciers hid in jagged, slaty peaks, direfully folded and faulted, pitching with snowfields and greenery strewn on their desert tali, sheer from the roar below here. Old nature, grand style, is getting busy.

FROM CHAPTER XIII, "BUTTING BLINDLY INTO STORM"

August 16. Not a wink all night. We divided the last caribou steak, and wrung water from our blankets to make tea, which Miller wouldn't drink as we had no sugar. But we felt cheerier. The raw dawn shifted weary glints on the dull blue glaciers of the front-range. "What to do," thought I, "but to go on zwiebacking?" I did. Miller cut wood. The baking over, we chased twenty caribou that had peeked at us, and hit back for the river. The flood hadn't fallen, but was spreading out into a hundred channels, so we waded it back to camp. King crossed on Big Buck to get the wood, and it was very funny to see him buck in midstream with Fred on his back too—the animated old woodpile.

Simon was lazing by the fire, protected from the scud by a willow thatch importantly called a "Fuegian wind-break" by the Professor. He ran at me with all kinds of tales how we could get up some glacier—the one visible from here with the serac of dirty ice-blocks, under the highest point of the front range. The strange sacks of "mountain stuff" which seemed such a useless burden on the trail, were open, and weird Arctic clothing was passed around. I have drawn a pair of red stockings, with tassels, two pair of Arctic socks (like mittens for the feet), hand mittens, a pair of grimy drawers, and one of the green eiderdown sleeping bags.

Now, we can't all wander about in the McKinley fogs. Some one of the five must stay to read the barometer at the base camp under the front range, whither we move tomorrow up this stream. The Shantung silk tent holds only four, and there aren't enough green sleeping-bags—weighing just four pounds each, unless wet—to go around. The Professor won't say who must stay behind, which seems to lie between Simon and Miller. I want Miller to climb, and told the Professor that it was a good deal to risk our lives with the kid, whose eyesight and hearing are defective, and is slower than old Ned. "Yes, Miller is more adaptable," was all he answered. Miller says he thinks that Simon has some previous agreement to be taken on the mountain; but I doubt that.

Now the Professor says that he expects "a man to volunteer to stay behind," which is the devil of a scheme. Yet vaguely he adds that whoever shows up worst on the first day's climb, goes back. Whew! How can such vacillation get our confidence? He's simply afraid, or unable, to decide anything beforehand. Of course, Simon has corralled a rucksack and a green sleeping-bag, and is importantly hammering the heads on the ice axes. One he has already used to chop willows. Miller saw, and cursed him. I'm in the tent, mending those grimy drawers. The rest are out in that Fuegian wind-break. No one knows it's my birthday. What's the use?

August 17. We enter the fog to attack the virgin peak of Mt. McKinley, unknown and unexplored from all sides. Thus, without proper reconnoitering, we have jammed our heads into the 10,000-foot range, which walls the main mountain mass. It seems to curve, and join the right-hand, or south haunch of the main dome, whose face has appeared quite perpendicular. Below that face, between it and our outer range, and at right angles to our direction, flows Peters' Glacier (named by Brooks). We think that it heads into a curving wall, connecting front range and main mountain, by which we hope to reach an arête of the peak. But so reticulated with ridges and hung with glaciers are these heights, that I doubt if any one of us has a clear idea of just where we are going to hit; or will have, till clear weather comes. This is our base camp, and we're ready to make a ten- or twelve-day attack on the old mountain without descending. Yet August is the Alaska rainy season, and it may drizzle on till the September frosts, which will mean checkmate by fresh snows on the mountain.

The outlook is cheerless: we're discouraged; the low clouds rain on, and on, and on. Grub-packs and pack-covers are saturated. A spirit of "Oh, let it go, it's wet anyhow," pervades camp. The ground is littered with old boots, smelly sacks, unwashed dishes, and slabs of caribou, which Fred has discarded after careful sniffs. Handfuls of fly-blows crust the meat bags.

Yet the Professor talks of pushing up the glacier anyhow, tomorrow. He has been out reconnoitering with King, and announces he's found a way for horses across the moraine to the ice. I took a turn over the black hill, which splits the ice-foot in twain, and we call the "nunatak." Saw nothing, nothing, but crazy cataracts of mud water, in crazier gorges.

August 19. And still rain. "Simon," said the professor this morning through the drizzle, "go down to the stream and read the barometer" which meant that we're going to hit up the glacier. Nothing was said about who should stay behind; still no one dares ask the Professor his schemes.

We breakfasted on meat tainted from its mildewy sack and stewed in its absorbed water, and plunged upward into the fog toward the unknown ice. No one stayed behind. Each led a beast; crossed, re-crossed over sharp bowlders, down and up sheer, sliding talus, to stumble with feet and hoofs grueled by bowlders hurtled along under the brown foam of glacier streams. Finally over sharp moraine, like the Andes in miniature—to a luminous smooth lip of foggy ice.

We started up. It grew suddenly steep. Big Gray stumbled and fell, but was righted before rolling over. The ice whitened; leveled. The horses nosed a few lateral crevasses, nickered, jumped them with awkward care. Gradually, huge seracs (icefalls) swam through the lightening mist, and a castellated black ridge struck down to bisect the glacier into two amphitheatres. The Professor turned into the left hand and nearer one, against Fred's protest. From our futile talks, I had got too hazy ideas of where we were aiming to speak up. Between two upper seracs, fresh snow hid the crevasses, and the fog thinned. The Professor went ahead, sounding with his ice axe. It was slow, ticklish work, winding back and forth over cracks that might, or might not, let you through to wait for the last trump—you couldn't tell till you tested them. The horses snorted; balked; leaned back, legs quivering, till we beat a terrorized jump out of each. I had on sneakers, and was thinking what a testimonial could be made to the rubber company for wearing them to 7,000 feet on McKinley, when the Dark Gray bungled a leap, and lost his hind quarter down a crevasse. All hands unpacked him, and hauled him by saddle tie-ropes. Now and then the other beasts imitated him. Higher and higher we felt a way; piloting each horse in turn across each crevasse, quadrilling—at last over clean ice, netted with cracks—to a dome-like summit. Beyond, the glacier dipped down all around to vague icefalls hanging upon paste-white walls banded with brown irony veins; and to the left and north, but not toward McKinley, a possible-to-climb talus slope flanked the dizzy ridge. The Professor drew a brass aneroid from his money belt, and muttered, "Seventy-five hundred feet."

Fred, Miller and I, cramped in the silk tent, are trying to fill the oil stove to give the beans another boil. (Simon only half cooked them.) We are talking weather, ice, and glacial erosion. Under us are wet blankets, wetter tarpaulins, wettest ice. It is suffocating hot; disordered food, clothing, instruments, all are steaming. Outside, some attempt has been made to sort the stuff, but it's rather hopeless; pounds have been added to the rucksacks, and the sugar is syrup. The smell of meaty, mildewed cotton pervades the air. The Professor and Simon have gone out to reconnoitre the talus between the glaciers, following a route to shore (off the ice) explored by Fred and me, roped.

We're all five to sleep here tonight, some one outside, as the tent, being meant for one man, holds only four. Just now, Simon took our breaths away by volunteering, and is rigging up a sort of couch out on the glacier, like a funeral pyre, of sacks, blankets, and boxes. The tent is guyed down with ice axes. We have one teaspoon among us. Yes, it's the real Alpine thing, this. Good night.

August 21. Four inches of snow fell last night, and twice I unloaded the tent wall, which was pressing down and wetting us. . . . Toward noon, Fred and I felt our way northeast up the glacier, rounding the hill of dirty ice-blocks, visible from so far down the valley. The Professor went exploring south, along the ridge leading evenly to the highest point of the far range, but condemned for its length and indirectness as a route to the supposed head of Peters Glacier.

Unroped in the driving snow, King and I wound among the sheer crevasses of the serac, where you could look down from four to four thousand feet. We poked with ice axes, crawled from little ridge to ridge of hard snow. We gained the foot of a col joining the ridge that bisected the glacier. It looked possible to climb; at least, everything else was perpendicular. We started, when out from the white gloom below, and refracted to a spiritual nearness, tinkled a horse bell. So Simon, afraid to be left behind, had brought up the horses despite the storm. We kept on harder; turning to the left around the spur, shinning the upper walls of crevasses where the glacier became almost hanging; higher, higher, till we topped the soiled snow-blocks, and steps had to be cut in the crevassed cliffs. More quadrilling to gain steep snow-bridges, and one huge crevasse where if you slipped you shot into the eternal like slush down a gable. I missed a jump on the first try, and slid back—a little. Towering ever above, swam the wall, now to waver to sheerness, now settling to a human angle, with the refractive trick of all snowy places even in clear weather in Alaska. So we plugged blindly on in the storm, where no foot had ever trod, up the scaffold of the highest peak on the continent.

The storm seemed to thin. Light, like the first streak of winter dawn, settled upon the long ridge opposite. Suddenly, what we believed to be the top of our slope stretched itself a full thousand feet higher into the sky; and steeper,

steeper. "Look, look!" I cried, and if the ridge had crumbled with us into the valley, we should have still stood staring.

That was enough for Fred. It was after four o'clock. Rock had ended. Sheer, hard névé, covered with six inches of fresh snow, down which balls were even now grooving trails, alone filled the heaven. The aneroid said 9,000 feet. Fred crawled to the edge of the granite nub, to gaze straight down the most disturbing distance yet, into the abandoned amphitheatre of yesterday. When I look into such places, I have a feeling—not vertigo, not exactly fear, that worries me. I think too fast and too much, and of impulses which are not quite sane. So, down we slid, again defeated, Fred recklessly, I carefully bridging the crevasses; past the Humboldt cliffs, where the snow shut in denser than ever, and the long white ridge became a dark, magic line over the shadowy glacier.

Four horses were shivering on the gravel humps near camp. Miller was in the tent, making pea soup. From a distance, Simon and the Professor approached wearily. "We didn't think that you'd go so far," said the Professor, when we told that our ridge could be climbed, possibly with heavy packs. He paid little attention. "But you see," he discouraged, "even if it can, we don't know what's beyond. The problem is . . . " etc., and he went on to tell how he and Simon had looked into a valley beyond the long ridge toward Mt. Foraker, where the slopes were better, he said, and "we can get around to the main mountain on the divide between them"—(McKinley and Foraker, doubtless)—and where the rock was "much better, dark, apparently slate, and not that treacherous granite." Then he ordered to pack up and return the whole outfit down to the barometer camp!

Just now, after cleaning all the soggy food and stuff out of the large tent, and crawling into our steaming bags in the old, comfortable way—feet on dunnage, heads on pants and sweater wrapped in poncho to extend the wall and get the drip—Simon made Fred and me very, very tired. "Well," said the kid, with most transparent bravado, "now I think that our chances for getting to the top of McKinley are brighter than ever. We'll get around to the south side of this glacier tomorrow, where the Professor explored, and we're practically certain of finding a good way to the summit of this front range."

Neither Fred nor I spoke. That sort of insincerity makes me boil. As if it would do any good in such a storybook, arctic traveler-fashion, to *lie* in order to keep up our spirits. Pretty examples of courage men must be to rig up a fool's paradise around them to give them nerve. Victory lies first with whom best faces the darkest side of the picture, and fights upward from the worst. Wonder if Simon wasn't parroting the Professor.

Editor's afterword: In late August Cook's team reached a high point of about 11,000 feet, stopped by cliffs that rose several thousand feet. Their chosen route, now called the Northwest Buttress, wouldn't be successfully climbed until 1954.

7

The Wilderness of Denali

by Charles Sheldon

In the early 1900s, as prospectors and pioneering mountaineers were being lured into the Denali region by gold and summit fever, respectively,
an easterner named Charles Sheldon (1867–1928) came north to the Alaska
Range on a different sort of quest: a big-game hunt. What Sheldon found
proved far more valuable than any trophy animal. Denali's wilderness and
wildlife sparked the idea for a park-refuge unlike any other in the nation.

By all accounts a talented hunter, passionate naturalist, devout conservationist, and astute political lobbyist, the Vermont-born and Yale-
educated Sheldon was drawn to the Denali region in 1906 by his desire
to hunt and study Alaska's wild white sheep. For a guide he wisely chose
Harry Karstens, a transplanted Midwesterner who had come north at
age nineteen, seeking gold. Known to be a first-rate explorer and
outdoorsman, Karstens would later participate in the first ascent to
Denali's 20,320-foot summit and become the pioneering superintendent of Alaska's first parkland. Joined by horsepacker Jack Haydon,
Sheldon and Karstens searched for Dall sheep on the northern side of
the Alaska Range. Though their quarry initially proved elusive, Sheldon
eventually found the sheep. He also found wilderness and big-game
populations unlike any other he had known, and together they inspired
an historic vision: the protection of Alaska wild lands and wildlife in a
combination park and game preserve. In a journal entry dated January
12, 1908, Sheldon even named this park-refuge: Denali National Park.

After his departure in 1908, Sheldon would never return to the region, but the Denali country would remain a vital part of his life. On
returning to New York, he began a campaign that would culminate,
more than eight years later, with the creation of Alaska's first—and still
most famous—conservation unit. Legislation to establish Mount
McKinley National Park passed Congress in February 1917 and was
signed into law by President Woodrow Wilson. Nearly 100 miles long
and 25 miles wide on average, the park protected almost 1½ million
acres of wildlife habitat. In 1980, the park would be expanded to 6 mil-

lion acres and given the name that Sheldon had so dearly desired: Denali.

Sheldon later wrote an account of his travels in *The Wilderness of Denali,* published in 1930 by Charles Scribner's Sons. The excerpts below are taken from chapters 2 and 6, which describe his initial hunt for Dall sheep in 1906.

FROM CHAPTER 2, "DENALI, 1906"

July 27. Going on, I penetrated short distances among the mountains and here and there climbed the slopes, scanning the surface everywhere, but could not find a sign of sheep. These mountains, covered with abundant feed, seemed ideal sheep ranges, but neither a sheep track nor any dung pellets could be found, nor was anything resembling a trail visible on the slopes. It was perfectly clear that for some reason this region directly [north] of Denali is inhospitable for sheep.

But I was in some degree compensated for my disappointment when I approached the base of the great mountain, for feeding on its basal slope were two cow caribou. Winding me at once, they galloped or trotted in an easterly direction until lost to sight among the canyons. So, my first start up Denali was made while caribou were fleeing before me.

I climbed the spur that flanks the east edge of the moraine of Peters Glacier and continues to the outside range. At the point where I climbed up, I found a tin cylinder half full of alcohol, a tower, a leather-covered valise box, two or three empty cans, a tent pole or two, and some wood that had been brought up there on horses. These proved to be part of the equipment left by Frederick A. Cook's party, which three years previously had attempted the ascent of Denali by following up Peters Glacier.

The slope became steeper as I zigzagged upward for nearly three hours until, having climbed a thousand feet in soft snow, I was obliged to stop where it rose almost perpendicularly. My aneroid barometer recorded 8,900 feet. As the clouds lifted, leaving the vast snow-mantled mountain clear, I seated myself and gazed for more than an hour on the sublime panorama. There was not a breath of wind, and no sound except the faint murmur of the creek far below, and the cannonading and crashing roar of avalanches thundering down the mountain walls.

Great masses of ice kept constantly breaking away from far up near the summit. Starting slowly at first, they increased in momentum and size, accumulating large bodies of snow and ice, some of which during the rapidity of the descent were ground into swirling clouds, resembling the spray of cataracts.

When the sliding material pitched off the glacier cap and struck the bare walls below, enormous fragments of rock were dislodged and carried along with the mass, which finally fell on the dumping ground of the moraine. Then, before the clouds of snow had disappeared from the path of the avalanche, the rumbling of the echoes died away and silence was again supreme. During the four hours that I was there, nineteen avalanches fell—some of them of enormous proportions. Eleven were near by and visible throughout their descent.

Behind me reared the tremendous glacier cap in all its immensity. To my left Peters Glacier filled the deep valley between the north face of the mountain and a high adjoining range; to my right was the northeast ridge of Denali; and, as far as I could see, on both sides of me were the spired crestlines of the outside ranges.

Directly below was the newly formed moraine of Peters Glacier, the glacier itself appearing like a huge white reptile winding along the west side. Not yet smoothed by the elements, this moraine was one confused mass of drumlins, kettle holes, eskers, and kames. Many miniature lakes glistened in the depressions; patches of green grass and dwarf willows along the water courses, with flowers and lichens, added a wealth of color to its desolate surface. Along the base of the mountain was the dumping ground of the avalanches—a wild disorder of debris.

Through bisected ranges of mountains I could see the rolling piedmont plateau, filled with hundreds of bright lakes, and still beyond could look over the vast wilderness of low relief all clothed in timber, until the vision was lost in the wavy outlines of rolling country merging into the horizon. Far to the northwest Lake Minchumina, reflecting the sun, fairly shone out of the dark timber-clad area surrounding it.

Alone in an unknown wilderness hundreds of miles from civilization and high on one of the world's most imposing mountains, I was deeply moved by the stupendous mass of the great upheaval, the vast extent of the wild areas below, the chaos of the unfinished surfaces still in process of moulding, and by the crash and roar of the mighty avalanches.

The sun was low; a dark shadowy mantle was cast over the wild desolate areas below; the skyline of the great mountain burned with a golden glow; distant snowy peaks glistened white above sombre-colored slopes not touched by the light of the sun, which still bathed the wide forested region of the north. A huge avalanche ploughed the mountainside not a hundred and fifty yards to my left, while clouds of snow swept about me.

Awakening to the realization that I had been and was still in a path of danger, I slowly made the descent.

While wandering about the foot of the slope I observed a few very old tracks of rams, indicating that sheep, though they do not live within it, occasionally cross this area. Golden eagles had been in sight all day; bear diggings were numerous even on the lower slopes, where ground squirrels, conies, and marmots were plentiful; as were also fresh tracks of caribou. While returning I shot a fine marmot, and when outside the ranges I saw a band of cow caribou feeding on the ridges and two or three single bulls descending into the timber.

Reaching camp long after midnight, I was saddened by the thought that in order to find sheep I must move to new country. Nothing could have been more satisfactory than to have found them inhabiting these mountains. Hunting and stalking rams under the great dome would have been romantic indeed.

FROM CHAPTER 6, "HEAD OF THE TEKLANIKA"

August 17. As the rain continued my hopes sank, for time was passing and I had to content myself with watching a dozen ewes and lambs not ten minutes' walk from camp. At 3 P.M. however the rain ceased, the mist cleared, and I was soon tramping north down the river to inspect the great mountain [Sable Mountain] on the opposite side. To the southwest, seventy-five ewes were visible; to the east a few sheep, too far off to determine the sex. Having gone a mile, the glasses showed twelve sheep high up near the north end of the mountain of many colors—Cathedral Mountain I called it. Viewed from half a mile nearer, all were seen to be rams. Still nearer, and the glasses revealed that some of them had large horns. Big rams! After an arduous exploration of the country for more than eighty miles, including many days of toilsome tramping over rough mountains, at last I had found old rams! I could scarcely believe it, but after going a little nearer, the glasses confirmed it. Among thirteen rams, nine had strikingly big horns. Two more rams, one with a good head, came over the crest, but the others assumed a threatening attitude and would not permit these to join the band.

Seating myself, I studied the mountain with the field glass in the hope of finding a reasonable route for stalking the rams. The slope was exceedingly steep, the canyons were deep, the talus in places seemed almost perpendicular. Here and there between areas of talus were strips of slippery grass ground. The rams were near the crest, well toward the north end of the mountain, feeding on the edge of a deep canyon whose sides of shattered rock rose up in precipices, furrowed here and there with depressions that possibly might be ascended. But these routes of approach were below the rams and could not be undertaken with any hope of success. It was impossible to circle the crest directly above the rams because it was split by the head of the canyon, leaving a gap of high unscalable cliffs. Only one possible route seemed available, and even this, since part of the approach would be in plain sight of the sheep, was extremely doubtful. Half a mile to the south of the rams I could keep out of sight while ascending the slope, until well up near the heads of the intervening canyons, and then stalk across the open slope directly toward them. It was obvious that along such a route the probability of success would be doubtful, but on the other hand, the next day the rams might be far away. I realized also that the success or failure of the whole trip might depend on the result of this stalk, and that, since my time was so limited, the risk was worth taking. Moreover, my several years' experience in hunting sheep in Alaska and Yukon Territory had taught me that with proper caution it is sometimes possible to approach sheep, even when in plain sight. This encouraged me to make the attempt. Descending from the high bluff bordering the river, extreme caution was necessary while crossing the three hundred yards of bars and four intervening channels, which at that time of the day, owing to the rapid melting of the glaciers, were rushing and roaring at maximum height. As any of the rams could easily detect me when moving on the flat, I slowly crawled to the first channel, and after a look at the rams through the field glasses, plunged at a selected moment into the river. Once wading, I could not stop until across, and to cross these channels without being seen by the rams was not only doubtful, but was by far the most dangerous part of the whole stalk. The moosehide moccasins afforded a weak foothold and several times, when nearly up to my hips in the swirling icy water, its leaping combers dancing around me, I was nearly swept off my feet. The chances were that such an accident would mean death. A long time was consumed in reaching the fringe of spruces at the base of the mountain, but it was finally accomplished without being observed by the rams. Once, while crossing the bar, I saw the two new rams, chased by three of the others, suddenly turn and run back over the crest. I knew that they were outsiders, prohibited from joining the others by the spirit of the band.

Not worried by the unlucky "thirteen," then quietly feeding in the same place, I went up rapidly through the spruces to a grassy slope and hidden from the rams climbed as quickly as possible, while rain, driven by a strong wind blowing from the sheep directly toward me, began to fall. Finally, when half a mile away, I turned and started directly toward them, the light rain beating on my face.

A magnificent new landscape was spread about me, the mountain panorama made wilder by the wind and rain; while banks of clouds, filling the lower depressions, caused the spired crestlines to loom as if suspended along a broken horizon. My position seemed almost to overhang the river below, from which the noise of the rushing torrents sounded with a dull continuous roar.

For an hour and a half my advance along that steep broken slope required all the caution and strategy that experience had taught me. Often in plain sight of the rams, necessitating the most careful watchfulness, I moved only when all the heads were down or turned away; at other times depressions shielded me from their eyes. The grassy slopes were steep and slippery, the broken rocks loose and likely to fall with disastrous noise. Two canyons were crossed, both with extreme difficulty and danger.

During all this time the rams were quietly feeding in the way character-istic of old ones. They appeared fat and heavy, with short thick necks that protruded when their heads were up. Their movements were sluggish and expressive of supreme confidence. Ewes are more active, their motions more jerky; they impress the stalker as more alert and watchful. But to one who knows sheep well, the apparently indifferent actions of the old rams are not deceptive. They quietly raise their heads to look, their gaze is calm, one or another is nearly always looking either up, down, or sidewise. The experi-enced stalker knows that their very unconcern implies that their senses of sight and hearing are employed in a way far more effective than are those of ewes, which depend more on the collective sense of the band than on that of the individual members. But, even when with his band, each ram watches for himself, independent of the others—watches more carefully than do ewes, and with vision as keen. A band of rams usually detects approaching danger much sooner than does a band of ewes.

My advance, slow and difficult, was one of increasing suspense. I had suc-ceeded in approaching so near that the chance of success would be ruined by the slightest mistake. Had one of the rams seen me in motion at any time during that stalk, at once all would have moved off. Many times one or another—sometimes several—were apparently looking right at me as I lay motionless on the slope. But even if they did see my bulk, not one suspected me as an enemy. Unless the stalker is very near, if he stands still, or if sitting upright remains motionless, sheep do not often become suspicious. But if they detect the slightest movement, they are suddenly alarmed. At any distance, even when motionless, the stalker must always avoid suspicious attitudes. This means that as he advances, he must continually observe the surface around him, and also the immediate background, in order that he may properly adjust his postures.

Before crossing the second canyon, I was only three hundred yards away, crawling on a slope of broken rock where it was necessary to feel carefully and select each knee and elbow rest. Finally, after mounting the opposite side of the canyon, I advanced foot by foot in the intervals of their watching. At other times many minutes were required to so arrange the small broken rocks as to prevent their falling or my slipping. As I climbed out of this canyon two marmots whistled, but on peering over the edge my anxiety was relieved by noticing that the rams were not disturbed. A golden eagle uttering shrill screams was soaring above the band but the rams paid no attention to it; nor did they to the querulous bleat of the conies or the chatter of ground squirrels. When I finally reached the brink of the canyon beyond which the rams were feeding, the rain had decreased to a drizzle but the wind was fairly strong. As the canyon walls were too precipitous to descend, my time for action had come.

Finding a slight depression at the edge I crept into it and lay on my back. Then slowly revolving to a position with my feet forward, I waited a few moments to steady my nerves. My two-hundred-yard sight had been pushed up, and watching my opportunity, I slowly rose to a sitting position, elbows on knees. Not a ram had seen or suspected me. I carefully aimed at a ram standing broadside near the edge of the canyon, realizing that the success of my long arduous trip would be determined the next moment. I pulled the trigger and as the shot echoed from the rocky walls, the ram fell and tried to rise, but could not. His back was broken. The others sprang into alert attitudes and looked in all directions. I fired at another standing on the brink, apparently looking directly at me. At the shot, he fell and rolled into the canyon. Then a ram with big massive wrinkled horns dashed out from the band and, heading in my direction, ran down into the canyon. The others immediately followed, but one paused at the brink and, as I fired, dropped and rolled below. Another turned and was running upward as I fired and missed him.

For a moment, after I had put a fresh clip of cartridges in the rifle and pushed down the sight, all was silence. I remained motionless. Then came a slight sound of falling rocks and the big ram appeared, rushing directly toward me—coming so fast that he crossed the slope to the brink of the canyon before I could get a bead on him. He dashed down the steep opposite side and came running up only twenty feet away, when I fired. He kept on, but fell at the edge of the canyon behind me. Two other big rams were following, but when I fired at him, they separated. One ran up the canyon and as he paused a moment, I killed him in his tracks. The other had gone below but at the sound of the shot, started back. When he reached the top I fired and he rolled down near the bottom. A smaller one ran up the slope near by, but I paid no attention to him.

Then another appeared on the edge of the canyon, where the first two had been shot. He had returned from the bottom of the canyon and seemed confused as to which way to run. Since his horns were large, I pushed up the two-hundred-yard sight, and brought him down. Another then came running out of the canyon directly toward me, and turned to go up the slope. As his horns were not very large, I let him go. The remaining three rams must have ascended through the bottom of the canyon for they were not seen again.

Seven fine rams had been killed by eight shots—and by one who is an indifferent marksman! My trip had quickly turned from disappointment to success.

The U.S. Biological Survey had entrusted me with the mission of securing the skulls of at least four adult rams, with some of their skins, for the study collection in the National Museum, and I desired four reasonably good trophies (the legal limit) for myself. Most of these were now before me.

The rain had stopped. I sat there smoking my pipe, enjoying the exhilaration following the stalk, while the beauty of the landscape about me was intensified by my wrought-up senses.

Although two of the rams, badly wounded, had fallen above the canyon, I could not see them, and finding a route to the bottom, mounted its farther wall. Near the top, I found the first ram lying on his side. While I approached, he simply sat up, looked at me with a wild expression in his eyes, and expanded his nostrils, but did not offer resistance, struggle, or utter a sound as I dispatched him. Then, going above to the next one, I found him also practically unable to move, and promptly put him out of misery. I was obliged to descend the mountain in the dark (about 10:30), and after fording the river reached camp about midnight.

A fire was soon burning, the soup quickly warmed, and tea made. After satisfying my hunger I sat close by the fire to dry my clothes, which had been completely soaked since first I waded the river in the morning. The wind had ceased, the sky had become cloudless, the air frosty and clear. The sparks of the fire shot straight up through the spruce trees, while ghostly shadows danced among them as if to emphasize the inky blackness beyond. By candle light at 1:30 in the morning I finished recording in my journal the success of that memorable day.

Editor's afterword: Over the next few days, Charles Sheldon butchered the sheep; hauled meat, skins, and skulls down Cathedral Mountain; treated skins and skulls for specimen preservation; took measurements; and studied their stomach contents. Then, reunited with his companions, he packed his specimens, left the Denali wilderness, and returned east. Sheldon's main work was now complete. But he also realized the need for a longer stay, to better understand the sheep's life history. On August 1, 1907, Sheldon returned for a second visit[i] that lasted until June 11, 1908. Besides studying sheep, he gathered facts on other species large and small and paid close attention to the landscape, the wildlife habitat, and the changing weather and seasons. He made friends with Denali's year-round residents and met the market hunters who supplied wild meat to the region's mining camps and towns; hunters who, if uncontrolled, would some day threaten Denali's wildlife populations. It was during this second visit to the Denali region that Sheldon began to envision a plan for its preservation.

Part III

Mountaineering

8

To the Top of the Continent

by Frederick A. Cook

Arguably the most enigmatic character to ever walk Denali's slopes, New York Dr. Frederick A. Cook (1865–1940) was a physician, an arctic explorer, a lecturer, a mountaineer, and an author—and, some would add, a notorious liar and convicted criminal. Already a veteran of polar expeditions, Cook organized his first climbing expedition to Denali in 1903—though his team, strangely enough, included no experienced mountaineers. Approaching from Cook Inlet, his six-man, fourteen-horse expedition made two attempts to reach the summit, but barely reached above 11,000 feet. Despite the failed attempts, Cook's party circumnavigated the Alaska Range's two highest peaks, Denali and 17,400-foot Mount Foraker, an amazing if unintentional feat that is still widely regarded as miraculous (and not repeated until the mid-1990s).

Cook returned to Denali in 1906 with a group that included two accomplished climbers, Belmore Browne and Herschel Parker. After two months of exploring the mountain's southern perimeter, the group retreated to Cook Inlet in August, convinced that Denali could not be climbed from the south. Just as the group was breaking up, a peculiar thing happened. Accompanied only by horsepacker Ed Barrill, Cook returned to the great peak for "a last desperate attempt." Upon his return to the coast a few weeks later, Cook sent a telegram back east, proclaiming, "We have reached the summit of Mount McKinley." That wondrous news was, of course, relayed to the press and made major headlines.

Browne and Parker almost immediately doubted Cook's claims. As Browne later explained, "I knew the character of the country that guarded the southern face of the big mountain, had travelled in that country, and knew that the time that Dr. Cook had been absent was too short to allow his even reaching the mountain. I knew that Dr. Cook had not climbed Mt. McKinley."

Over the years, as more and more evidence piled up against Cook,

Previous page: Denali National Park, Mt. McKinley, Pioneer Ridge, morning light (© Pat O'Hara)

most members of the mountaineering community (and the general public) came to agree with Browne. Today only a few holdouts—most notably members of The Frederick A. Cook Society—continue to believe Cook's claims.

Cook described both Denali expeditions in *To the Top of the Continent: Discovery, Exploration and Adventure in Sub-arctic Alaska. The First Ascent of Mt. McKinley, 1903-1906.* Included here are three excerpts in an abridged form. The first documents Cook's initial "defeat" on Denali in 1903; the second summarizes the party's return to the coast and future prospects of climbing the peak; the third is Cook's description of attaining Denali's summit in 1906—now widely regarded as a fanciful account.

PART I: THE EXPEDITION OF 1903

FROM CHAPTER V, "UP THE SLOPES OF MT. MCKINLEY FROM THE SOUTHWEST—THE FIRST DEFEAT"

With an abundance of fresh meat for the men and good grass for the horses and a great undulating treeless country before us, long marches were possible. On the evening of August 11th, we rose to a bluff as the setting sun softened the great waving sea of evergreen forests, extending into the unknown world of the Kuskokwim. Along our line of march the land now became much more irregular. The glacial rivers as we neared the big mountains increased in numbers and size, and the tree line ascended somewhat higher along the streams into the foothills. Heron Glacier was noted just below, pouring huge quantities of ice and rock and water out of the great gold-fringed clouds which hung on the lower slopes of Mt. Foraker, while its three peaks of ice were softened by a warm afterglow. From points near here we got the first glimpse of the top of Mt. McKinley. Its contour was a surprise to us for it indicated a double system of peaks not shown from the east or the west. We could see only the upper four thousand feet over the ice-crested shoulder of Mt. Foraker, a double system of gable roofs placed side by side with the eastern apex slightly higher. The slopes were shingled by plates of ice, which were continuous with the surface of a glacier carrying the drainage down from the median depression. Here was the roof of the continent; the prize of our conquest, seemingly within grasp, and our ambition, cooled by fifty-one days of wet feet, warmed to a new enthusiasm.

We pitched camp on the side of the vigorous stream that rushes out of the grottos of Heron Glacier. Through the waving leaves of the big cottonwood trees we watched the veiling and unveiling of the polished cliffs of Mt. Foraker, with its awe-inspiring cornices chiselled in graceful curves of alabaster. As the beans boiled and the aroma of the bacon and fresh bread drifted with the chill of twilight the echoes of the explosive noises of Heron Glacier sent a thrill of the arctic battlefield to our hearts.

A march of three days over whaleback ridges ploughed by vanished glaciers, took us to a point on a tributary of the Tatlathna River, about fourteen miles northwest of the crest of Mt. McKinley. Our camp was placed beside a foaming stream at an altitude of twenty-six hundred feet, along the edge of the last willows. A mile below we noted the zigzag of the upper line of the spruce forest which we had skirted for two hundred miles. To the east a succession of glacial benches rose gradually for about five miles to an altitude of four thousand feet and there began the sharp pyramidal foothills which are characteristic of this area. In wandering about the camp we saw a great deal of interesting life; mosquitoes and flies were absent, but bumblebees attacked us several times. There were squirrels and marmots, and the bears were so numerous that we never felt safe without firearms at hand. An occasional wolf-track was seen and one wolf was bold enough to come right into our camp. Caribou grazed about like domestic cattle, and moose were always expected in the willows. Mountain sheep were more common in the regions northeast and southwest of Mt. McKinley. Perhaps the most remarkable bit of life we saw here was a family of black foxes following us at long range like dogs and retreating to their earth mounds when we took up the chase.

While here a violent storm swept our camp and we were kept rather busy in holding up the tents and nursing a willow fire. The stream rose with alarming swiftness. Our tents were on a flat not more than three feet above the foaming stream. When we turned into our sleeping bags that night we felt anxious about that rising stream. Shainwald had such premonitions of a coming flood that he devised a safety signal. Placing a small log at a point near our level he attached to it a rope and this rope was taken in his tent and fastened to his toe. The wind blew violently that night and the rain poured down in torrents. Just before dawn Shainwald felt a jerk at his toe. He quickly called all, but we were already lying in pools and when we arose we stumbled into cold water. There was no great danger at this time but in the haste and bustle of moving camp to higher ground we were thoroughly awakened.

Our position was particularly favourable for a promising attack upon the southwest ridge of the big mountain. Before beginning the climb we decided to spend two days in rest and final preparation.

In fifty-four days we had marched a tortuous course of five hundred miles through swamps and forests, over glacial streams, up and down mountainsides, through a trackless country. We had travelled afoot while the horses carried our supplies. In this march we had hoped to get to the mountain by the first of August, but had been delayed a great deal through the illness of the horses during the early part of the trip. The season was now advancing rapidly; storms were beginning to pour down from Mt. McKinley with a great deal of rain; the temperature ranged from 45° to 60°F, and the glacial streams were much swollen. Still, our position seemed so favourable, and the ascent of the mountain appeared so easy from our point of observation, that we felt certain of reaching the summit within a few days.

Our days of rest were spent in making final preparations for the alpine work. We had carried with us a sufficient quantity of hard biscuits for the mountain ascent, but these biscuits had been so much in water and were so often crushed by accidents to the packhorses that they were worthless. We were now compelled to devise some kind of bread for the high altitude, because there bread could not be baked. It occurred to me that we might bake our bread in the usual way with the tin reflector, and then toast and dry it, after the manner of zweiback. For this purpose I detailed Dunn and Miller to go down the river a few miles where they could procure spruce wood, and within twenty-four hours they had successfully baked sufficient bread, and toasted and dried it thoroughly for mountain work. This I think is a new thing in mountaineering and it certainly proved excellent for our purposes.

Our mountaineering equipment was very simple and extremely light. As food for each man we allowed pemmican, 1¼ pounds per day; zweiback, 4 oz. per day; sweetened condensed milk, 4 oz. per day; and some tea. We had also a small quantity of cheese and erbswurst; both of these, however proved unsatisfactory. Pemmican, bread, tea, and sweetened condensed milk seemed to satisfy all our wants. For fuel we had wood alcohol to be burned in aluminum stoves, and also petroleum to be burned in a Primus stove. The latter proved by far the more successful. We carried no dishes except a few cups, spoons, pocket knives, and one kettle, in which we melted snow to get water for our tea.

There was nothing unusual about our clothes, except a large eiderdown robe (the down adhering to the skin of the birds). The robe was so arranged that it could be made into either a sleeping bag or an overcoat. Our tent was made of silk, after a special pattern which I devised for polar work. It was large enough for three men and weighed three pounds. Each man carried a regular alpine axe, and in his rucksack he was to carry his sleeping bag, glacier rope made of horsehair, provisions, and a general outfit for a ten days' stay in the mountains. This weighed forty pounds.

Mt. McKinley presented a formidable face from our camp. The upper ten thousand feet were, during the day, usually wrapped in dark clouds. The best view was obtained when the sun was lowest, and by far the most impressive view was during the long hours of the blue twilight. In the bright light the mountain seemed dwarfed. The foothills, the glacial depressions, and the striking irregularities were then run together into a great heap of mingled snow and rock, but the feebler play of light at dawn and sunset brought out all of the sharp edges, the great cliffs, the depressions, the lesser peaks, and the difficult slopes. To the northeast there was a long ridge with a gradual ascent, but this ridge seemed impossible as a route to the summit because of several lesser peaks, which appeared to bar the way. To the southwest there was a more promising ridge, also interrupted by a spur, which however we hoped to get around. The western face of the great peak between these ridges, above twelve thousand feet, was an almost uninterrupted cliff of pink granite, so steep that snow could not rest upon it. Hence the only way to the summit from the west as we understood it at that time was along the southwesterly ridge.

Aiming for this ridge, we moved our entire camp with the horses along the southern bank of the river to a point on the main stream where it came from a huge moraine. Crossing here, we ascended into a narrow valley four thousand feet, and there pitched our camp. Here the grass was abundant, and the outlook for an easy ascent was good, but the rain came down incessantly. On the following day, with five horses, the entire party pushed over a series of moraines to a glacier which started from an amphitheatre. The ice travelling was quite difficult for the horses; deep snow and numerous crevasses made the task tedious and very dangerous. We pitched our camp at an altitude of seven thousand three hundred feet on the glacier near a part of the wall of the amphitheatre to the southwest, the only place where the slope permitted an ascent. During the night a great deal of snow fell, and on the following morning we left our horses, and in the snowstorm ascended this slope to eight thousand three hundred feet, only to find that farther progress was absolutely cut off by a chasm the cliffs of which we afterward learned led down with a sheer drop of two thousand feet into the bed of Peters Glacier. The horses were sent to the last camp while we remained on the glacier another night and explored the area for a route out of the gathering basin; but the only outlet was toward Mt. Foraker.

Defeat for our first attempt was now evident. There was no way over the gap in the shoulder upon which we had risen. We were, however, able from here to get an occasional peep between the clouds into a new world of great action and sublime beauty.

We therefore descended out of a region of perennial snows into one of perpetual rains at four thousand feet. The base camp was quickly taken down and packed and then we started for the golden lowlands where the sun was seen to shine as we looked between the clouds. Rising to a commanding foot-hill southward we were able to see that there would be great difficulties in rising out of the lower country to the glaciers that looked promising from above, so we now decided that the few remaining days of the closing season would be better spent by an ascent over the ice of Hanna Glacier.

In this sudden descent from eight thousand feet to three thousand feet we noted a languid, feverish feeling, a weakening as if convalescent from a serious illness. We soon learned to accept this descent of spirits with the descent of slopes as an aftermath of every climb.

FROM CHAPTER IX, "DOWN THE SUSITNA—
AROUND THE ALASKA RANGE"

Though our mountaineering ambitions were hopelessly frustrated, we had succeeded in pushing around and through the Alaska Range over unexplored country. We therefore added a good deal of material to the annals of pioneer research. Before leaving the cloud piercing spires of Mt. McKinley we had planned to make a rapid reconnaissance of its eastern approaches and thus obtain data for a future expedition.

Mt. McKinley from the east gives a much clearer impression of great alti-tude. We could not see the lower ten thousand feet, but the upper slopes though difficult are more nearly accessible than those of the west. The upper ten thou-sand feet are rounded like a beehive, and three spurs offer resting places for glacier ice, over which it was thought a route to the summit might perhaps be found.

The season had now so far advanced that if we cared to avoid being detained for the winter, we saw that we must take to our rafts quickly and descend the Chulitna River [and then the Susitna, to Cook Inlet]. We had still to raft sixty miles of an unknown stream. Our supply of provisions was nearly exhausted, we were hatless and almost shoeless, and our clothing was torn into rags.

Returning to the rafts at noon we quickly packed our belongings to start down-stream.

We arrived at Tyonok on September 26th, just four months after our start. In that time we had walked over seven hundred miles, and by boat and raft we had travelled three hundred miles; we had explored a good deal of new territory; we had ascended Mt. McKinley to eleven thousand four hundred feet, encircled the McKinley group, and had made a fair geological and botanical collection. Altogether we had done all that determined human effort could in the short interval of an Alaskan summer.

Mt. McKinley offers a unique challenge to mountaineers, but its ascent will prove a prodigious task. It is the loftiest mountain in North America, the steepest mountain in the world, and the most arctic of all great mountains. Its slopes are weighted down with all the snow and ice that can possibly find a resting place, but unlike Mt. St. Elias, the glaciation is not such as to offer a route over continuous ice. The area of this mountain is far inland, in the heart of a most difficult and trackless country, making the transportation of men and supplies a very arduous task. The thick underbrush, the endless marshes, and the myriad vicious mosquitoes bring to the traveller the troubles of the tropics. The necessity for fording and swimming icy streams, the almost perpetual cold rains, the camps in high altitudes on glaciers in snows and violent storms bring to the traveller all of the discomforts of the arctic explorer. The very difficult slopes combined with high altitude effects add the troubles of the worst alpine climbs. The prospective conqueror of America's culminating peak will be amply rewarded, but he must be prepared to withstand the tortures of the torrids, the discomforts of the North Pole seeker, combined with the hardships of the Matterhorn ascents multiplied many times.

PART II: THE EXPEDITION OF 1906

FROM CHAPTER XIV, "TO THE TOP—
THE WORLD IN WHITE AND THE HEAVENS IN BLACK"

Long before dawn we rolled out of the sleeping bags, crept out of the tent, and then placing the robes about our shivering shoulders we studied the brightening blue of the topmost pinnacle of the Alpine North Pole. I never saw a more impressive spectacle. The peak loomed up like a giant mountain in the curiously deceptive light before dawn. In reality it was but two thousand feet above our camp, a mere fraction of the altitude of the great mountain, but in our enfeebled condition the peak appeared as high and as difficult as the entire uplift from the first camps. As the darkness merged into twilight the sky brightened, but as the sun rose the sky darkened and the cold increased.

With numb fingers and teeth chattering we packed our sleeping bags and a light emergency ration in the rucksacks, and then with a grim determination we started for the culminating peak. The sun soon rose far above the green lowland beyond Mt. Hayes and moved toward the ice-blink caused by the extensive glacial sheets north of the St. Elias group. Our route was over a feathery snowfield which cushioned the gap between rows of granite pinnacles.

During most of this part of the ascent we were in frosty shadows where the cold pierced to the bone, but when we did rise into the direct sunbeams there was a distinct warm sensation. Ten yards away, however, in another shadow, the air was as cold as during the polar night. The sunbeams seemed to pass through the air without leaving behind a trace of heat, similar to the effect of an electric spark through space.

A magnificent spread of an other-world glory ran in every direction. A weird world in white, with stars fading in gloomy blackness. Far below were milky waves of clouds and still farther down ugly gaps of indigo into which the vapours settled to their last resting place. At the present writing I am tempted to enlarge on the awe-inspiring grandeur of this scene, but at the time we were too miserable to spend even visual energy on mere scenic effects.

An advance of twenty steps so fagged us that we were forced to lean over on our ice axes to puff and ease the heart; another twenty steps and another rest, and so on in a life-racking series of final effort.

The last few hundred feet of the ascent so reduced our physical powers that we dropped on to the snow, completely exhausted, gasping for breath. We had gone so near the limit of human endurance that we did not appreciate the proud moments of the hard-earned success. Glad enough were we to pull the eiderdown robes about us, and allow our thumping, overworked hearts, as well as our lungs, labouring in less than half an atmosphere, to catch up. We puffed and puffed, and after a while the sickening thump under the left fifth rib became less noticeable. Breath came and went easier, and then the call of the top was again uppermost. It was an awful task, however, to pick ourselves up out of the deep snow and set the unwilling muscles to work pulling up our legs of stone. The mind was fixed on the glitter of the summit, but the motive force was not in harmony with this ambition.

Just below the summit we dropped over an icy shelf on the verge of collapse. After a few moments we gathered breath and courage and then for the last stage the lifeline tightened with a nervous pull. We edged up along a steep snowy ridge and over the heaven-scraped granite to the top. AT LAST! The soul-stirring task was crowned with victory; the top of the continent was under our feet. Our hands clasped, but not a word was uttered. We felt like shouting, but we had not the breath to spare. The thing that impressed me first was the noble character of Edward Barrille, the bigness in heart and soul of the man who had followed me, without a word of complaint, through hopelessness to success; and then after several long breaths the ghastly unreality of our position began to excite my frosted senses.

Curious experience this. It was September 16th, the temperature 16° below zero, the altitude twenty thousand three hundred and ninety feet. The Arctic Circle was in sight; so was the Pacific Ocean. We were interested mostly, not in the distant scenes, but in the very strange anomaly of our immediate surroundings. It was ten o'clock in the morning, the sky was as black as that of midnight. At our feet the snow glittered with a ghastly light. As the eye ran down we saw the upper clouds drawn out in long strings, and still farther down the big cumulus forms, and through the gap far below, seemingly in the interior of the earth, bits of rugged landscape. The frightful uncanny aspect of the outlook made us dizzy. Fifty thousand square miles of our arctic wonderland was spread out under our enlarged horizon, but we could see it only in sections. Various trains of morning clouds screened the lowlands and entwined the lesser peaks. We could see narrow silvery bands marking the course of the Yukon and the Tanana, while to the south, looking over nearby clouds, we had an unobstructed view. Mt. Susitna, one hundred miles away in a great green expanse, was but a step in the run of distance. The icy cones of the burning volcanoes Redoubt, Illiamna, and Chinabora, the last two hundred miles away, were clearly visible with their rising vapours. Still farther the point of Kenai Peninsula, and beyond, the broad sweep of the Pacific two hundred and fifty miles away!

A record of our conquest was, with a small flag, pressed into a metallic tube and left in a protected nook a short distance below the summit. A round of angles was taken with the prismatic compass. The barometers and thermometers were read, and hasty notes jotted down in our notebook. Most impressive was the curious low dark sky, the dazzling brightness of the frosted granite blocks, the neutral gray-blue of space, the frosty dark blue of the shadows, and, above all, the final picture which I took of Barrille, with the flag lashed to his ax, as the arctic air froze the impression into a relief which no words can tell.

9

The Conquest of Mount McKinley

by Belmore Browne

No one played a greater role in Denali's pioneer mountaineering era than Belmore Browne (1880–1954). Between 1906 and 1912, he and longtime climbing partner Herschel Parker made three attempts to reach Denali's summit—and on their last expedition, they came within a few hundred yards of the top. Except for the untimely arrival of a ferocious mountain storm, the names of Browne and Parker would be as widely recognizable as those of Bradford Washburn, Hudson Stuck, or Frederick Cook—perhaps even more so. In climbing circles, Browne has long been ranked among the greatest of Denali mountaineers. As Washburn comments in his book *Mount McKinley,* "Mountaineers have greatly admired Belmore Browne and his gallant companions [of 1912] over the years, not because they set a new altitude record for North America, or for their near-ascent of McKinley . . . but for the very quality of their undertaking, their daring spirit, their inspiring determination. And the fact that they told the whole simple heartbreaking truth about what actually happened. Even in their tragic defeat, the trio displayed a standard of fairness and nobility that is still applauded . . ."

Born on New York's Staten Island, Browne was at heart a Westerner and outdoorsman who loved to hunt, paint, write, climb, and explore wilderness. In 1905, while traveling by train to Alaska, he happened to meet another Easterner: Herschel Parker. A Columbia University physics professor and talented alpinist, Parker invited Browne to join a Denali climbing expedition he was organizing with Cook. One year later, that team vainly attempted to climb Denali from the south. As the group was breaking up, Cook decided to make "a last desperate attempt." Accompanied only by horsepacker Edward Barrill, he returned to the mountain—and reappeared a few weeks later, claiming success.

Browne immediately doubted Cook's claim. In 1910, he and Parker returned to disprove Cook's claim and make their own second attempt. In Browne's words, their expedition successfully retraced Cook's route "peak by peak and snowfield by snowfield, to within a foot of the spot" where Cook had taken his alleged summit photograph; this turned out to be a spot below 10,000 feet, some 20 miles from Denali's summit. Failing again themselves to reach the top of the continent, Browne and Parker would return in 1912 for a third and last try.

The excerpt included here describes the final ill-fated summit assault of Browne, Parker, and teammate Merl La Voy. This abridged account is taken from Belmore Browne's book *The Conquest of Mount McKinley*, first published in 1913 by Putnam's and reprinted in 1956 by the Houghton Mifflin Company. The June 28 excerpt begins with the team leaving its 16,615-foot camp.

∎

FROM CHAPTER XXVI, "THE CONQUEST OF MOUNT MCKINLEY"

The morning of our final climb dawned clear as crystal. As I came out into the stabbing cold to report on the weather, the whole expanse of country to the northeastward stretched like a deep blue sea to where the rising sun was warming the distant horizon.

True to our schedule we left camp at 6 A.M. Not a sound broke the silence of this desolate amphitheater. At first the snow was hard and required little chopping. We moved very quietly and steadily, conserving our strength for possible exertions to come. At regular half-hour intervals La Voy and I exchanged places, and the steady strokes of our axes went on with scarcely an intermission.

Between changes both Professor Parker and I checked off our rise in altitude, and to our surprise we found that, although we thought we were making fairly good time, we were in reality climbing only 400 feet an hour. Close to the top of the big ridge 1,000 feet above our camp we ran into soft snow and we fought against this unexpected handicap at frequent intervals during the day. When we reached 18,500 feet we stopped for an instant and congratulated each other joyfully, for we had returned the altitude record of North America to America, by beating the Duke of the Abruzzi's record of 18,000 feet made on Mount St. Elias. Shortly afterward we reached the top of the big ridge. Sentiment, old associations, and a desire for a light second breakfast halted us in the lee of some granite boulders. We had long dreamed of this moment, because, for the first time, we were able to look down into our battleground of 1910, and see all the glaciers and peaks that we had hobnobbed with in the "old days." But the views looking northeastward along the Alaskan Range were even more magnificent. We could see the great wilderness of peaks and glaciers spread out below us like a map. On the northern side of the range there was not one cloud; the icy mountains blended into the rolling foothills which in turn melted into the dim blue of the timbered lowlands, that rolled away to the north, growing bluer and bluer until they were lost at the edge of the world. On the humid south side, a sea of clouds was rolling against the main range like surf on a rocky shore. The clouds rose as we watched. At one point a cloud would break through between two guarding peaks; beyond, a second serpentine mass would creep northward along a glacial gap in the range; soon every pass was filled with cloud battalions that joined forces on the northern side, and swept downward like a triumphant army over the northern foothills. It was a striking and impressive illustration of the war the elements are constantly waging along the Alaskan Range.

On the southern side hang the humid cloud banks of the Pacific Coast, the very farthest outpost of the cloud armies of the Japan current; on the north stands the dry, clear climate of the interior, while between, rising like giant earthworks between two hostile armies, stands the Alaskan Range.

We absorbed these beauties as we wound back and forth between the granite boulders on the top of the ridge, and as we advanced the clouds began to thicken on the southern side, but through the deep blue chasms between, the well-remembered contours of the peaks we had explored in 1910—Beard, Hubbard, and Huntington—seemed like the faces of old friends.

As we advanced up the ridge we noticed a shortness of breath and Professor Parker's face was noticeably white, but we made fast time and did not suffer in any other way. At a little less than 19,000 feet, we passed the last rock on the ridge and secured our first clear view of the summit. It rose as innocently as a tilted snow-covered tennis-court, and as we looked it over we grinned with relief—we *knew* the peak was ours!

Just above us the first swell of the summit rose several hundred feet, and we found hard crust and some glare ice where our ice-creepers for the first time began to be of use. Up to our highest camp we had used rubber "shoe-packs" with leather tops, but on our last climb we wore soft tanned moccasins covered with "ice creepers" of the Appalachian Mountain Club design.

From the time that we had topped the ridge the great northern summit of Mount McKinley had claimed our attention. It rose directly opposite to us and every detail of its ice and rock stood out in bold relief against the northern sky. Report has it that the Lloyd Mount McKinley party [the Sourdough Expedition] had reached this peak or one of its northern shoulders and there raised a pole above a pile of rocks.

On our journey up the McKinley Glacier far below we had begun to study this peak. As we advanced closer and closer, each pinnacle of the Northern Ridge stood out in turn against the sky until on the last days close to the southern summit every rock and snow slope of that approach had come into the field of our powerful binoculars. We not only saw no sign of a flagpole but it is our concerted opinion that the Northern Peak is more inaccessible than its higher southern sister.

During our ascent of the ridge and the first swell of the final summit the wind had increased, and the southern sky darkened until at the base of the final peak we were facing a snow-laden gale. As the storm had increased we had taken careful bearings, and as the snow slope was only moderately steep all we had to do was to "keep going uphill." The climbing was now about of the same steepness as that we encountered in scaling the ridge above our camp, and as the snow was driving in thicker clouds before the strengthening wind we cut good steps. The step chopping reduced our progress once more to the 400-foot-an-hour speed.

The slope we were attacking was a round dome that came to a point, forming the top and beginning of the northern heel. Before the wind and snow blotted the upper snowfields from view, we had a good view of the inside of the horseshoe which sloped down to wicked-looking seracs that overhung a snowfield far below. Our one thought therefore was to keep well to the north so that in case we got lost in a blizzard there would be less chance of our descending among the crevasses at the top of the drop off. To accomplish our desire we cut our steps in zigzags of about the same length.

When we started up the last slope above the first swell of the final dome, we were at an altitude of 19,300 feet. At 19,300 feet La Voy had begun his turn of chopping, and as the lower portion of the summit was less steep than the upper slopes we succeeded in rising 500 feet during our combined turns at leading.

As I again stepped ahead to take La Voy's place in the lead I realised for the first time that we were fighting a blizzard, for my companions loomed dimly through the clouds of ice-dust and the bitter wind stabbed through my "parka." Five minutes after I began chopping my hands began to freeze, and until I returned to 18,000 feet I was engaged in a constant struggle to keep the frost from disabling my extremities. La Voy's gloves and mine became coated with ice in the chopping of steps.

The storm was so severe that I was actually afraid to get new, dry mittens out of my rucksack for I knew that my hands would be frozen in the process. The only thing to be done was to keep my fingers moving constantly inside of my leather-covered wool mittens.

When my second turn was three-fourths finished, Professor Parker's barometer registered 20,000 feet. It would have been possible for him to set back the dial and get a higher reading, but beyond this point it would have been dangerous to read the instrument had he been able to. The fury of the storm and the lashing clouds of steel-like ice particles would have made it next to impossible to read the dial.

On reaching 19,000 feet my barometer had registered within 100 feet of Professor Parker's, but as we rose higher my instrument—probably due to false compensation—had dropped with great rapidity to 17,200 feet, or little higher than our camp between the two peaks! From then until I returned to camp it was useless, but on the following day it "recovered its composure" and registered the same as Professor Parker's. Professor Parker's barometer behaved with absolute regularity throughout our whole trip, and as we had been able to study the last slopes carefully and could approximate accurately our speed in climbing, our calculations would place the summit at 20,450 feet or 150 feet higher than the United States Government triangulation. On leaving, and returning to, our base camp, both our barometers and a third that [teammate Arthur] Aten had read twice daily during our absence agreed closely; and furthermore all three agreed closely with Brooks's and Reaburn's contour lines.

After passing the 20,000-foot level, the cold and the force of the wind began to tell on me. I was forced several times to stop and fight with desperate energy the deadly cold that was creeping up my hands and feet. My estimate at the time for the last quarter of my time was 50 feet. As I stepped aside to let La Voy pass me I saw from his face as he emerged from the snow cloud that he realised the danger of our position, but I knew too that the summit was near and determined to hold on to the last moment.

As Professor Parker passed me his lips were dark and his face showed white from cold through his "parka" hood, but he made no sign of distress and I will always remember the dauntless spirit he showed in our most trying hour. The last period of our climb on Mount McKinley is like the memory of an evil dream. La Voy was completely lost in the ice mist, and Professor Parker's frosted form was an indistinct blur above me. I worked savagely to keep my hands warm, and as La Voy's period came to its close we moved slower and more slowly. Finally, I pulled my watch from my neck inside my "parka" hood, and its hands, and a faint hail from above, told me that my turn had come. In La Voy's period we had ascended about 250 feet.

As I reached La Voy I had to chop about twenty feet of steps before coming to the end of the rope. Something indistinct showed through the scud as I felt the rope taughten and a few steps more brought me to a little crack or *bergschrund*. Up to this time we had been working in the lee of the north heel of the horseshoe ridge, but as I topped the small rise made by the crack I was struck by the full fury of the storm. The breath was driven from my body and

I held to my axe with stooped shoulders to stand against the gale; I couldn't go ahead. As I brushed the frost from my glasses and squinted upward through the stinging snow, I saw a sight that will haunt me to my dying day. *The slope above me was no longer steep!* That was all I could see. What it meant I will never know for certain—all I can say is that we were close to the top!

As the blood congealed in my fingers I went back to La Voy. He was getting the end of the gale's whiplash, and when I yelled that we couldn't stand the wind he agreed that it was suicide to try. With one accord we fell to chopping a seat in the ice in an attempt to shelter ourselves from the storm, but after sitting in a huddled group for an instant we all arose—we were beginning to freeze!

I turned to Professor Parker and yelled, "The game's up; we've got to get down!"

And he answered, "Can't we go on? I'll chop if I can." The memory of those words will always send a wave of admiration through my mind, but I had to answer that it was not a question of chopping, and La Voy pointed out our back steps—or the place where our back steps ought to be, for a foot below us everything was wiped out by the hissing snow.

Coming down from the final dome was as heartless a piece of work as any of us had ever done. Had I been blind, and I was nearly so from the trail chopping and stinging snow, I could not have progressed more slowly. Every foothold I found with my axe alone, for there was no sign of a step left. It took me nearly two hours to lead down that easy slope of 1,000 feet! If my reader is a mountaineer he can complete the picture!

Never in my life have I been so glad to reach a place as I was when I reached the top of the first swell below the summit.

Had the cold that was creeping stealthily upward from the tips of La Voy's and my hands and feet once taken hold, we would have frozen in a few minutes, and the worst part of our fight on the summit was the fact that we were fighting a cruel danger that was *unseen!* In the canon of the Yentna in 1906, where Barrill and I had been forced to take our lives in our hands ten times in less than an hour, it was a fair open fight against the rushing water, but in a fight against a blizzard you are struggling blindfolded against a thousand stabbing ice daggers.

Our troubles were not over, however, when we reached the base of the final dome, for here there were no steps, and in descending through the hissing clouds of ice-dust I was led by the wind alone. Again I might have accomplished as much while blinded, for my only guide was the icy blast striking my right shoulder. Had the wind shifted we would have perished, but after what seemed hours a dim shape loomed through the storm—it was the highest rock on the great ridge and our route was now assured. Finding the first rock ended our first struggle on Mount McKinley's summit for in descending we kept in the protecting lee of the great ridge. When the gale quieted enough to let us, we talked! We cursed the storm that had driven us back. La Voy said that we had done enough in getting on top of the mountain, and that we had climbed the peak because it was only a walk of a few minutes from our last steps to the final dome. This was true, but unfortunately there is a technicality in mountaineering that draws a distinction between a mountain top and *the* top of the mountain—we had not stood on *the top*—that was the only difference! We reached camp at 7:35 P.M. after as cruel and heart-breaking a day as I trust we will ever experience.

On the following day we could not climb. Almost all our wearing apparel down to our underclothes was filled with the frost particles that had been driven into our clothing by the gale.

I have spent my life in the open and through the handling of sailing craft have learned to approximate the velocity of wind as accurately as the next man. Professor Parker and La Voy, too, were both men who had had much experience in the judging of wind. The *most conservative* of our estimates of the climatic conditions we fought against was a wind of fifty-five miles an hour and a temperature of 15° below zero. During the entire climb La Voy and I were free from any ill effects from altitude with the exception of moderate shortness of breath, and Professor Parker suffered little more. La Voy and I both found that the use of our arms in step cutting was far more exhausting than leg work. I rolled and smoked a cigarette at 18,000 and 19,000 feet, and enjoyed the tobacco as I do in lower altitudes. Had the storm allowed me to, I would have smoked on top of the mountain. La Voy had never used tobacco in any form. Professor Parker is a light smoker and discontinued the use of tobacco while he was at high altitudes.

The drying out of our clothing was a difficult task as we had only one alcohol stove. To add to our difficulties La Voy and I both developed an attack of snow-blindness from our siege of step cutting, and all day long the stabbing pains shot through our temples. Fate too ordained that the peak should be clear, although long "mare's tails" of snow stretching out to the north told us that the gale was still lashing the summit.

FROM CHAPTER XXVII, "THE END OF THE LONG TRAIL"
Throughout the long day after our fight with the summit we talked food and weather conditions. We had now given up all thought of eating pemmican [a

high-energy food consisting of dried meat and melted fat, which proved in-
digestible at high altitude] and were living, as in fact we had been living since
leaving our 15,000-foot camp, on tea, sugar, hardtack [an unleavened bread],
and raisins. Our chocolate was finished. We had cached our pemmican as we
advanced according to the daily amount we were able to choke down, and
we found on studying the matter that *we had lost ten days' rations in useless pemmican since leaving our 13,600-foot camp!* In our highest camp alone we had lost
four days' rations! We were not only harassed by the thought of the food we
had lost, but also by the memory of *the useless weight we had carried.* Moreover,
we were forced to eat more of our hardtack and raisins in an attempt to gain
the nourishment we had been deprived of by the loss of our pemmican.

This complication reduced us to four meagre days' rations, which meant
that we could only make one more attempt on the summit of Mount McKinley,
and that attempt must be made on the following day.

The reader will realise with what breathless interest we studied the weather
conditions. What had caused the storm on the summit? we asked each other.
Was it a general storm sweeping in from the Susitna Valley, or was it a local
tourmente caused by change of temperature? Similar questions filled our minds,
and we decided to leave at 3 A.M. on our next attempt.

The following day, strengthened as far as our insipid food would allow, and
with our eyes patched up by boracic acid, we started on our final attack.

The steps made on the previous day helped us and in four hours and a half
or by 7:30 A.M. we had reached an altitude of 19,300 feet at the base of the
final dome. From this point we could see our steps made on the first attempt
leading up to the edge of the final dome, and from this point we also secured
the photograph of the summit that appears in this book.

But our progress up the main ridge had been a race with a black cloud
bank that was rolling up from the Susitna Valley, and as we started towards our
final climb the clouds wrapped us in dense wind-driven sheets of snow. We
stood the exposure for an hour; now chopping a few steps aimlessly upwards,
now stamping backward and forward on a little ledge we found, and when
we had fought the blizzard to the limit of our endurance we turned and without
a word stumbled downward to our ridge. I remember only a feeling of weakness and dumb despair; we had burned up and lived off our tissue until we
didn't care much what happened! In a crevice on the highest rock of the main
ridge we had left our minimum thermometer; it, a few cans of frozen pemmican, and our faithful old shovel, are the only traces of our struggle on the
Big Mountain.

We reached camp at 3 P.M. and after some hot tea we felt a wild longing to

112

leave the desolate spot. Packing our necessities carefully we shouldered our light loads and struck off down the glacier. I turned on the edge of the glacier bench for a last look at our old camp. Stuck deep in the snow our battered shovel showed black above a foot-trampled blue, while above, the roar of the wind came down from the dark clouds that hid the summit.

Editor's afterword: The trio rejoined Arthur Aten at base camp on July 4; two days later, the team witnessed an avalanche like no other they had seen. A deep rumbling came from the Alaska Range and the earth around them began to roll. A few minutes later, the entire western flank of Mount Brooks—about ten miles from camp—began to avalanche. Plunging down the mountain like a gigantic wave, the snowslide tumbled thousands of feet onto the glaciers below, creating an enormous white cloud that Browne estimated to be 4,000 feet high. Months later, the climbers learned that the earthquake that caused the immense avalanche had been connected to an earlier eruption of Mount Katmai (hundreds of miles away). Unknown to Browne and the others, that same avalanche tore apart large sections of their route above base camp, ripping off huge chunks of ice and bedrock and turning the Northeast Ridge (later renamed Karstens Ridge) into a jumble of ice blocks. Had members of the expedition been descending the ridge when the ground shook, in all likelihood they would have been killed. Ironically, the pemmican diet and stormy weather that drove the climbers down may also have saved their lives by forcing them off the upper mountain before the earthquake struck.

10

Mount McKinley: The Conquest of Denali

by Bradford Washburn

Born in Cambridge, Massachusetts, in 1910, lifelong New Englander Bradford Washburn has maintained a long-distance love affair with the Denali region for more than sixty years. A celebrated scientist, photographer, author, lecturer, cartographer, explorer, and mountaineer, Washburn is widely recognized as the world's leading authority on Mount McKinley—a name he prefers to Denali, because it is the officially recognized one. In many quarters, this longtime director of the Boston Museum of Science (now its honorary director) is affectionately nicknamed "Mr. McKinley." And with good reason: Since his first photographic and aerial mapping flights over the peak in 1936, he has devoted much of his life to its study and exploration.

Washburn has spent more than 200 days on the mountain's slopes, visited it in every month except February, and stood on its summit three times, including once (in 1947) with his wife, Barbara, the first woman to reach the roof of the continent. In 1960, he produced his highly acclaimed Mount McKinley map, still considered a cartographic work of art. And his photographic record of the mountain remains unmatched. He showcases many of his photographs in *Mount McKinley: The Conquest of Denali,* which Washburn co-authored with David Roberts, a mountaineer, world traveler, and writer who has earned critical acclaim for both his climbing and writing.

Over the years, Washburn has also acted as McKinley's visionary, recommending several new routes to the mountain's top. His remarkable vision was first demonstrated in 1947, when he publicly proposed a new path to the summit in *The American Alpine Journal.* Naming it the West Buttress Route, Washburn predicted that this new path—and not the Muldrow Glacier followed by early expeditions—would be the safest, easiest, and quickest way up McKinley, if an expedition received aerial support. Sure enough, most modern McKinley mountaineers, assisted by airplane transport to the Kahiltna Glacier, have followed the West Buttress.

Even before his first trips to McKinley, Washburn had been thrilled by the stories of its early mountaineers, such as Belmore Browne, Hudson Stuck, and the Alaska "Sourdoughs." More than any other group of climbers, past or present, those four miners-turned-mountaineers symbolize the pioneering spirit and adventurous nature of what is often called the Alaskan mystique. During the past ninety years, their ascent has become legendary.

Washburn's description of the 1910 Sourdough Expedition, "Attack from the Northeast," is included here. It originally appeared as Chapter 5 of *Mount McKinley: The Conquest of Denali,* published in 1991 by Harry N. Abrams, Inc., Publishers.

C ook's McKinley and North Pole explorations instantly stirred up a tempest of activity among those who really wanted to be the first on Mount McKinley' summit—and at the same time to prove that Cook and Barrill could not possibly have made the top. While Herschel Parker and Belmore Browne were finalizing their plans for another determined attack from the southeast, an extraordinary all-Alaskan expedition was taking shape in Fairbanks—in midwinter. Its objective was simple and direct: to have Alaskans climb their own mountain first and "to prove that Doc Cook was a goddam liar!"

The question of whether or not Cook had reached the top of McKinley was one of the main topics of barroom conversation throughout Alaska as soon as his book appeared in February 1908. Fairbanks in those days was a frontier town, populated largely by prospectors and the people who outfitted them and supplied their diverse and practical needs. They were just plain fed up with the streams of classy "outsiders" who kept coming to Alaska to explore their wilderness and climb their mountains. These "sourdoughs" were a tough, competent, self-sufficient, ingenious bunch. A number of them had sized up McKinley and its approaches from the north and northeast after Judge Wickersham had tried to climb the mountain in 1903, for it was only thirty miles away from their mining claims in the Kantishna area—just a stone's throw from the present site of [the wilderness lodge] Camp Denali.

Charlie McGonagall was one of the toughest, yet smallest, of these unique explorers. In search of gold, he had often hiked southward from Moose Creek, past Wonder Lake, across the McKinley River (whose source is the meltwater of Muldrow Glacier), and over the rolling tundra upland to Cache Creek. From there he had climbed, solo, all the way along the creek to its trident of upper

115

forks. Entirely by chance, he once selected the central fork and followed it, in an easy scramble up a barren rock valley that emerged at an amazing little pass. There, to his astonishment, he found himself looking out across the vast, smooth ice surface of Muldrow Glacier, a full twenty-six miles above its terminus. This pass, the first of the keys that opened the route to the top of McKinley from the Northeast, now bears Charlie McGonagall's name. He found no gold there, "just a lot of snow and ice and rotten granite." But, looking up the glacier from his pass, he saw that, for several miles above where he stood, Muldrow was "as smooth as Wall Street, the easiest sort of walking."

After McGonagall had discovered this pass, two other events of vital importance to McKinley's climbing history took place, in the summer of 1906 and the early winter of 1908. At that time Charles Sheldon, the great naturalist, and Harry Karstens of Fairbanks had camped and collected biological specimens throughout the northern foothills of the Alaska Range. On August 5, 1906, Sheldon and Karstens climbed to the top of a "rounded summit," almost certainly today's Stony Hill on the Denali Highway [actually, the Denali Park Road]. From its top, in perfect weather, they "obtained a magnificent view of Denali, free from clouds, towering above the adjacent snowy peaks." Sheldon reported: "I could now view its double summit from the east, and distinctly see the great Muldrow Glacier falling down its eastern side from the snowfield between the two domes. The view from 'Bog Hill' was magnificent and more complete of Denali than any I have yet seen. The south peak near the western extremity of the south dome is the highest point. A glacier [the Harper Glacier of today] descends between the south and north summit domes. I believe that if the top of this glacier [today's Denali pass] can be reached along its south edge, the mountain can be ascended. From my position it looked possible. But the difficulties may be found below on parts of the mountain I could not see." Sheldon reached this conclusion as he and Karstens stood only a stone's throw from where Dr. Cook had made the same observation on September 5, 1903.

On January 14, 1908, Sheldon and Karstens visited Tom Lloyd at his claim on Glen Creek, eight miles east of Kantishna, where he and McGonagall and Billy Taylor were prospecting for gold: "From the crest of the high [4,000-foot] ridge behind Lloyd's cabin extended a magnificent unobstructed view, reaching along the Alaska Range east and west of Denali," wrote Sheldon. "While standing there with Tom Lloyd, I told him of the double ridge summit and of the great icefall [now Harper Icefall] descending easterly from the basin between them, and asserted my belief that if no technical difficulties should be found below the upper areas, the great mountain could be climbed from the ridge bordering the north side of the glacier."

By 1909, this background of information was well known to most of the Kantishna miners, along with the remarks of [earlier explorers] Brooks, Cook, and Dunn. Sheldon and Karstens were certain that the way to the top of McKinley was clear above the halfway point, and McGonagall had found a pass that led to Muldrow Glacier. At that time, only a scrap of the route—from about 9,000 to 12,000 feet—remained unseen. Is it any wonder, then, that exciting things happened among a group of semi-inebriated sourdoughs one evening in the fall of that year?

The conversation at the saloon started with the usual discussion about Cook and McKinley, now kindled to white heat by the new Peary-Cook polar controversy. The barside chatter finally erupted into a $5,000 bet placed by Bill McPhee, owner of the saloon, that McKinley would be climbed by somebody before July 4, 1910. Nobody at the saloon liked "easterners" very much, and the whole Cook mess had infuriated everyone. If Cook hadn't done it, some other goddamned outsider like Abruzzi or Parker or Browne soon would. Although no gold was to be found at Charlie McGonagall's pass, why not make an honest buck by winning Bill's bet and thwart those outsiders at the same time? Five thousand dollars is no little sum today, and even amid all the gold-talk of Fairbanks in 1909, it was a very tempting prize. It did not take long for a group of enterprising miners to take up McPhee's challenge.

The organizer and leader of the now famous "Sourdough Expedition" to Mount McKinley was its weakest, flabbiest member, Tom Lloyd. His partners were an experienced, rugged group of prospectors: Peter Anderson, William R. ("Billy") Taylor, and Charlie McGonagall. Others who traveled with the climbers to the base camp were Robert Horne, William Lloyd, and Charles E. Davidson, later to become surveyor-general of Alaska.

Their departure was front-page news in the *Fairbanks Daily Times* of December 22, 1909, which carried the report under the headline "Cheers are Given as Climbers Leave." It was a "thrilling sight." From outside the Pioneer Hotel Horne led off with a "sturdy team of dogs," followed by three horse-drawn sleds, driven by Taylor, Tom Lloyd and Davidson, and McGonagall. Billy Lloyd closed the ranks with a mule-drawn sled.

Crazy as this expedition sounds, it was very carefully planned. The sour-doughs started out "outfitted as no McKinley expedition was ever before outfitted, and with less 'junk' with them than an Eastern excursion party would take along for a one-day's outing in the hills." Billy Taylor, when asked years later what they ate, replied succinctly: "Bacon, beans, flour, sugar, dried fruit, and butter." This menu was supplemented in the lowlands by caribou or moose they shot along the way and ate in "steaks or stews." On the mountain, when

117

climbing, they stuck to doughnuts and hot chocolate. Each man wore heavy winter underwear, bib overalls, a heavy woolen shirt, a windproof canvas parka, and heavy mittens—the typical, practical garb of dog drivers along a winter trail in the Yukon. Their gear was simple, rugged, inexpensive—and it worked.

Although there is no formal daily record of events from this expedition, Tom Lloyd kept a very interesting diary up to the head of Muldrow Glacier. And the details of the journey from there to the summit have emerged over the years from interviews with the two men who made the climb: Billy Taylor (by Norman Bright) and Charlie McGonagall (by myself), filled out by lengthy chats I had with Harry Karstens, who had heard the whole story firsthand from all the participants.

From Fairbanks to the foot of McKinley is a very long way—well over 150 miles along the course of the winding trail. But it is relatively level and much easier going in the dead of winter when all the bogs and rivers are frozen solid—and there are no mosquitoes. The party took plenty of time on this long trek to Kantishna. It was very cold in January and the days were very short—the sun rose around eleven and set just after one. They also visited many miner friends along the way; at fifty degrees below zero, it is more pleasant to spend the night in a snug cabin than in a tent.

After leaving the Kantishna "diggings," the party dogsledded across Wonder Lake and set up camp on Februray 14, in the last good timber on the banks of the McKinley River, twenty-eight miles north of McKinley and 1,800 feet above the sea. Here they discovered the remains of an old camp and a note on a blazed tree: "Alfred H. Brooks, August 21, 1902." Parker and Browne also found this abandoned camp, Lloyd's tent and all, during their expedition to McKinley two years later.

After a few days of resting and planning at Lloyd's Glen Creek cabin, they crossed the gentle hills to Cache Creek and set up a comfortable base camp on February 27, at the "last willows," four miles below Muldrow Glacier and 2,900 feet above sea level. While they were here, a violent argument broke out between Davidson and Tom Lloyd. The subject is not known, but one story holds that a fist fight ensued. The following day Davidson, Horne, and Billy Lloyd pulled out of camp and headed north, leaving the party without its one experienced surveyor and photographer. Hudson Stuck later remarked that, as a result, from this point on the trip was a "sporting adventure" rather than a serious expedition.

At any rate, as the violence of the winter waned and the sun rose higher in the sky, the remaining members of the party pushed onward up Cache Creek and over McGonagall Pass. On March 13 they reached their first camp on the glacier, at the corner opposite Gunsight Pass, below the First Icefall, at an altitude of about 6,500 feet. They called it "Pothole Camp," and it is pictured in the *New York Times Magazine* of Sunday, June 5, 1910—an 8-by-10-foot wall tent, complete with a tin stovepipe and wooden ridgepole, surrounded by a high wall of snow blocks to protect it from the wind.

Another picture in the *Times,* easy to identify and also clearly taken from this camp, shows that they worked their way around the First Icefall on the right (northwest) side of the glacier, a steep snowy side hill that must have been miserable dogsledding. From there they made a huge move all the way past the Great Icefall, to their final camp at the upper end of the Muldrow. According to both McGonagall and Taylor, they managed to cross most of the big crevasses by using a "portable bridge" of long, light, dead spruce logs which they carried along for the purpose. Everyone fell repeatedly into the smaller cracks but "always managed to get out" somehow, unharmed.

Their final camp was established on March 18 at 10,900 feet, apparently excavated right into the hillside at the bottom of the ridge later named for Harry Karstens. A photograph taken of the view toward Mount Silverthrone from this site and published in the *New York Times* leaves no doubt as to its location.

The next challenge the men faced was to negotiate the crest of this 3,600-foot ridge of snow and ice that climbed steeply upward to the great basin of Harper Glacier, which led directly to McKinley's twin summits. After taking one good look at the ridge, and possibly making a brief attempt to climb it, the team decided to establish no more camps above "Tunnel Camp," since backpacking would be murderous. Their goal would be to make the summit climb in a fantastic 9,000-foot dash, up and back in a single day. Nowadays we talk of "alpine-style" climbing as if it's a new idea, but this climb, if it could be done, would be the first and most extraordinary alpine-style dash ever.

But the wise sourdoughs didn't want to make their summit bid too soon. They wanted to have a well-stocked camp to which they could retreat in case of a big storm, and they wanted to prepare the great ridge by creating a giant staircase that they could go up fast and descend speedily in case of bad weather near the top.

It is astonishing when one reads the brief notes that recorded the activities of the next few days to see how many trips were made up and down the glacier—all the way back to Cache Creek, fifteen miles away. Because most of the dogs were needed by other miners, the climbers had only half a dozen to help them. As a result, they had to do a lot of backpacking up "Wall Street Glacier" (their name for Muldrow), hauling not only their food and equipment forward, but also lots of firewood for their sheet-iron Yukon stove.

Charlie McGonagall looked back on the final week as one of seemingly endless step-cutting. They had no alpine ice-axes, just stafflike walking sticks, a shovel to excavate steps, and a regular axe to use when it was too icy for the shovel. Day after day they dug and chopped that 4,000-foot staircase— first completing it to the end of the ridge (at what is now known as Browne Tower, at 14,600 feet) and then making trips up and back to clear fresh-blown snow from the steps to keep them ready for the great day.

It came finally, on April 1, 1910. Rising at five, already in broad daylight now that it was spring, the team started up the staircase. Alas, far up the ridge the clouds rolled in, and the men were forced to return to camp, frustrated and discouraged. But after one more stormy day, the skies cleared, and on April 3, after a breakfast of bacon and beans, the doughty three-man team was off again, this time before dawn, at three in the morning. Billy Taylor took a "sack with six doughnuts and a thermos of hot cocoa to eat on the trail" and reported that the others did the same. They also dragged along a fourteen-foot dried spruce flagpole, tied to a short handline. Said McGonagall, "On the glacier below we packed it, but up on the ridge it was too long to carry and it throwed you off balance."

They made the 3,600 vertical feet to Browne Tower in less than three hours and then traversed the lower plateau of Harper Glacier (15,000 feet above sea level). Then they tackled the worst slope of all—now known as the Sourdough Gully—which climbs at angles from forty to fifty-five degrees for 2,200 feet, all the way from the gently sloping plateau to the crest of the final ridge of the North Peak at 18,200 feet.

Why did they climb the North Peak (19,450 feet) instead of the South Peak (20,320 feet)? Apparently they thought all along that the North Peak was the higher. It certainly does look like the top from anywhere near Wonder Lake or Kantishna, and, seen from Browne Tower, it looks much higher than the South Peak. They also knew that the South Peak was not visible at all from the Kantishna mining camps, and they wanted their friends to see their flag and "know damned well that we'd been there!"

In choosing their ascending order, Charlie McGonagall drew third place. Billy Taylor was second. Peter Anderson was the toughest and led most of the way. That they were able to hack their way up that gully was amazing for no preliminary work had been done there, and it was always steep and icy. It was a tremendous job of step-chopping and very delicate climbing with no rope ("we didn't bother with it") or belays of any sort. Once they reached the crest of the ridge the going was easy but the breathing much harder.

At 18,700 feet, just a few hundred yards short of the summit, they came to the final outcrop of rocks. There they decided to erect the pole, as it was the only place where it could be well secured at the bottom. Charlie McGonagall stayed there and worked on guying the pole. He secured it with "four guy-lines, just cotton ropes . . . fastened . . . to the little spurs of rocks" and nailed onto it "a piece of a candle-box with our names and the date." When asked why he hadn't gone to the top, he replied: "My job was to haul the pole and that was as far as it would go. Why go farther? There was a terrific view up there!" Pete Anderson and Billy Taylor reached the top at 3:25 P.M. "Colder than hell; it was 30 below. Mitts and everything was all ice," Taylor told Norman Bright. The view was stunning, but the lowlands were hidden by a sea of clouds. The two men agreed that they had spent two to three hours climbing to the summit and then descending the narrow bridge to the flagpole—Charlie got very cold waiting. And then it took a long time for the three of them to se-cure the flagpole to everyone's satisfaction.

That they descended the gully with no rope, no ice axes, and nothing but "creepers" [crude crampons] on their rubber-soled "shoepacs" is a miracle—but they finally returned safely to camp at nine o'clock that night, after eigh-teen hours on the trail. Billy Taylor brought back three of his six doughnuts. He hadn't found time to eat them.

The next day they hustled all the way down to base camp, and then headed home to the Kantishna and back to work. Lloyd said of his team: "Bill Taylor is a big man and strong as a horse. . . . Pete Anderson is a tower of strength. . . . Everyone knows Charlie McGonagall. He has been a mail-driver in the North for years, and he is a wonderful fellow." The same, however, could not be said of Tom Lloyd. His only prize was won for getting it all started. For once he had reached the tunnel camp at the bottom of Karstens Ridge he retreated to base camp and immediately after the climb hightailed it back to Fairbanks. And there, on April 11, *he declared that all four of them had reached the top of both peaks of McKinley together!* The news was broadcast the next day with banner headlines in the *Fairbanks Daily Times* and on April 14 in the *New York Times*—echoes of Dr. Cook made by the very man who had planned the expedition to prove that Cook was the "King of Fakers."

The other three members of the party were furious when the news hit Kantishna. By the time they returned to Fairbanks early in the summer, doubts about everyone's story naturally had begun to circulate, both in Alaska and "outside." Even Charles Sheldon and Herschel Parker wondered. Billy Taylor later said: "We three didn't get out until June and by then they didn't believe *any* of us had climbed McKinley!"

But Alaskans *had* climbed McKinley's North Peak. They had done it alone and in their own way. What they did is still recorded as one of the most extraordinary exploits in all of mountaineering history. And they had proof of their success—that flagpole!

Editor's afterword: A final blow to the Sourdoughs' weakening credibility in the wake of Lloyd's lies was apparently struck in 1912, when Belmore Browne and Herschel Parker reported they saw no evidence of the fourteen-foot flagpole during their attempt to climb McKinley. Because Browne and Parker carefully documented their own ascent, great credibility was given to their point of view. As Parker put it, "Dr. Cook didn't have anything on the Lloyd party when it comes to fabrications." Case closed. Or so it seemed at the time. The Sourdough story became generally accepted as nothing more than an Alaskan tale, until the following year.

In 1913, after a decade of unsuccessful attempts to reach the pinnacle of North America, the expedition led by Episcopal missionary Hudson Stuck spotted the Sourdoughs' flagpole while en route to the summit. The climbers made their exciting discovery from the Grand Basin (now known as the Harper Glacier), located between the North and South Peaks. In *The Ascent of Denali,* Stuck recalled: "While we were resting, we fell to talking about the pioneer climbers of this mountain who claimed to have set a flagstaff near the summit of the North Peak, as to which feat a great deal of incredulity existed in Alaska for several reasons, and we renewed our determination if weather permitted when we had ascended the South Peak, we would also climb the North Peak to seek for traces of this earlier exploit on Denali. All at once Walter [Harper] cried out: 'I see the flagstaff!' Eagerly pointing to the rocky prominence nearest the summit—the summit itself covered with snow—he added: 'I see it plainly!' [Harry] Karstens, looking where he pointed, saw it also and, whipping out the field glasses, one by one we all looked, and saw it distinctly standing against the sky. With the naked eye I was never able to see it unmistakably, but through the glasses it stood out, sturdy and strong, one side covered with crusted snow. We were greatly rejoiced that we could carry down positive information of this matter." It is especially worth noting that Stuck's party was the only group ever to verify the flagpole's existence. The next expedition to climb the North Peak, two decades later in 1932, failed to find any evidence of the pole. Except for the one chance sighting, the Sourdoughs' story might always have been regarded as a tall tale. But thanks to the efforts of the 1913 expedition, this group of skookum miners was finally and deservedly given credit for what Stuck called "a most extraordinary feat, unique—the writer has no hesitation in claiming—in all the annals of mountaineering." Ninety years later, the Sourdoughs' achievement is still recognized as extraordinary. And certainly unique.

Following is a second Washburn excerpt from his book, *Mount McKinley: The Conquest of Denali*. Excerpted from Chapter 14, "Going to Extremes," this text considers some of the challenges remaining on McKinley and why the peak, in Washburn's words, continues "to tempt the world's top mountaineers."

The exploration of the great mountains of the world passes through a series of phases that seems to be identical on every continent and in every range.

At first, the mere investigation of the region around a virgin peak and the approaches to its base requires months or years to complete. During this basic reconnaissance, the pioneers constantly study the heights in hopes of locating the weakest spots in the mountain's armor. Often when great peaks are studied this intensively by an experienced team, several climbable routes and approaches may be found. When the job is done, the team always reports the shortest, easiest, safest route as the one by which to attempt the first ascent.

This first approach is usually along a ridge, as ridges are by their very nature the safest routes—and often the shortest. You can fall off a ridge, but if you are climbing along one, you are usually safest from avalanches, the objective dangers over which you have no control no matter how good a climber you are. Here the judgment of the leader or whoever makes these primary decisions is of vital importance to the safety of the whole party.

When a peak has been climbed once, its attraction diminishes dramatically for those who enjoy only virgin ground. (These people are having less and

123

less enjoyment in the mountain ranges of our world today.) For most of those who savor real adventure, however, almost all of the world's mountains, large or small, have several ridges leading to their summits. When one of these has been climbed, the next one is likely to be the shortest and safest of the remaining unclimbed routes.

Once all of the ridges have been climbed, attention tends to center on the valleys and faces between them, unless at the very start one of the valleys proved to be the best route of all. On McKinley the wisest route turned out to be a combination of two valleys linked by a very safe ridge: Muldrow Glacier, Karstens Ridge, and Harper Glacier.

As the focus moves to the faces that lie between the obviously safe routes, the accident potential increases enormously. Some faces are relatively safe, but those that are dominated by unstable walls of ice or snow are lethal trouble spots. Here the climber's safety is no longer in any way related to competence. His life depends on whether or not an avalanche sweeps his route while he is on it. This sort of Russian roulette is being played more and more frequently throughout the world today. Many shrewd players of this chancy game study the walls they want to climb for days or weeks, trying to determine how often they are swept by avalanches. If the face of the ice wall that dominates the route regularly falls off only once each week, then the safest time to enter the corridor of death is immediately after the last avalanche. Then the big problem is how long the climb will take.

Such a situation exists today on McKinley's magnificent East Face—a 9,000-foot wall of granite ribs, dominated by several very active walls of unstable ice. The great Traleika Icefall at the bottom of this face is so steep and moving so fast that it epitomizes the roulette game. Only one party has ever tried it, in 1971. Miraculously, its members managed to thread their way up through the icefall—and back down—without accident, but on the descent they repeatedly found sections of their uphill route wiped out by the collapse of huge ice pinnacles. The climb was so uniformly dangerous that the team did not want to risk relaying supplies up through the 3,000 feet of this icy Niagara to the safer going above, from which a successful summit attempt would be possible. Now we have superbly detailed stereo pictures of every inch of this route and they have been thoroughly studied by top climbers, as McKinley's East Face would be a great prize. But nobody has yet wanted to make a second attempt at that icefall—and nobody has yet wanted to set foot in the great avalanche-cones above it that guard the approaches to the dramatic yet climbable and safe granite ridges that separate them. History, however, is certain to repeat itself. Someone, probably soon, will climb that wall, complex and dangerous as are its approaches.

The climbers today who are attempting these new routes up McKinley and its satellites are an extraordinary breed. Although they come from all over the world, many of the very best are from America's West and Alaska. Certainly, they all have better clothing, food, and equipment than the "pioneers" of only fifty years ago. They have also learned how to use this new gear with superb effectiveness. But most of the new routes that they are forging today are so steep and technically so difficult—even when they are safe—that none of the best climbers in the last generation would have considered them at all possible. In fact, they would not have even thought of attempting this sort of climb.

Twenty years ago none would have dared to apply California's Yosemite techniques to the frigid walls of Alaska's peaks or the Himalaya. If there were no little ledges or shoulders where you could camp for the night on one of these walls, you simply did not try to climb them. In Yosemite it is possible to bivouac for the night slung in a featherweight hammock hitched to a few pitons hammered judiciously into the oft-overhanging rock—but not in Alaska. Nevertheless, it is now being done on all these Alaskan walls, sometimes in the winter. And so, one by one, new routes are being climbed successfully today by a handful of experts whose abilities, physical stamina, and resourcefulness transcend the wildest dreams of the leaders of only a few years ago.

But what drives people to do this sort of thing? As a big peak is finally dissected to a point where virtually all the basic routes have been climbed somehow by somebody, others begin to attempt what the French call *variantes*. These routes follow the majority of the path that has been climbed before but then fork off up a new gully or a succession of hitherto unclimbed ledges to rejoin the old route higher up on the climb. All of these variations are incredibly difficult, some very exposed, and some dangerous. Their divergence from the basic first ascent is often too brief to rate them as a new climb, but they give a special sense of achievement and joy to those who do them.

The psychology behind all this is very simple: those of us who compete want to do our thing a bit better than or a bit differently from those who have gone before. Whether it's the individual who strives to whittle a second off the record for the mile run or the person who climbs Everest alone in five days without oxygen, this drive for what is different, or new, or better is an integral part of the human psyche. As the limits of possibility accepted by each generation are overcome and new goals replace them, the elite group that is pressing at these frontiers becomes smaller, ever more competent, and often far more willing to put their lives on the line to achieve success.

If a virgin peak may be considered to be in its youth, McKinley is now approaching old age in this scheme of things. As possible new routes on its slopes have dwindled to a handful and involve more unavoidable danger, climbers have turned to its satellites for new challenges—the undeniable thrill of climbing on rock and ice that nobody before has ever touched, of experiencing vistas that no one in all the passage of time has seen. This thrill of discovery lies at the heart of all human endeavor, and in the mountains it is no different from anywhere else—except that the game, if played to the extreme, involves danger as well as difficulty, and those who play the game out at the pioneer fringe of the Alaska Range can no longer do so unless they are endowed with extraordinary skill, stamina, and judgment.

And why does McKinley tempt the world's top mountaineers, when the Alps, the Andes, or even exciting parts of the Himalaya are far easier to approach? What tempted Riccardo Cassin, Lionel Terray, Doug Scott, and Dougal Haston? Why did Barbara and I devote half our lifetimes to charting this range and delving deeply into its secrets?

The answer is simple. There are few mountains of any size, anywhere on earth, that share McKinley's pristine beauty or offer the fascination of its rugged and exquisite wilderness approaches, its lush lowlands and rushing, icy rivers, its flora, and its as–yet–unspoiled wildlife. Whether you first glimpse it at dawn from the gateway of the Chulitna Canyon or at twilight across Wonder Lake, you are caught spellbound by its grandeur and its aloofness from everything else that surrounds us in the hectic confines of our lower world.

Why do people want to struggle through the wilderness to McKinley's summit, knowing well in advance the inevitable physical miseries and downright dangers the struggle will involve, from the mosquito-ridden tundra of its approaches, through its crevasse-gutted glaciers, to the last granite crags that support its drifted peak?

The magnets that draw people to McKinley in ever-growing numbers, year after year, are different for everyone. Hudson Stuck, who had lived and worked in its shadow for years, said that he would rather climb it than discover the richest gold mine. Pete Anderson and Billy Taylor climbed it to win a miners' bet. Dr. Cook attempted it because its conquest would bring him the fame that would finance his trip to the North Pole. Belmore Browne loved the struggle with the wilderness in any form, forest or glacier, ridge or canyon:

McKinley epitomized this love. Hemmed in by the increasing complexities of civilization, we all feel a special joy in coming face-to-face with the best that nature has to offer.

And every one of us who has climbed to the crest of McKinley's final wind-swept drift will remember Robert Tatum's very personal thrill of pausing there to look "out the windows of Heaven."

Two thousand years ago, Aristotle understood better than most of us do today each person's ceaseless urge to press forward the frontiers of our knowledge:

> *The Search for the Truth is in one way hard,*
> *and in another easy,*
> *For it is evident that no one of us*
> *Can ever master it fully, nor miss it wholly.*
> *Each of us adds a little to our understanding of Nature,*
> *And from all the facts assembled arises a certain grandeur.*

11

The Ascent of Denali

by Hudson Stuck

Hudson Stuck (1863–1920) came to Alaska in 1904, the year after Dr. Frederick Cook and Judge James Wickersham had launched the first serious attempts to reach the top of the continent. Largely unknown in mountaineering circles, Stuck by his own admission was "no professed explorer, or climber or 'scientist,' but a missionary. . . . " More concerned with men than mountains, he had traveled north to work with Alaska's Natives. As archdeacon of the Yukon, he visited settlements throughout Interior Alaska year-round, while traveling by foot, river boat, and dog team.

Yet Stuck's passion for missionary work was nearly matched by a deep-seated enthusiasm for mountaineering. Though a self-professed "amateur in these matters," he had climbed as a boy in the hills of Scotland, then later in the Canadian Rockies and on 14,410-foot Mount Rainier. Among the supplies he brought to Alaska was his complete set of climbing gear.

Almost from the start, Stuck found himself tempted by North America's highest peak, exclaiming, "I would rather climb that mountain than discover the richest gold mine in Alaska." Seven years after his arrival, Stuck resolved to reach Denali's summit, or at least make a serious attempt, and in 1913 he set out to do what eight previous expeditions had failed to accomplish: reach the top of the continent.

For companions, he chose three men experienced in dealing with ice and snow, though none was a mountaineer. Stuck's first choice was Harry Karstens; lured north from Illinois by the Klondike gold rush, he'd built a reputation as a first-rate explorer, woodsman, and backcountry traveler. The other two were Robert Tatum and Walter Harper, both twenty-one years old. Tatum, from Tennessee, worked with Stuck at the Episcopal mission in Nenana, while Harper, part Native Alaskan, had served as Stuck's attendant, interpreter, dog team driver, and boat engineer. Two Indian teenagers named Johnny and Esaias helped during the team's approach.

The party began its expedition at the village of Nenana—about ninety miles northeast of Denali—in mid-March and began moving up the mountain's north side, via the Muldrow Glacier, on April 18. They would reach the summit fifty days later, on June 7.

Hudson Stuck recounted his party's remarkable expedition in *The Ascent of Denali: A Narrative of the First Complete Ascent of the Highest Peak in North America* (first published by Charles Scribner's Sons in 1914 and reprinted in 1989 by the University of Nebraska Press's Bison Books). Two abridged selections are included here: excerpts from Chapter 1 show the logistical demands of an early twentieth-century expedition; Chapter 5 describes the team's stay on the summit.

FROM CHAPTER 1, "PREPARATION AND APPROACH"

The resolution to attempt the ascent of Denali was reached a year and a half before it was put into execution: so much time was necessary for preparation. Almost any Alaskan enterprise that calls for supplies or equipment from the outside must be entered upon at least a year in advance. The plan followed had been adopted long before as the only wise one: that the supplies to be used upon the ascent be carried by water as near to the base of the mountain as could be reached and cached there in the summer, and that the climbing party go in with the dog teams as near the 1st March as practicable. Strangely enough, of all the expeditions that have essayed this ascent, the first, that of Judge Wickersham in 1903, and the last, ten years later, are the only ones that have approached their task in this natural and easy way. The others have all burdened themselves with the great and unnecessary difficulties of the southern slopes of the range. [Actually, the Sourdoughs also approached from the north.]

Unfortunately, the equipment and supplies ordered from the outside did not arrive in time to go in with the bulk of the stuff. Although ordered in February, they arrived at Tanana only late in September, just in time to catch the last boat up to Nenana. And only half that had been ordered came at all—one of the two cases has not been traced to this day. Moreover, it was not until late the next February, when actually about to proceed on the expedition, that the writer was able to learn what items had come and what had not. Such are the difficulties of any undertaking in Alaska, despite all the precautions that foresight may dictate.

The silk tents, which had not come, had to be made in Fairbanks; the ice axes sent were ridiculous gold-painted toys with detachable heads and broomstick handles—more like dwarf halberds than ice axes; and at least two workmanlike axes were indispensable. So the head of an axe was sawn to the pattern of the writer's out of a piece of tool steel and a substantial hickory handle and an iron shank fitted to it at the machine shop in Fairbanks. It served excellently well, while the points of the fancy axes from New York splintered the first time they were used. "Climbing irons," or "crampons," were also to make, no New York dealer being able to supply them.

One great difficulty was the matter of footwear. Heavy regulation-nailed alpine boots were sent—all too small to be worn with even a couple of pairs of socks, and therefore quite useless. Indeed, at that time there was no house in New York, or, so far as the writer knows, in the United States, where the standard alpine equipment could be procured. As a result of the dissatisfaction of this expedition with the material sent, one house in New York now carries in stock a good assortment of such things of standard pattern and quality. Fairbanks was ransacked for boots of any kind in which three or four pairs of socks could be worn. Alaska is a country of big men accustomed to the natural spread of the foot which a moccasin permits, but we could not find boots to our need save rubber snow-packs, and we bought half a dozen pairs of them (No. 12) and had leather soles fastened under them and nailed. Four pairs of alpine boots at eleven dollars a pair equals forty-four dollars. Six pairs of snow-packs at five dollars equals thirty dollars. Leather soles for them at three dollars equals eighteen dollars; which totalled ninety-two dollars—entirely wasted. We found that moccasins were the only practicable foot gear; and we had to put *five* pairs of socks within them before we were done. But we did not know that at the time and had no means of discovering it.

All these matters were put in hand under Karsten's direction, while the writer, only just arrived in Fairbanks from Fort Yukon and Tanana, made a flying trip to the new mission at the Tanana Crossing, two hundred and fifty miles above Fairbanks, with Walter and the dog team; and most of them were finished by the time we returned. A multitude of small details kept us several days more in Fairbanks, so that nearly the middle of March had arrived before we were able to make our start to the mountain, two weeks later than we had planned.

Karstens having joined us, we went down to the mission at Nenana (seventy-five miles) in a couple of days, and there two more days were spent overhauling and repacking the stuff that had come from the outside. In the way of food, we had imported only erbswurst, seventy-two four-ounce packages; milk chocolate, twenty pounds; compressed China tea in tablets (a most excellent tea with a very low percentage of tannen), five pounds; a specially selected grade of Smyrna figs, ten pounds; and sugared almonds, ten pounds—about seventy pounds' weight, all scrupulously reserved for the high-mountain work.

For trail equipment we had one eight-by-ten "silk" tent, used for two previous winters; three small circular tents of the same material, made in Fairbanks, for the high work; a Yukon stove and the usual complement of pots and pans and dishes, including two admirable large aluminum pots for melting snow, used a number of years with great satisfaction. A "primus" stove, borrowed from the *Pelican's* galley, was taken along for the high work. The bedding was mainly of down quilts, which are superseding fur robes and blankets for winter use because of their lightness and warmth and the small compass into which they may be compressed. Two pairs of camel's-hair blankets and one sleeping bag lined with down and camel's-hair cloth were taken, and Karstens brought a great wolf robe, weighing twenty-five pounds, of which we were glad enough later on.

Another team was obtained at the mission, and Mr. R.G. Tatum and the two boys, Johnny and Esaias, joined the company, which, thus increased to six persons, two sleds, and fourteen dogs, set out from Nenana across country to the Kantishna on St. Patrick's Day.

Travelling was over the beaten trail to the Kantishna gold camp, one of the smallest of Alaskan camps, supporting about thirty men.

Our immediate task now lay before us. A ton and a half of supplies had to be hauled some fifty miles across country to the base of the mountain. Here the relaying began, stuff being taken ahead and cached at some midway point, then another load taken right through a day's march, and then a return made to bring up the cache. In this way we moved steadily though slowly . . . toward an opening in the range six or eight miles to the east of the great mountain. This opening is known as Cache Creek. Passing the willow patch at its mouth, where previous camps had been made, we pushed up the creek some three miles more to its forks, and there established our base camp, on 10th April, at about four thousand feet elevation. A few scrubby willows struggled to grow in the creek bed, but the hills that rose from one thousand five hundred to two thousand feet around us were bare of any vegetation save moss and were yet in the main covered with snow. Caribou signs were plentiful everywhere, and we were no more than settled in camp when a herd appeared in sight.

Our prime concern at this camp was the gathering and preserving of a sufficient meat supply for our subsistence on the mountain. It was an easy task. First Karstens killed a caribou and then Walter a mountain sheep. Then Esaias happened into the midst of a herd of caribou as he climbed over a ridge, and killed three. That was all we needed. Then we went to work preparing the meat. Why should any one haul canned pemmican hundreds of miles into the

131

greatest game country in the world? We made our own pemmican [a concentrated fat-rich food] of the choice parts of this tender, juicy meat and we never lost appetite for it or failed to enjoy and assimilate it.

On the 11th April Karstens and I wound our way up the narrow, steep defile for about three miles from the base camp and came to our first sight of the Muldrow Glacier, some two thousand five hundred feet above camp and six thousand three hundred feet above the sea. That day stands out in recollection as one of the notable days of the whole ascent. There the glacier stretched away, broad and level—the road to the heart of the mountain, and as our eyes traced its course our spirits leaped up that at last we were entered upon our real task. One of us, at least, knew something of the dangers and difficulties its apparently smooth surface concealed, yet to both of us it had an infinite attractiveness, for it was the highway of desire.

FROM CHAPTER V, "THE ULTIMATE HEIGHT"

We lay down for a few hours on the night of the 6th June, resolved to rise at three in the morning for our attempt upon the summit of Denali. At supper Walter had made a desperate effort to use some of our ten pounds of flour in the manufacture of "noodles" with which to thicken the stew. We had continued to pack that flour and had made effort after effort to cook it in some eatable way, but without success. The sourdough would not ferment, and we had no baking powder. *Is* there any way to cook flour under such circumstances? But he made the noodles too large and did not cook them enough, and they wrought internal havoc upon those who partook of them. Three of the four of us were unwell all night. The digestion is certainly more delicate and more easily disturbed at great altitudes than at the lower levels. While Karstens and Tatum were tossing uneasily in the bedclothes, the writer sat up with a blanket round his shoulders, crouching over the primus stove, with the thermometer at -21°F outdoors. Walter alone was at ease, with digestive and somnolent capabilities proof against any invasion. It was, of course, broad daylight all night. At three the company was aroused, and, after partaking of a very light breakfast indeed, we sallied forth into the brilliant, clear morning with not a cloud in the sky. The only packs we carried that day were the instruments and the lunch. The sun was shining, but a keen north wind was blowing and the thermometer stood at -4°F. We were rather a sorry company. Karstens still had internal pains; Tatum and I had severe headaches. Walter was the only one feeling entirely himself, so Walter was put in the lead and in the lead he remained all day.

We took a straight course up the great snow ridge directly south of our camp and then around the peak into which it rises; quickly told but slowly and most laboriously done. It was necessary to make the traverse high up on this peak instead of around its base, so much had its ice and snow been shattered by the earthquake on its lower portions. Once around this peak, there rose before us the horseshoe ridge which carries the ultimate height of Denali, a horseshoe ridge of snow opening to the east with a low snow peak at either end, the centre of the ridge soaring above both peaks. Above us was nothing visible but snow; the rocks were all beneath, the last rocks standing at about nineteen thousand feet. Our progress was exceedingly slow. It was bitterly cold; all the morning toes and fingers were without sensation, kick them and beat them as we would. We were all clad in full winter hand and foot gear—more gear than had sufficed at 50° below zero on the Yukon trail. Within the writer's No. 16 moccasins were three pairs of heavy hand-knitted woollen socks, two pairs of camel's-hair socks, and a pair of thick felt socks; while underneath them, between them and the iron "creeper," were the soles cut from a pair of felt shoes. Upon his hands were a pair of the thickest Scotch wool gloves, thrust inside huge lynx-paw mitts lined with Hudson Bay duffle. His moose-hide breeches and shirt, worn all the winter on the trail, were worn throughout this climb; over the shirt was a thick sweater and over all the usual Alaskan "parkee" amply furred around the hood; underneath was a suit of the heaviest Jaeger underwear—yet until high noon feet were like lumps of iron and fingers were constantly numb. That north wind was cruelly cold, and there can be no possible question that cold is felt much more keenly in the thin air of nineteen thousand feet than it is below. But the north wind was really our friend, for nothing but a north wind will drive all vapor from this mountain. Karstens beat his feet so violently and so continually against the hard snow to restore the circulation that two of his toenails sloughed off afterward. By eleven o'clock we had been climbing for six hours and were well around the peak, advancing toward the horseshoe ridge, but even then there were grave doubts if we should succeed in reaching it that day, it was so cold. A hint from any member of the party that his feet were actually freezing—a hint expected all along—would have sent us all back. When there is no sensation left in the feet at all it is, however, difficult to be quite sure if they be actually freezing or not—and each one was willing to give the attempt upon the summit the benefit of the doubt. What should we have done with the ordinary leather climbing boots? But once entirely around the peak we were in a measure sheltered from the north wind, and the sun full upon us gave more warmth. It was hereabouts, and not, surely, at the point indicated in the photograph in Mr. Belmore Browne's book [*The Conquest of Mount McKinley*], that the climbing party of last year was driven back by the blizzard that descended upon them when close to their goal. Not until we had stopped for lunch and had drunk the scalding tea from the thermos bottles, did we all begin to have confidence that this day would see the completion of the ascent. But the writer's shortness of breath became more and more distressing as he rose. The familiar fits of panting took a more acute form; at such times everything would turn black before his eyes and he would choke and gasp and seem unable to get breath at all. Yet a few moments' rest restored him completely, to struggle on another twenty or thirty paces and to sink gasping upon the snow again. All were more affected in the breathing than they had been at any time before—it was curious to see every man's mouth open for breathing—but none of the others in this distressing way. Before the traverse around the peak just mentioned, Walter had noticed the writer's growing discomfort and had insisted upon assuming the mercurial barometer. The boy's eager kindness was gladly accepted and the instrument was surrendered. So it did not fall to the writer's credit to carry the thing to the top as he had wished.

The climbing grew steeper and steeper; the slope that had looked easy from below now seemed to shoot straight up. For the most part the climbing-irons gave us sufficient footing, but here and there we came to softer snow, where they would not take sufficient hold and we had to cut steps. The calks in these climbing-irons were about an inch and a quarter long; we wished they had been two inches. The creepers are a great advantage in the matter of speed, but they need long points. They are not as safe as step-cutting, and there is the ever-present danger that unless one is exceedingly careful one will step upon the rope with them and their sharp calks sever some of the strands. They were, however, of great assistance and saved a deal of laborious step-cutting.

At last the crest of the ridge was reached and we stood well above the two peaks that mark the ends of the horseshoe.

Also it was evident that we were well above the great North Peak across the Grand Basin. Its crest had been like an index on the snow beside us as we climbed, and we stopped for a few moments when it seemed that we were level with it. We judged it to be about five hundred feet lower than the South Peak.

But still there stretched ahead of us, and perhaps one hundred feet above us, another small ridge with a north and south pair of little haycock summits. This is the real top of Denali. From below, this ultimate ridge merges indistinguishably with the crest of the horseshoe ridge, but it is not a part of it but a culminating ridge beyond it. With keen excitement we pushed on. Walter, who had been in the lead all day, was the first to scramble up; a native Alaskan,

134

he is the first human being to set foot upon the top of Alaska's great mountain, and he had well earned the lifelong distinction. Karstens and Tatum were hard on his heels, but the last man on the rope, in his enthusiasm and excitement somewhat overpassing his narrow wind margin, had almost to be hauled up the last few feet, and fell unconscious for a moment upon the floor of the little snow basin that occupies the top of the mountain. This, then, is the actual summit, a little crater-like snow basin, sixty or sixty-five feet long and twenty to twenty-five feet wide, with a haycock of snow at either end—the south one a little higher than the north. On the southwest this little basin is much corniced, and the whole thing looked as though every severe storm might somewhat change its shape.

So soon as wind was recovered we shook hands all round and a brief prayer of thanksgiving to Almighty God was said, that He had granted us our hearts' desire and brought us safely to the top of His great mountain.

This prime duty done, we fell at once to our scientific tasks. The instrument-tent was set up, the mercurial barometer, taken out of its leather case and then out of its wooden case, was swung upon its tripod and a rough zero established, and it was left a while to adjust itself to conditions before a reading was attempted. It was a great gratification to get it to the top uninjured. The boiling-point apparatus was put together and its candle lighted under the ice which filled its little cistern. The three-inch, three-circle aneroid was read at once at thirteen and two-tenths inches, its mendacious altitude scale confidently pointing at twenty-three thousand three hundred feet. Half an hour later it had dropped to 13.175 inches and had shot us up another one hundred feet into the air. Soon the water was boiling in the little tubes of the boiling-point thermometer and the steam pouring out of the vent. The thread of mercury rose to 174.9° and stayed there. There is something definite and uncompromising about the boiling-point hypsometer; no tapping will make it rise or fall; it reaches its mark unmistakably and does not budge. The reading of the mercurial barometer is a slower and more delicate business. It takes a good light and a good sight to tell when the ivory zero-point is exactly touching the surface of the mercury in the cistern; it takes care and precision to get the vernier exactly level with the top of the column. It was read, some half-hour after it was set up, at 13.617 inches. The alcohol minimum thermometer stood at 7°F all the while we were on top. Meanwhile, Tatum had been reading a round of angles with the prismatic compass. He could not handle it with sufficient exactness with his mitts on, and he froze his fingers doing it barehanded.

The scientific work accomplished, then and not till then did we indulge ourselves in the wonderful prospect that stretched around us. It was a perfectly clear day, the sun shining brightly in the sky, and naught bounded our view save the natural limitations of vision. Immediately before us, in the direction in which we had climbed, lay—nothing: a void, a sheer gulf many thousands of feet deep, and one shrank back instinctively from the parapet of the snow basin when one had glanced at the awful profundity. Across the gulf, about three thousand feet beneath us and fifteen or twenty miles away, sprang most splendidly into view the great mass of Denali's Wife, or Mount Foraker, as some white men misname her, filling majestically all the middle distance. It was our first glimpse of her during the whole ascent. Denali's Wife does not appear at all save from the actual summit of Denali, for she is completely hidden by his South Peak until the moment when his South Peak is surmounted. And never was nobler sight displayed to man than that great, isolated mountain spread out completely, with all its spurs and ridges, its cliffs and its glaciers, lofty and mighty and yet far beneath us. On that spot one understood why the view of Denali from Lake Minchumina is the grand view, for the west face drops abruptly down with nothing but that vast void from the top to nigh the bottom of the mountain. Beyond stretched, blue and vague to the southwest, the wide valley of the Kuskokwim, with an end of all mountains. To the north we looked right over the North Peak to the foothills below, patched with lakes and lingering snow, glittering with streams. We had hoped to see the junction of the Yukon and Tanana Rivers, one hundred and fifty miles away to the northwest, as we had often and often seen the summit of Denali from that point in the winter, but the haze that almost always qualifies a fine summer day inhibited that stretch of vision. Perhaps the forest fires we found raging on the Tanana River were already beginning to foul the northern sky.

It was, however, to the south and east that the most marvelous prospect opened before us. What infinite tangle of mountain ranges filled the whole scene, until gray sky, gray mountain, and gray sea merged in the ultimate distance! The near-by peaks and ridges stood out with dazzling distinction, the glaciation, the drainage, the relation of each part to the others all revealed. The snow-covered tops of the remoter peaks, dwindling and fading, rose to our view as though floating in thin air when their bases were hidden by the haze, and the beautiful crescent curve of the whole Alaskan range exhibited itself from Denali to the sea. To the right hand the glittering, tiny threads of streams draining the mountain range into the Chulitna and Sushitna Rivers, and so to Cook's Inlet and the Pacific Ocean, spread themselves out; to the left the affluents of the Kantishna and the Nenana drained the range into the Yukon [River] and Bering Sea.

Yet the chief impression was not of our connection with the earth so far below, its rivers and its seas, but rather of detachment from it. We seemed alone upon a dead world, as dead as the mountains on the moon. Only once before can the writer remember a similar feeling of being neither in the world or of the world, and that was at the bottom of the Grand Cañon of the Colorado, in Arizona, its savage granite walls as dead as this savage piece of ice.

Above us the sky took a blue so deep that none of us had ever gazed upon a midday sky like it before. It was a deep, rich, lustrous, transparent blue, as dark as a Prussian blue, but intensely blue; a hue so strange, so increasingly impressive, that to one at least it "seemed like special news of God," as a new poet sings. We first noticed the darkening tint of the upper sky in the Grand Basin, and it deepened as we rose. Tyndall observed and discussed this phenomenon in the Alps, but it seems scarcely to have been mentioned since.

It is difficult to describe at all the scene which the top of the mountain presented, and impossible to describe it adequately. One was not occupied with the thought of description but wholly possessed with the breadth and glory of it, with its sheer, amazing immensity and scope. Only once, perhaps, in a lifetime is such vision granted, certainly never before had been vouchsafed to any of us. Not often in the summertime does Denali completely unveil himself and dismiss the clouds from all the earth beneath. Yet we could not linger, unique though the occasion, dearly bought our privilege; the miserable limitations of the flesh gave us continual warning to depart; we grew colder and still more wretchedly cold. The thermometer stood at 7° in the full sunshine, and the north wind was keener than ever. My fingers were so cold that I would not venture to withdraw them from the mittens to change the film in the camera, and the other men were in like case; indeed, our hands were by this time so numb as to make it almost impossible to operate a camera at all. A number of photographs had been taken, though not half we should have liked to take, but it is probable that, however many more exposures had been made, they would have been little better than those we got. Our top-of-the-mountain photography was a great disappointment. One thing we learned: exposures at such altitude should be longer than those below, perhaps owing to the darkness of the sky.

When the mercurial barometer had been read the tent was thrown down and abandoned, the first of the series of abandonments that marked our descent from the mountain. The tent pole was used for a moment as a flagstaff, while Tatum hoisted a little United States flag he had patiently and skillfully constructed in our camps below out of two silk handkerchiefs and the cover of a sewing-bag. Then the pole was put to its permanent use. It had already

137

been carved with a suitable inscription, and now a transverse piece, already prepared and fitted, was lashed securely to it and it was planted on one of the little snow turrets of the summit—the sign of our redemption, high above North America. Only some peaks in the Andes and some peaks in the Himalayas rise above it in all the world. It was of light, dry birch and, though six feet in length, so slender that we think it may weather many a gale. And Walter thrust it into the snow so firmly at a blow that it could not be withdrawn again. Then we gathered about it and said the Te Deum.

It was 1:30 P.M. when we reached the summit and two minutes past three when we left; yet so quickly had the time flown that we could not believe we had been an hour and a half on top. The journey down was a long, weary grind, the longer and the wearier that we made a detour and went out of our way to seek for Professor Parker's thermometer, which he had left [from a previous expedition] "in a crack on the west side of the last boulder of the northeast ridge." That sounds definite enough, yet in fact it is equivocal. "Which is the last boulder?" we disputed as we went down the slope. A long series of rocks almost in line came to an end, with one rock a little below the others, a little bit out of line. This egregious boulder would, it seemed to me, naturally be called the last; Karstens thought not—thought the "last boulder" was the last *on* the ridge. As we learned later, Karstens was right, and since he yielded to me we did not find the thermometer, for having descended to this isolated rock, we would not climb up again for fifty thermometers. One's disappointment is qualified by the knowledge that the thermometer is probably not of adequate scale, Professor Parker's recollection being that it read only to 60° below zero F. A lower temperature than this is recorded every winter on the Yukon River.

A thermometer reading to 100° below zero, left at this spot, would, in my judgment, perhaps yield a lower minimum than has ever yet been authentically recorded on earth, and it is most unfortunate that the opportunity was lost. Yet I did not leave my own alcohol minimum—scaled to 95° below zero, and yielding, by estimation, perhaps ten degrees below the scaling—there, because of the difficulty of giving explicit directions that should lead to its ready recovery, and at the close of such a day of toil as is involved in reaching the summit, men have no stomach for prolonged search. As will be told, it is cached lower down, but at a spot where it cannot be missed.

However, for one, the writer was largely unconscious of weariness in that descent. All the way down, my thoughts were occupied with the glorious scene my eyes had gazed upon and should gaze upon never again. In all human probability I would never climb that mountain again; yet if I climbed it a score more times I would never be likely to repeat such vision. Commonly, only for a few hours at a time, never for more than a few days at a time, save in the dead of winter when climbing is out of the question, does Denali completely unveil himself and dismiss the clouds from all the earth below him. Not for long, with these lofty colds contiguous, will the vapors of Cook's Inlet and Prince William Sound and the whole North Pacific Ocean refrain from sweeping upward; their natural trend is hitherward. As the needle turns to the magnet so the clouds find an irresistible attraction in this great mountain mass, and though the inner side of the range be rid of them the sea side is commonly filled to overflowing.

Only those who have for long years cherished a great and almost inordinate desire, and have had that desire gratified to the limit of their expectation, can enter into the deep thankfulness and content that filled the heart upon the descent of this mountain. There was no pride of conquest, no trace of that exultation of victory some enjoy upon the first ascent of a lofty peak, no gloating over good fortune that had hoisted us a few hundred feet higher than others who had struggled and been discomfited. Rather was the feeling that a privileged communion with the high places of the earth had been granted; that not only had we been permitted to lift up eager eyes to these summits, secret and solitary since the world began, but to enter boldly upon them, to take place, as it were, domestically in their hitherto sealed chambers, to inhabit them, and to cast our eyes down from them, seeing all things as they spread out from the windows of heaven itself.

12

Minus 148°:
The Winter Ascent of Mt. McKinley

by Art Davidson

In 1965, a year after his passion for mountaineering had lured him to Alaska, Colorado native Art Davidson joined the Osaka Alpine Club on an expedition to Denali. Following a new route up the mountain's South Buttress, the team put three Japanese climbers on the summit, including twenty-nine-year-old expedition leader Shiro Nishimae. While walking the mountain's slopes, Nishimae and Davidson tried to imagine the great peak in winter. By the mid-1960s, nearly all of Denali's major faces and ridges had been ascended, including those once considered impossible. No longer was The High One a mysterious place to climb—except in winter. No one had even seriously considered a winter attempt until Nishimae and Davidson turned their dream of ascending Denali during its still-unknown season into a reality.

One and a half years later, in late January 1967, Davidson, Nishimae, and six other climbers were transported by plane into the Alaska Range. Expedition members included team leader Gregg Blomberg, a Denver mountaineering instructor; Anchorage orthopedic surgeon George Wichman, the team doctor; Ohio biologist John Edwards; Dave Johnston of Anchorage, a self-described "climbing bum" with a forestry degree; Frenchman Jacques "Farine" Batkin, one of Europe's top climbers; and Swiss-born Ray Genet, a future Denali legend who talked himself onto the team despite minimal climbing expertise.

Just three days into their 1967 climb, the team suffered a tragedy: Batkin fell into a crevasse and died. After much soul searching, the team decided to continue, and on February 28, Davidson, Johnston, and Genet reached Denali's summit. Forced to descend in darkness, the three chose to bivouac at 18,200-foot Denali Pass, rather than continue down to high camp at 17,200. That night, a severe storm moved in, bringing hurricane-force winds and wind chills far below -100° Fahrenheit.

The following excerpt is taken from Art Davidson's book *Minus 148°: The Winter Ascent of Mt. McKinley,* originally published in 1969 and reprinted in 1986 by Cloudcap Press in Seattle. Davidson recounts the arrival of high winds at Denali Pass and the summit party's initial struggle for survival. At this point, the expedition is split in two. Blomberg, Edwards, Nishimae, and Wichman wait at 17,200 feet, while Davidson, Johnston, and Genet are stranded at Denali Pass. To give a more complete picture of the circumstances, Davidson includes some journal entries written by Gregg Blomberg, Shiro Nishimae, and John Edwards, three of the four men isolated lower on the mountain. (Note: The parachute mentioned had been left by an earlier expedition in which supplies had been airdropped onto Denali, a strategy no longer allowed.) The following is from the chapter concerning the events of March 1, titled "-148°."

17,200 FEET: GREGG, JOHN, SHIRO, GEORGE

Gregg's diary

A frightening thing is developing, but let me start from this morning. Shiro got up early, and although there was some wind we decided to give it a go. We started off with Shiro and George and John and me roped in twos. From the time we started it was apparent we wouldn't get far. The winds aloft were howling. After a few hundred yards John pooped out, and I went ahead to tell the others. When I caught them George unroped to go back with John, and I roped in with Shiro. The idea was to go up and see that the others were all right. When we approached the pass it was evident why the others had not descended. The wind was howling like crazy. I tried to lead up to the pass but was turned back by the wind. We then traversed to a spot that we thought was directly under their bivouac site. Shiro went up and tried twice, but the wind was so fierce it was impossible. The wind was coming from our direction, and if we went one step too far it meant not getting back again.

Shiro tried another place . . . the same . . . We retreated rapidly. Once, when Shiro had come back, I asked him what he saw. He said: "Three sleeping bags. They are in their sleeping bags." When we were just about back in camp he told me all he saw was one sleeping bag lying up against the rock and flapping in the wind. Shiro surmises the three are on the leeward side of the rock, covered with the parachute, with possibly two in one bag. All I know is that they must have made it back to the bivouac site, and are in a bind. If we could have reached them—they were less than a hundred feet away—we could have told them that the wind wasn't so bad on this side of the pass. We could have told them to make a try.

It's a bad situation . . . winds up to a hundred miles per hour, possibly more. It's a whiteout up there. . . . I pray at this point that they make it through. . . . They must make it through.

Much later Shiro confided: "When I saw only one sleeping bag I was certain they were dead. I told Gregg I saw three. He is very emotional. I thought maybe dangerous to alarm him. He might lose his mind."

DENALI PASS: ART, DAVE, PIRATE

The wind woke us. The wildly whipping parachute billowed and snapped with reports like those of a bullwhip or rifle. The wind blasted against the rocks we were nestled among with a deafening eruption of noise; crosscurrents in the storm fluctuated its pitch to a groan or a prolonged whine. A dull, aching pressure along my backside was the cold, pressed into me by the wind.

I twisted in my sleeping bag to grope for the loose section of parachute thrashing me from behind. The moment I caught it my hands were pierced with cold; groggy with sleep, I'd forgotten that the nylon, like everything else outside our sleeping bags, was about -40°. The cold sank into my fingers while the parachute, jerking and cracking erratically, resisted my attempts to anchor it. As soon as I managed to gather the slack material under me, the weight of my body holding it down, I shot one hand under an armpit and the other into my crotch for warmth. I was out of breath from the effort.

Drawn tighter, the parachute made less noise, and I was able to relax for a few moments. My fingers, aching inside from being deeply chilled, began to gradually rewarm with strong tingling sensations. I pressed the length of my body against Dave to be warmer on that side, and I felt Dave shift inside his bag, trying to press against me. I snuggled close to him and lay quietly for a long time, hoping I'd fall asleep again, as if not thinking about the wind and cold would make them disappear.

I couldn't sleep, and the wind only grew more vicious. I tried to ignore the cold along my backside, away from Dave, but when the first shiver ran through my body I turned to check the sleeping bag where it touched my back. To my horror it was no thicker than its shell, two pieces of nylon. The wind had pushed the down away. I could hardly believe it possible that the parachute, designed to resist wind, was letting the wind eat through it and into my sleeping bag.

The parachute began cracking again. "Oh, hell," I mumbled. The cracking meant a portion of the parachute had broken loose again. Feeling I didn't have the strength for another attempt at anchoring it, I curled up in my bag, shivering occasionally, waiting for something to happen; I didn't know what. After what seemed like several minutes but was probably only a matter of seconds, I heard Pirate trying to tie down the parachute.

"Art." Pirate's voice sounded far off and unfamiliar. "Help me hold it."

Hearing his voice made me realize that the three of us had been awake for more than an hour before anyone had spoken. Burrowed into my sleeping bag, I didn't want to budge from its security, false as it was, for even a moment. While I was deciding whether to help Pirate or prolong my rest, I felt Dave get to his hands and knees and begin wrestling with the parachute, which was now pounding his head and back as it billowed and cracked back in rapid succession. Yanking and cursing, Dave managed to pull part of it around him again, only to have it whip off as soon as he settled down into his bag.

"Look, we gotta get outa here!" Dave yelled.

"Where? We'd never make it down!" I said, grabbing onto the piece of parachute that Pirate was clinging to. "Maybe it's a morning wind that'll die down."

"Morning wind?" Dave looked at me with disbelief. "It's a bloody hurricane, you fool! I'm checking the other side of the rocks."

"Awwghaaaaa. . . ." Pirate growled, staring up into the wind.

Instead of getting completely out of his bag, Dave tied the drawstring at the top tight around his middle. With his legs still in the sleeping bag and his arms free, he lurched toward the crest ten feet away. I was horribly apprehensive. If he lost his grip on the rocks he could easily be blown off the mountain. On the other side we'd never hear him again if he called for help. How far was he going? Maybe he'd be hidden behind a rock where we wouldn't be able to find him if we needed his strength. Besides the logic of my fear, I recoiled against Dave's leaving because it seemed to break our trust; it violated a fundamental law of survival—stay together.

"Dave!" I cried. "Wait! I think it's safer here."

"Stay if you want!" he hollered back. "This wind's bad, and I'm gettin' out of it!"

"Where are you going?" Dave didn't hear me. "It's exposed over there!" He had disappeared over the crest.

Since my mittens were too bulky to grip the parachute, I pulled thick wool socks onto my hands; my fingers were nearly numb already. I was astonished as I looked up to see Pirate holding the parachute with his bare hands. Just as I yelled at him to get something over them, one of my socks started to slip off. Pulling it back on, I shifted position, and the wind seized the wind parka I had been sitting on. Inside its main pocket was the tape recorder I had been using for the psychological testing, but at that moment I was more concerned about the loss of the half dozen cookies I'd stashed in the pocket. One moment the parka had been next to me, then I saw it whirling through the air, fifty, a hundred feet up, sailing in the direction of McKinley's summit.

With Dave gone, his loose end of the parachute caught the wind, and this threatened to rip the entire piece of nylon from our grip. We gave up trying to wrap the parachute around us; the pull on our arms wrenched our whole bodies as we clung to it to keep it from escaping. The parachute was our only shelter.

"My hands are bad!" Pirate's voice was weak, almost a whimper. His face was drawn into a hideous, painful grin. Ice caked his beard.

"Bring them in!" I yelled, though his head was only inches from mine. His fingers felt like chunks of ice against my stomach.

"They're stiff!"

"Move them!" I reached for a better grip on the parachute. It slipped. I lunged. Pirate caught it as it whipped past him. He winced in pain.

"Aw, the hell with it!" Pirate sighed. As he let loose, the parachute twisted through the air. It snagged on a rock. I saw it starting to rip, then it was gone.

For the first time, I noticed the sky. It was a blue wall, smashing into the mountain. Thin pieces of cloud shredding—everything grew blurred. My eyes were watering and stinging from squinting into the wind. Compared to anything I had ever experienced, this wind was like another element. It was as if gravity had shifted and instead of holding us down, was pulling us across the landscape.

Pirate began digging his hands in under my parka. The top of my bag had fallen open to the wind. As I pulled it shut, I fell against Pirate. We grabbed each other.

"Hold onto me!"

"Art, let's get into one bag."

"How? There's no room. . . . Give me your hands." I felt his icy fingers grabbing the skin around my middle. My bag had opened again, and to keep the wind from getting to me Pirate pushed himself over the opening. I just leaned against him, trying to catch my breath. Shivering, teeth chattering, my whole body was shaking with cold.

"Pirate, it's no good!" Wind was coming into my bag. We were both losing our warmth. "Each in his own bag . . . it's better."

"I can't feel my fingers!"

"Put 'em between your legs."

"I don't want to lose my hands!"

I remembered Dave. If it was less windy on the other side of the rocks, he

144

would have come back to tell us. If it was just as windy, I thought he would have returned to be with us. Something must have happened to him. But maybe he had found a sheltered corner. How could he abandon us?

"Pirate, let's try the other side!"

"Naw . . . the wind's everywhere!"

We huddled together, hunched upright in our sleeping bags, wedged tightly between two rocks. Whenever we relaxed the wind caught us, started us sliding along the ice which gradually sloped away, and forced us to push and fight our way back up into the rocks. Leaning against Pirate didn't make me any warmer, but it was comforting—I wasn't alone. We didn't talk. I could breathe more easily with my head inside my bag. I wondered what the others were doing down in the cave. Shiro's cough, Gregg's foot, John's swollen ear—it was too frightening to think about.

Beneath me I felt the ice sliding. Slipping onto my side, I brought an arm out in time to grab Pirate's knee. I pulled myself back against the rocks. My arms trembled from exhaustion. Pirate stared blankly out of his bag. His head turned slowly toward me with a groggy nodding motion. Was he slipping into a stupor? I wondered whether I looked as awful.

"It's no use here," I sighed.

I could barely keep myself up against the rocks. There was nothing I could do for Pirate. Maybe Dave had found a safe spot. I had to check the other side of the rocks, but that would be deserting Pirate. Yet there was no way I could help it. How could I just leave him? I had to do something for myself!

"I'm going over." He didn't move. "Pirate," I yelled, "I'm going over after Dave!"

His head shook from side to side as he half mumbled, half shouted, something I couldn't understand. I grabbed at the rock above me and pulled myself up the slope. Another rock; its sharp cold cut through the wool socks. Another pull. I reached the crest. To my tremendous relief I saw Dave crouched on the ice only about fifteen feet away. His back was toward me.

"Dave!" He couldn't hear me. I worked a little closer to him. The wind threatened to throw me off the crest. Beyond lay bare glacier where I'd never catch anything to hold onto if I was blown from the rocks.

"Dave!" This time he turned and saw me. I was out of breath and must have been gasping as much as yelling. "Is it better where you are?"

"What? . . . It's the same. Go back!"

I didn't want to go back, and waiting here on the crest was impossible because it was completely exposed to the wind. Before I'd decided which way to go, a cross-current gust caught me. I grabbed for rocks. One came loose. I caught another one nearer Dave. Somehow the sock on my left hand had blown off. I shoved the bare hand into my sleeping bag. The other hand held onto a rock. The wind flung and tossed my body as though it were weightless.

My right hand ached with cold from gripping the rock, and my forearm began cramping from the strain. I couldn't go back into the wind, but neither could my right hand cling to the rock much longer. The only other rock I could reach was three feet to my left, near Dave. My numb right hand had become so dead that I couldn't feel the rock it held onto. My shivering body seemed on the verge of going into convulsions.

I tried to think. If I lost my grip, I'd be blown across the ice. My mind was racing. I had to grab for the rock near Dave with my left hand: it was bare, no mitten or sock. It would be frozen. I had to. Suddenly, my bare hand shot out to grab the rock. Slicing cold.

I saw Dave's face, the end of his raw nose, frostbitten. His mouth, distorted into an agonized mixture of compassion and anger, swore at me to get a glove on. I looked at my hand. It was white, frozen absolutely white.

I pulled my body onto the rock. Dave was only five or six feet away on the ledge he had chopped in the slightly sloping ice.

"Christ, Art." His voice cracked. "You froze your hands!"

I pushed off from the rock, letting the wind throw me against Dave. He flung his arms around me. All I could do was lie across him, wheezing and shaking, trying to catch my breath.

"Man," he said, "we gotta dig in!"

17,200 FEET: GREGG, JOHN, SHIRO, GEORGE
John's journal

The pass was roaring windy, and we had our first real concern for the summit party. . . . Change of wind. Raven flew down buttress! Hypothesis concerning summit party: perhaps they had not gone to the summit the previous day, and had gone today. . . . Weather worsening all afternoon. Flying clouds, but mountain looked magnificent all afternoon. Blue shadows, yellow snow. . . . Shiro saw one sleeping bag against the bivouac rocks. At the time Gregg thought Shiro had seen three, but had misheard under the roar of the wind, and was rather profoundly disturbed when back in camp Shiro said he had seen only one. . . . Very tired and anxious for the three. I am pretty sure they will break out despite the weather and come down tonight despite the whiteout. If not, we are in serious trouble indeed.

[Pilot Don] Sheldon flew in late this afternoon, low around the igloo, with landing lights on. Some discussion as to the significance of this flight, but probably only a reconnaissance before the storm. Had Ray been in radio contact with Anchorage and given an emergency to Sheldon, or was this flight on his own or on someone else's account before the onset of the storm? George very apprehensive about storm. Solemn. There is not much we can do about it but wait for the others to move down. But if they don't? I have no great apprehension for the three above yet. I think they will fight their way down, that is, if they are all well. Art's altitude sickness? But then we may have seven days before Sheldon can take us out.

Gregg's diary continued

It's evening. We all stayed in case there is need to help one of the others down. The wind has descended to this altitude, and we are huddled in the snow cave with a large mouth covered by a tent, weighed down by rocks which we hope will hold. If they come down tonight, we will be crowded, but we will be a happy crowd. If they make it back tonight, we will descend tomorrow as quickly as possible. The wind is from the southeast, right into the tent, but it will hold unless things get worse. Those guys only had a bunch of lunch, one stove full of gas, a pot, their sleeping bags, and the parachute with which to cover themselves up.

Please God, let us hear their voices. Let them descend unharmed. Give them a break in the wind and the wisdom and stamina to use it.

What can we do? I suppose the best is the prayer above. I am thankful that Shiro wanted to come down yesterday, or we would have probably been caught in the same trap. How proud and stupid we all are.

Edi [Gregg's wife], you can't imagine how I long to be in your arms, to lay my head in your lap while you stroke my hair. This is nothing new. I have been longing to be with you since I started. I think you can tell by this journal. All my love, honey. Don't worry. I'll still call you about the fifth of *this month*. Good night. Pray for a happy morning.

With the provisions and personal reserves they have they could probably last two more days at the longest, but practically speaking they must make it down tonight or tomorrow morning at the latest. If they had only known today that the wind wasn't as bad on this side of the pass. Oh, pray to hear their voices urgently wanting to come inside.

On the bright side, they are the strongest of us. Dave and Art have plenty of experience. Ray has good sense. They're all tough as nails. With a tiny break in the wind, they can't help but make it! Thank God the wind is dying down here, and pray it is there. Oh Lord, what anguish we are all suffering for our friends' safety.

DENALI PASS: ART, PIRATE, DAVE

Dave cradled Pirate's feet against his belly and massaged them gently until they began to rewarm.

"Dave," I said, "you know you saved us out there." My words sort of hung in the air. They sounded hollow, and Dave bit at his lip self-consciously. I didn't say more, but my eyes followed Dave with admiration and a kind of love as he tucked Pirate into his bag and then reached for the stove.

For more than an hour I had clung to the ledge on the ice, feeling the frostbite blisters swell on my hands and watching helplessly while Dave dug a cave in the ice. Just before he had completed it, Dave had collapsed from exhaustion; by then Pirate had pulled himself together, and despite his hands and feet, which were beginning to swell with frostbite blisters, he had somehow made it over the crest to finish hollowing out the cave. Dave had recovered enough strength to help me through the small hole in the ice which was the entrance to our new home.

Now inside our cave, Dave leaned on his elbows, and steadying the stove with one hand, he prepared some food with his free hand. In this cramped chamber under the ice cooking was more miserable than it had ever been in the last four weeks; Dave had quietly accepted the job because his were the only hands capable of working the stove. At least he had found some good food to fix—four pound-and-a-half cans of ham, bacon, and peas which had been cached by a previous expedition among the rocks we had bivouacked against. Since our pot had blown away, he heated the ham in its own can, then used the can to melt water in.

Flattened against the wall while Dave cooked in the middle, I realized how small our cave was. At the wide end there was barely enough room for our shoulders, and at the narrow end our feet in our sleeping bags were heaped on top of each other. Because of the rocks behind us, Dave and Pirate had been unable to make the cave long enough for us to stretch out completely. Over our feet the ceiling was about a foot and a half above the floor; toward the larger end there was just enough height to turn or lie on our sides with one shoulder touching the ice on the floor and the other touching the ice on the ceiling. We were quickly learning that our every movement bumped the next person. This cave certainly wasn't pleasant or comfortable by ordinary standards, but it kept us safe from the wind, and that was all that mattered, for the moment.

Dave looked for his journal and found it missing. We had lost too much to the wind—the use of four hands and two feet, an incalculable amount of body warmth, two packs with half our food in them, the parachute, my wind parka, and—perhaps our greatest loss—the foam pads which would have insulated us from the ice and helped to keep our bags dry. Yet we felt secure. We were supplied with enough gas to make water for another day, maybe two more days if we stretched it. With four lunches left, and three remaining cans of food, we needn't worry about starving.

That night ham and hot water were a feast, not filling, but delicious nonetheless; it was our first warm food since leaving the cave down at 17,200 feet more than thirty hours before. My hands had become so inflexible that Dave had to place each bite of ham—there were five of them—in my mouth, then tip the can to my lips to let me drink. Eating made us giddy with pleasure and almost got us feeling warm.

We were actually exultant, not from any sense of conquering the wind, but rather from the simple companionship of huddling together in our little cave while outside in the darkness the storm raged through Denali Pass and on across the Alaska Range.

We agreed that the wind coming out of the northwest was funneling through the pass at least 130 miles per hour. We remembered that a wind of such velocity, combined with the -30° [to] -45° air temperature outside our cave, created an equivalent wind-chill temperature somewhere off the end of the chart; the last figure on the chart was minus 148°.

"One hundred and forty-eight degrees below zero."

It was frightening to say, but the worst was over, we thought. In the morning the wind should slack off; we would descend, greeting the others at 17,200 feet with the news that we had made the summit; we would get off the mountain and go home. We wanted to believe the climb was over, that in a couple of days everything would be warm and easy again. Yet the wind, howling and pounding the slope overhead, reminded us that we couldn't move until it died down. We talked of the cave as our refuge, but the suspicion that we were being held captive in the ice must have entered each of our minds as we fell asleep listening to the wind.

Editor's afterword: Not until March 7—six days later—would the wind die enough to allow Davidson, Johnston, and Genet to leave their cave and resume their descent; the four others had already headed down the mountain. Approaching Windy Corner (elevation 13,200 feet), they were surprised, thankful, and a bit annoyed to discover that a massive rescue mission had been launched to save them. After all they'd been through, the three men felt the rescue operation was unnecessary and didn't like being responsible for such a big commotion. Still, they were reassured to know others were concerned enough to risk their own safety. And there was the frostbite to consider: All three were descending on half-frozen feet.

The trio was reunited with Edwards and Blomberg in Talkeetna, while Nishimae and Wichman later joined their teammates in Anchorage. Afterward, all except Nishimae (who returned to Japan) went to Fairbanks for postclimb medical testing. Their examiners "shook their heads in disbelief at the human wrecks the mountain had sent back to them," Davidson wrote. During their five weeks on Denali, the three who'd reached the summit lost, on average, thirty-five pounds each. Five of the seven surviving climbers had some frostbite. And for periods ranging from a few hours to several days, all expedition members experienced a sense of isolation and unreality normally associated with severe psychosis.

Scientists also later determined that winds on Denali's upper slopes had exceeded 150 miles per hour, with temperatures of -50° F. The resulting wind-chill temperatures during the life-threatening days at Denali Pass had been much, much colder than even minus 148°.

13

Wager with the Wind:
The Don Sheldon Story

by James Greiner

Some 115 highway miles north of Anchorage is Talkeetna, a small (population about 400 people) end-of-the-road community that is home to
an eclectic mix of dog mushers, trappers, miners, log cabin builders, re-
tirees, tourism entrepreneurs, mountain guides, and bush pilots. Over
the past quarter-century, Talkeetna has become popularly known as the
"Gateway to Denali," largely because of its air taxi services. Nowadays,
Talkeetna's pilots annually transport a thousand or more climbers to and
from the Kahiltna Glacier, starting point for most Denali mountaineering expeditions. They also take large (and growing) numbers of tourists
on flightseeing trips into the Alaska Range. Over the years, many of these
"Denali Flyers" have become household names in Alaska: Lowell Thomas Jr., Doug Geeting, Jim Okonek, Cliff Hudson. But the most famous—and first—of Talkeetna's flyboys was Don Sheldon.

Born in Colorado and raised in Wyoming, Sheldon came to Alaska
in 1938 and soon found his way to Talkeetna. Inspired by the likes of
legendary glacier pilot Bob Reeve and a firm believer that "going by
airplane was better than beating yourself to death on a pair of snowshoes," he soon learned to fly. After a stint in the Air Force during World
War II and some postwar commercial-piloting jobs in the Lower 48,
Sheldon returned to Talkeetna in 1948. Three years later he met Bradford
Washburn, who needed a skilled pilot for his ongoing studies of Denali.
The two formed a long-lasting partnership, based on mutual respect and
a shared love for high places.

A fast learner, Sheldon quickly became the region's premier glacier
pilot. In 1954 he made the first commercial flight into the Kahiltna
Glacier; from then until his death from cancer in 1975, he flew hundreds of mountaineers into the Alaska Range and participated in numerous rescue missions. He, as much as anyone, helped open Denali
to the mountaineering masses and laid the groundwork for Talkeetna's

air-taxi industry. During his twenty-seven-year Talkeetna career, Sheldon also transported trappers, hunters, miners, and others to remote wilderness sites. Though he beat up many planes—four were destroyed in crashes—Sheldon never injured himself or a passenger.

Longtime Alaska outdoors writer James Greiner wrote a biography of Sheldon a year before the pilot's death. (Greiner himself would die in 1992 after a long battle with cancer.) The following story, "Mount McKinley's 'Highest Airport,'" is excerpted in shortened form from Greiner's book *Wager with the Wind: The Don Sheldon Story*, published by Rand McNally & Company in 1974.

A s the decade [of the sixties] began, climbing in the McKinley Group was attaining a decidedly international flavor. Today, as in the past, Sheldon estimates that 15 percent of the climbers he caters to come from Japan. The laughing, mostly non-English-speaking groups of Oriental climbers have become commonplace on the gravel main street of Talkeetna. Sheldon's tiny front-porch office is festooned with expedition flags of Japanese origin, and a huge unopened bottle of sake reposes in a remote corner of the desk that holds his base radio gear. He seems to have an instant rapport with the Orientals. Like magic, he finalizes the complex logistics and liaison arrangements for expeditions without speaking a word of Japanese and is even able to joke and laugh with the climbers over subjects of mutual interest. On the wall near his desk is an outdated calendar issued by the Mitsubishi Aircraft Company of Tokyo, and he is fond of pointing to the picture of the sleek twin-engined plane on its cover and grimacing in mock disdain, a tenuous attempt at humor that Sheldon always brings off with perfection.

During the spring and early summer, the sagging plank floor of the Talkeetna Air Service hangar is strewn with the unrolled sleeping bags of transient climbers and piles of additional gear in the process of being sorted. It is the temporary home of Sheldon's clients, and the subject of mild criticism by other business people of Talkeetna, especially those who own motels. The hangar affords a large area in which to sort ice axes, crampons, jumars, pitons, carabiners, climbing ropes, expensive down clothing, handmade boots, daily food rations, and other seemingly endless items of gear that are essential to all mountain-climbing expeditions. Best of all, the hangar, called the "Talkeetna Hilton," is free of charge. Mountaineers, who usually operate on tight budgets, really appreciate Sheldon's hangar hotel. And with the climbing crews close at hand Sheldon can assemble them for a fast departure when the weather breaks in his favor.

In 1960, Talkeetna was fast learning to accept the climbers. True, they were a motley lot of mixed extraction, but unlike the average tourist, they exuded a professional sincerity. These men often got their first look at McKinley from Talkeetna's main street. Impressive at any time, the view is especially awesome when the mountain, reflecting the sun's rays from its snow-covered surface, glows pink against the pale-blue evening sky. With few exceptions, the huge mountain to the northwest signified the happy termination of long planning, meticulous preparation, and high expectation, and they were now anxious to accompany Sheldon on the second-to-last step toward their goal.

The enigma of the mountain climber is virtually insoluble. These men with the sparkling eyes and sun-crinkled features share one common bond— the desire to reach out and grasp the ultimate challenge. To the climber, the higher and more difficult the mountain the more desirable the challenge becomes.

That they go to the mountain with full recognition of the risks involved is a fact of life totally beyond credibility to the nonclimbers of the world, and critics have mumbled about the need for bonding all climbing parties as insurance against the expense of retrieving them from the mountain. Usually mere record breaking has little part in what makes them tick, but in the history of climbing, there have been men who admittedly seemed more interested in getting there fast than in enjoying what happened on the way. John Day was such a man.

John Day's lifelong ambition was to be recognized as an Olympic-class athlete, but he had always just barely missed his goal. Earlier, guided by the legendary Hal Waugh, he had spent a mountain of effort and a river of money trying to shoot an Alaskan brown bear of world-record size. He had failed.

Afflicted with a slightly crippled back, the wealthy owner of the Gold Rey Ranch, near Medford, Oregon, was 51 years old and in excellent physical condition when he arrived in Talkeetna in mid-May. With him was his hired climbing crew, consisting of the Whittaker twins, Jim and Lou, from Seattle [also on the team was 46-year-old Peter K. Schoening, an engineer and veteran of the Himalayas]. Jim Whittaker three years later would establish his name in the top rank of the mountaineering world by becoming the first American to stand at the summit of Everest. Both of the tall, rugged Whittakers were active mountaineers and guides on Mount Rainier in their home state of Washington.

Day, the Whittakers, and Schoening came to Sheldon, who would place them at the starting gate for their race to the top of the mountain that towers into the cold pale-blue Alaskan sky almost 14 times the height of the Empire State Building.

A damp chill hung in the early-morning air of May 13 as the silver Cessna 180 became airborne over the small dirt airstrip in Sheldon's backyard.

At an indicated airspeed of 120 miles per hour, the 60-odd miles between Talkeetna and the South Face of McKinley quickly slipped beneath wings that now reflected the subtle shadings of a carpet of green spruce, meandering streams, and countless small lakes. Leaving the wooded lowlands, Sheldon applied climb power to establish his approach to the 10,200-foot level near Kahiltna Pass. When viewed from the air, Kahiltna Pass appears as a long, steep alleyway of snow, bordered by rocky crags that cast their shadows across its floor. The overall effect is one of highly deceptive gentleness, and on clear days such as this one, when the winds are calm, an aura of peaceful solitude prevails.

With his landing spot in sight, Sheldon's right hand made a smooth throttle adjustment, which gentled the engine. With the lessening of engine noise came an awareness of the sound of the wind rushing by the aircraft. All eyes were forward watching the surface of the glacier. From a distance, the floor of the glacier looked like an undisturbed carpet of snow, but the surface actually consisted of countless ridges of varying size, sharp outcroppings of rock, and numerous blue-green crevasses up to several hundred feet deep. Sheldon knew how to land here. At 80 miles per hour the Cessna responded, and with a slight hissing sound and a series of moderate bumps, the skis found the glacier surface, and the plane's tail dropped.

At 10,200 feet above sea level, the climbers stepped into a brilliant world of sun and snow that seemed thousands of miles from the summertime of Talkeetna, a brief 30 minutes in the past. Almost immediately, the Day party was ready to begin its assault on McKinley's South Summit via the West Buttress. John Day was anxious to grapple with the mountain, and the four-man expedition departed after bidding a terse farewell to Sheldon. They started their climb immediately without even setting up a base camp.

After turning the plane and taking off downslope, Sheldon returned to Talkeetna. Four hours later, on a support flight for another group, he overflew the pass and was surprised to see that the Day party was nearing a place called Windy Corner, 3,000 feet above their starting point.

At the time the Day party began their rush toward the South Summit, there were three other groups on the mountain: a five-member team from Waseda University in Japan, a larger Japanese expedition from Meiji University, and a five-member crew climbing under the banner of the Mountaineering Club of Alaska. Slightly ahead of the Day party, this group, all from Anchorage, consisted of Mrs. Helga Bading, [team leader] Paul Crews, Andrew Brauchli, Dr. Rodman Wilson, and Charles Metzger. Sheldon had taken both Japanese teams as well as the Anchorage group to the mountain and was flying supply drops to all three.

Helga Bading, who could not adjust to the low oxygen levels at 16,400 feet, had stayed in camp while the balance of her party climbed the last leg to the summit. On a whim, the Anchorage team brought along their tiny transceiver so they could broadcast from the summit.

The group from Anchorage reached the South Summit [May 17] at 7:15 P.M. and were closely followed by John Day's crew. Both parties shook hands, planted their expedition flags, and took the usual pictures. The meeting of the Day Expedition and the Mountaineering Club of Alaska team represented the first time in the history of McKinley climbing that two teams stood at the South Summit simultaneously. After spending a half-hour at the highest of all vantage points on the North American continent, the Anchorage team began their descent. John Day and his companions stayed a while longer to take more pictures.

By 9:30 P.M., the Anchorage climbers were in 18,200-foot Denali Pass. They noticed that Day's crew had already started down and was "about 40 minutes behind them," descending a steep, crevassed section of the mountain. Then without warning, the mountain turned victory to chaos. One of Day's crew had become careless and slipped. The others had allowed the rope that joined them to become slack, and one by one, they were all pulled off their feet, to begin a plunge of 500 feet down the steep face of the mountain. As they fell, they futilely attempted to arrest their plunge with ice axes, but their descent had become a deadly game of crack-the-whip.

The Anchorage team, a considerable distance away, heard muffled shouts from above but did not see the actual fall. When they were finally able to pinpoint the trouble, they saw only that the Day crew was piled in a heap at the foot of the sheer wall. By shouting questions, they were able to ascertain that there were injuries and that the Day team wanted a tent. Paul Crews, who was less exhausted than his comrades, ascended to the site of the accident with a Logan tent, which he slit across the bottom and erected over John Day, who seemed to be the most badly injured. It was at this point that the tiny radio transceiver became critically important, for it was their only communication link with the outside world.

At 6:00 A.M. on May 18, after a night of exhausting effort to do what they could for the Day team, Paul Crews sent a message to Tenth Rescue in Anchorage. He indicated the extent of the injuries suffered in the fall. (Day had badly torn ligaments in his left leg, and his hands and feet were badly frozen.) Crews requested an air evacuation for Day and fresh radio batteries for the tiny transceiver. An hour later, Crews detailed the worsening condition of Helga Bading. Sheldon was alerted by Tenth Rescue. He gassed the Super Cub and placed emergency medical supplies, more radio batteries, some food, sleeping bags, and a Primus stove behind the front seat. Sheldon knew that the Day party would need additional supplies if they were forced to stay on the mountain for any length of time.

After donning a light down jacket, his knit watch cap, and his ever-present felts and overshoes, he departed Talkeetna in the Super Cub and by plan flew to the North Face of McKinley. As he had expected, this side of the mountain was still wrapped in clouds and was shielded somewhat from the abating 100-knot winds of the past 3½ days. Calling upon his superb knowledge of cloud formations around the mountain, he climbed through multiple layers to an altitude of 19,000 feet above the North Face and finally topped out of the thick, swirling cloud layers . . . [then] spiraled downward for a break-through-the-clouds look. As he lost altitude in the multilayered clouds, he was able to hold the course he wanted by reference to his compass. Finally he broke through the bottom of the lower layers.

Sheldon had done an uncanny bit of flying and navigating. He had pinpointed the accident scene exactly. Banking the Super Cub gently, he grimaced as he viewed the broken trail left by the tumbling Day team. The ugly scratches streaked the snow slope down the 40-degree face of the West Buttress for a good 500 feet, from just below the crest of Denali Pass nearly all the way to the small level plateau behind the 17,230-foot crest of the upper step of McKinley's West Buttress.

Before leaving the area, Sheldon was shocked by one last horror. Approximately 200 yards from the scene of the fall lay the charred and "still-steaming" wreckage of a plane, identifiable only by the upthrust tail assembly and skeletal shape of the incinerated wings. Sheldon would later learn that the plane, a Cessna 180, had been flown by William Stevenson, an Anchorage contractor. Stevenson had been flying over a lower climbing camp, and curious, had climbed upward to see what was occurring at 17,200 feet. But the area over the accident site was too confined for the Cessna. Trying to turn in the tight confines of the basin, he had stalled his airplane and spun to his death. The plane had burned immediately, and Stevenson's passenger [Air Force Sergeant Robert Elliot] died with him.

Making one final circle, Sheldon popped the door upward, admitting a frigid blast of air, latched it to the wing, reached behind him, and dropped the extra supplies, which were recovered by the Day party. Then, he radioed home.

"Talkeetna base, this is 8898 Delta. I'm at 18,000 and there's been bad trouble here. Some guy piled a 180 up, and it burned. I'm going to Summit for gas en route Talkeetna."

Crews' radioed report from the mountain on May 18 had alerted the world to the multiple tragedy. Climbers from Anchorage, Seattle, Portland, and elsewhere on the West Coast had begun offering their services for a rescue effort that would dwarf any before or since. Several of the large commercial airlines brought these climbers to Anchorage free of charge, and the Army ferried many of them to Talkeetna. Almost overnight, Sheldon's red, sag-roofed hangar building had become the temporary home of almost 100 rescuers. Sheldon, between flights to the accident scene, ferried these men to the base of the mighty Kahiltna Glacier on McKinley, the main staging area for the rescue efforts. Due to the onset of ugly weather, Sheldon had decided that even though he could not land at the disaster site with his Super Cub, he could saturate the lower levels with climbers.

Helga Bading's condition had become much worse during the two days that had elapsed since she had opted to stay at the lower level while the rest of her companions went to the South Summit. She was now incoherent and could not keep food in her stomach. Oxygen, a supply of which had been airdropped the night before, could not overcome the terrible effects of the weak air, and she was being rapidly consumed by a condition called cerebral edema, known simply as altitude sickness prior to late 1960. . . . Her companions knew that if she were to live, she would have to be moved soon to a lower altitude, where the oxygen content of the air was higher. It was late evening of May 19 when they radioed the increasing seriousness of her condition.

Tenth Rescue called Sheldon to ask if he could meet the stricken woman near the 14,000-foot level on the mountain the next day. Sheldon said that he would try. After making this commitment, he felt the first stirrings of the strange loneliness that he has experienced so often during his life. All subsequent decisions would be his alone. Those decisions would affect both his own life and Helga Bading's life, which was now almost totally dependent upon him.

No one, including Sheldon, had ever made a landing near the 14,000-foot level on McKinley. He knew that pilots who fly at these heights, unless properly equipped, suffer hypoxia, the insidious disease of oxygen starvation. In the anemic air at this altitude, the engine of any fixed-propeller aircraft would lose about 45 percent of its total power capabilities. In addition to the lower power capabilities of the airplane, the pilot must exercise extreme care in selecting a landing site that will allow for a reduced-power, gravity-assisted takeoff with the added load of a bulky passenger. The powerful, unpainted six-place Cessna would not meet this challenge due to its high empty weight, and the only choice he had left was the small two-place Piper Super Cub, upon which he had depended so often before.

On the morning of May 20, Sheldon was up at about 4:00 A.M. as usual, after a brief three-hour nap. He found that the weather had broken substantially, and the sky around the mountain was now relatively free of clouds. He made his move at midmorning.

"On the 19th, Jack Wilson of Gulkana, Jim Gibson of Kenai, and George Kitchen along with Ted Huntley, both of Anchorage, had flown in to lend a hand. The thought of landing at 14,000 feet didn't particularly bother me, though I knew I would have a weight problem with the Super Cub. I also knew that I had a power problem with it. I had flown over the top of McKinley in it on many occasions, so ceiling was no consideration, but performance at high altitude is mainly dependent upon the weight you're carrying. I had to haul my own oxygen gear and survival equipment in case I didn't get there in one piece. I asked George Kitchen to fly cover for me for the same reason."

After carefully stowing these bare essentials of equipment, along with a generous bundle of fresh spruce boughs and willow wands, in the rear of the Super Cub, Sheldon began to think about gassing the plane. This consideration would be most important. He knew that too much gas in his tanks might negate a high-altitude takeoff, especially with a passenger in the airplane. Too little fuel could leave him stranded with a dead engine somewhere between the mountain and Talkeetna.

"A landing above 14,000 feet was no sweat, providing I could find a decent piece of steep snow-covered ice to do it on. It was the takeoff that was the big problem. All of the basics of glacier landings would apply, but even with the loss of power I knew I'd get up there, I had to play the weight factor real close. I figured what would be the best fuel load and gassed her up."

Sheldon's landing site [located at just above 14,000 feet on the West Buttress Route, as suggested by Bradford Washburn] had every right to look small, for it was situated on a tiny, shelflike field of snow that tilted upward to the east. It ended abruptly at the foot of a steep slope leading to the top of McKinley, and its lower end deteriorated into a broken jumble of evil-looking crevasses, followed by a staggering cliff. The entire usable surface was only about 2,000 feet long—but it was steep and smooth, and it was where it was needed.

Reducing power slightly, Sheldon flew lower over the tiny area and dropped a line of spruce boughs along the surface upon which he would land. These dark branches would be critical in the actual landing during the next go-around, for he would not be able to gauge his height above the unblemished snow without them.

"The worst part was that this had to be a one-shot deal—no second chance, no nuthin'. Once I lined up on short final here, I would be committed to a landing, like it or not. I knew that I'd have to paint it on or slide backward into the crevasses."

Fortunately, there was little turbulence, and as Sheldon lined up the Super Cub, he had the spooky feeling that he was on a collision course with the mountain, which filled his entire field of vision and rose high above it. Then he reached the point of no return, and his eyes watered with intense concentration.

During the next few fleeting seconds, with the Super Cub under full power, time stood still. As the shadowy crevasses flickered beneath his skis, he pulled the nose up sharply to match the angle of the snow surface that leaped upward before him. The Super Cub screamed in protest in the thin air as he felt for the snow surface with his skis. Then they touched with a metallic hiss, and he was climbing upslope. The plane bounced gently, and with the steepening face of the buttress leaping toward him, Sheldon kicked hard on the left rudder. The Super Cub turned abruptly, and he pulled the throttle back to idle. Sheldon was now parked crosswise on the slope, his left wing pointing downward at a severe angle. His skis held the plane, and he reached up to flip off the master switch. Then, to the popping sounds of cooling metal, he began to consider other pressing matters, such as drawing a deep breath.

Don Sheldon thus became the first man to ever land at the unprecedented altitude of 14,300 feet on the western flank of McKinley. Within an hour after touchdown, and sweating profusely with the heavy exertion of snowshoe-packing the fluffy snow, he had the tiny airfield flattened and flagged with orange survey tape and willow wands that he had brought with him. He then got Kitchen, who still circled above him, on the HF radio and told him to "come on in."

Just as Kitchen's Super Cub was finally placed on the high end of the short slope near Sheldon's, Paul Crews and Chuck Metzger, on the verge of total physical exhaustion, arrived on the scene pulling the sleeping-bag-swathed Helga Bading on a fiberglass sled that had been airdropped earlier by the Army. They had made the descent, over highly difficult and steep terrain, in 5½ hours and arrived at Sheldon's landing site during midafternoon.

Though she had regained consciousness because of the increased oxygen in the air at 14,300 feet, one glance told Sheldon that Mrs. Bading was in a condition very close to death, in the grip of what the press would term "moaning hysteria." Her skin showed the typical shadings of blue and green that accompany the condition that would soon be recognized as cerebral edema by the medical profession. That she was still alive was a credit to the efforts of both Dr. Rodman Wilson and the two team members who had brought her down to the 14,300-foot level. Dr. Wilson had cared for the woman with limited supplies at the 16,400-foot level, and though still in desperate condition, she was improving at the lower altitude.

After Sheldon and the others had gently loaded the woman aboard the Super Cub, he turned the plane to point it downslope and firewalled the throttle. He knew that this would be another one-shot affair. If he failed to get enough airspeed on the downhill run to fly the airplane, he would plunge into the crevasses or over the edge of the cliff beyond.

The tiny plane grudgingly gained airspeed, hurtling him toward the crevasse field. After what seemed an eternity, the Super Cub's tail came up. Easing back on the stick, he raised the plane's nose just as the last orange marker strip flitted beneath his left wing tip. He was airborne.

With the most difficult part of his first operation at the 14,300-foot strip accomplished, Sheldon set his course for Talkeetna. And now a final figure emerged out of the place from which these momentary heroes come—the obscurity of everyday life in Alaska. His name was Link Luckett, an employee of Hughes Helicopter Service in Anchorage. After returning to Talkeetna with Helga Bading and watching the Air Force medics load her aboard a military aircraft for the trip to Anchorage, Sheldon found Luckett waiting. The balding chopper pilot, flying one of his boss's Hiller two-place copters, had come to render aid and was heading for McKinley.

"Will you fly cover for me?" asked Luckett, after explaining what he had in mind to Sheldon.

"Yowsah, let's put the burn on her."

Luckett's tiny rotor-powered craft was assumed to have an absolute operating ceiling of 16,000 feet, and to assure maximum performance, he had off-loaded his battery (after starting his engine) and all of his emergency gear and had gone light on gasoline, allowing just enough fuel to reach the Day party and attempt rescue operations. . . . after what seemed an impossible time period to the circling Sheldon, Luckett miraculously set his fragile craft down on the snow near Day's camp. With this landing, at 17,230 feet, he established an altitude record for this tiny chopper and was the first rescuer to speak personally with the members of the ill-fated team. It was 7:00 P.M. on May 20.

Luckett found that the four men were indeed "fortunate" to be alive. Day's left leg was immobilized by badly torn ligaments, and his hands and feet were badly frozen. The leg had been neatly splinted by Dr. Wilson. Schoening's fingers were puffy and black with frostbite, and he had suffered a severe concussion in the fall. As a result of this concussion, he would remember little of the incident and would suffer memory lapses for some time. One of the Whittaker twins had also received head and neck injuries, and the other suffered frostbite and contusions. All of the men's faces were blistered by exposure, and the injuries had rendered the party immobile. Until this moment, they had been at the mercy of the mountain they had "conquered."

Luckett then instructed the climbers on how to pack down and mark a landing pad, after which he took off empty. Later, at 9:30 P.M., he returned to the scene, and watched by Sheldon who circled overhead, loaded and removed John Day. The climber who had raced with Denali rode uncomplaining, though in excruciating agony, to Sheldon's 14,300-foot landing strip.

Early in the morning of May 21, Luckett made his third and final landing at the top of the world and plucked Pete Schoening from the snow for the relay to 14,300 feet. Meanwhile, the Whittaker twins climbed down to the 14,300-foot level under their own power. Sheldon then relayed the four members of the Day party down to 10,200 feet [from where they were shuttled by other aircraft into town].

Although fatigued and weakened by the long period of superhuman effort, during which he had averaged only two or three hours of sleep per day, and the repeated exposure to the oxygen-weak air in which he had worked, Sheldon continued to remove 13 rescue climbers from the 14,300-foot strip and relay them to 10,200 feet. To accomplish the evacuation, he made a total of 18 landings between 3:00 A.M. on May 20 and noon of the next day. Prior to the marathon, he broke for one of his short naps between midnight and 2:00 A.M.

There followed a massive effort with both military and private aircraft to remove the remainder of the rescue teams from the mountain. Thus ended what the news media would herald as "one of the most daredevil and selfless feats in the long history of Alaskan aviation."

Part IV

Natural History

14

A Naturalist in Alaska

by Adolph Murie

In the early 1920s, biologist Adolph Murie (1899–1974) joined his older brother, Olaus, at Mount McKinley National Park to conduct the first studies of Denali-area wildlife since Charles Sheldon's 1906–1908 surveys. Both brothers would build decades-long relationships with the park; but Adolph would form an especially intimate bond with its wildlife and wilderness landscape, while becoming what some have called "the conscience" of then McKinley Park. Between the 1920s and 1970s, the younger Murie wrote scores of reports and several popular books about the park's mammals, birds, and general ecology. Those writings, combined with his studies of wolf-sheep relationships in the 1930s and 1940s, his many letters and commentaries in opposition to unnecessary park development, and his loud and prolonged call for the preservation of Denali's "wilderness spirit," had a powerful affect. Historian William Brown has called Murie "the single most influential person in shaping the geography and the wildlife-wilderness policies of the modern park."

Adolph Murie's influence was first manifested in his study of wolf-sheep interactions, during a time when Denali's wild sheep populations had crashed to alarmingly low numbers. Thanks in large part to his surveys, interpretations, and philosophies, McKinley Park's Dall sheep crisis ultimately led to a strengthening of ecosystem rather than "favored game" management, in which certain species (such as sheep) were given preference to others, which had to be "controlled"—especially wolves. The crisis also led to Murie's groundbreaking study of the East Fork Wolf Pack and his now famous book, *The Wolves of Mount McKinley.*

Later in his career, Murie the biologist and conservationist would become a staunch park activist. He argued against airplane tours, unnecessary road improvements, and helter-skelter development within park

Previous page: Adult male grizzly, Highway Pass area of Denali National Park
(© Bill Sherwonit)

boundaries, while encouraging wilderness preservation and park expansion to better protect wildlife ranges and habitat. In one letter to the superintendent, he urged, "since wilderness is recognized as one of the foremost values in the Park, it must be given special consideration in order to maintain its purity."

Murie wrote several books about Denali's wildlife. Besides the one on wolves, he authored *The Grizzlies of Mount McKinley; Birds of Mount McKinley National Park, Alaska;* and *Mammals of Denali. A Naturalist in Alaska* includes stories about nearly all of Denali National Park's best-known wildlife species and some of its more anonymous ones as well, from grizzlies and Dall sheep to foxes, mice, gulls—and wolverines. Following is an abridged version of Chapter 10, "Wolverine Trails," from *A Naturalist in Alaska,* which was first published in 1961 by Devin-Adair Co. and reprinted in 1996 by The University of Arizona Press.

One winter day many years ago my brother [Olaus] and I were mushing our dog teams up a narrow creek in northern Alaska. A region seldom visited, it was many days from the nearest habitation. The spruce trees bordering the creek were almost the last; over that high range ahead of us there would be no more. We were proceeding slowly up the winding creek when we saw a lone track on the smooth snow. We stopped the dogs, ready enough to halt, and snowshoed ahead to examine the trail. There were the telltale five toes, the broad rounded track, and the pattern, and we knew it was a wolverine's.

We noted that this wolverine had been loping down the middle of the creek and had come to a sudden stop. The mingled scents of humans, dogs, dried fish, and babies (we were traveling with an Eskimo family) from our entourage had floated to him, a bend or two ahead of us. I doubt that he had experienced such smells before, but he showed no curiosity. He had fled into the spruce woods bordering the creek.

Mushing dogs, with the dog fights, the trail breaking, and the wondering if the dog feed will last, is not without excitement, but what we remember about that arctic day is that trail on the creek bed. We had met a wolverine!

Since that day I have followed many trails, but I have gone for years without seeing a wolverine. Wolverines are seldom observed. Trappers long in the hills rarely meet them. Ernest Thompson Seton, the great naturalist, reported seeing only two during his lifetime. R. M. Anderson, over a long period of years devoted to travel and study in the North, saw sixteen, and most men of the North can readily recollect the few occasions when they have encountered one. The explanation lies partly in the relative scarcity of the animals. Although widely distributed, they usually are not abundant. Furthermore, they are wild and apprehensive, and they waste no time in making a safe retreat when they become aware of a peril. No doubt the wolverine has an excellent nose, and judging from my meetings with him, his vision is not lacking in acuteness. His keen senses, wildness, and alertness largely account for his obscure existence.

The wolverine's wildness is illustrated by the following incident. About six o'clock one evening, as I was driving down the highway in Mount McKinley National Park, I saw an animal galloping away from the road as though terrified. I recognized it as a wolverine, although it seemed unusually slender, probably owing to shedding. It continued its headlong flight until far up the slope, where it sat for a momentary look and then disappeared into a growth of willow. Its flight was exceedingly direct and strenuous.

On another occasion we saw a wolverine gallop up a long talus slope, again wildly hurrying from us. This one looked very much like a marmot, and I suspect that a marmot could easily be mistaken for a wolverine. But when he turned his head to one side to look back, as he frequently did, his long, flexible neck was obvious. He continued his flight to the top of the ridge, where he went out of view.

In appearance, the wolverine resembles a miniature bear. Heavily muscled, strong, and agile, it weighs twenty pounds or more. Charles Sheldon took one on the Toklat River in March 1908, which measured a little over forty-three inches in length, including the tail, and about fifteen inches high at the shoulders and weighed thirty-six pounds. The jaws are well developed and articulated in a deep groove in such a way that they cannot be pried from the skull. This close articulation, together with the heavy musculature, suggests that the jaws are capable for administering a powerful, crushing bite. The color of the fur is blackish brown, the head and tail being lighter than the body proper, except for the two broad, tan stripes which pass from the neck, back along the sides, to meet at the tail. It is much used for trimming parka hoods because of its attractiveness, and because it is supposed to gather less frost from the breath than do other furs, such as that of the wolf and the dog, which are also used for trimming hoods. It so happened that the wolverine fur trimming my own parka hood collected considerable frost, but possibly a wolf or dog trim would have collected even more.

In April 1949, Red Woolford and his partner trapped two male wolverines near Broad Pass [just east of McKinley National Park] about half a mile apart.

One of the animals was hog-tied and brought in alive, not without considerable effort. When I saw him, he was inside a dark shed, fastened to a chain. Because it was feared that a collar would slip over his rounded head, owing to his heavy neck muscles, instead of a collar a harness arrangement was made that circled his back and neck in such a way that it held him securely; it was on the order of a lap-dog harness but different in details. When we entered the shed, we were met by growls so deep and hoarse that I wondered if he was securely chained. As my eyes became accustomed to the dark, I saw this fierce animal facing us in threatening attitude, not at all daunted but ready to attack. Red ran the chain through a long metal pipe, which enabled him to lead him [the wolverine] outside and hold him off at a safe distance from us.

There was almost a continuous struggle as the wolverine tugged and fought. Of special interest were his rolling tactics. He kept rolling over on his back, and sometimes he rolled over and over so that the chain became twisted. Such behavior in a trap might possibly help pry it out of shape or loosen a foot. Red stated that once, when his hound rushed in to attack the wolverine, the latter assumed a position on his back as though ready to rip with claws and teeth, and he succeeded in grabbing the hound's nose. His readiness to roll over on his back suggests that it is a common defensive attitude. Possibly he would face a wolf in such a position.

When the wolverine was returned to the shed and proffered water, he drank freely, lapping like a dog. It has been stated that wolverines suck the water in like a cow, and perhaps they do at times. In the old books this animal has been called the glutton, and there are many stories in print attesting to its extravagant appetite. I asked about the appetite and was told that it was not especially large, that the amount eaten seemed about normal for the size of the animal. No doubt a hungry wolverine, like a hungry dog, will gorge itself, but perhaps, if food is regularly available, the quantities eaten will not be exorbitant.

Tracks are as much as most travelers see of the wolverine, especially tracks in the snow. The wolverine has indeed a kinship with winter. It is then that his trails enhance the snowy landscape and add a rare quality to a region.

There are many other animals in Mount McKinley National Park whose tracks we see in winter. The moose plows deep furrows, the weasel leaves an erratic line of jump marks, the ptarmigan forms a lacework of foot prints and wing and tail marks. All have their characteristics, although under some conditions these may be confusing.

But we are mainly concerned with the tracks of the wolverine. Like other animals it has several gaits, and, to my knowledge, little has been recorded about them.

The wolverine's muscular legs terminate in big feet with well-developed toes and claws. Therefore, the track is large, similar in size to that of the wolf, for which it is sometimes mistaken. Under favorable conditions the five toes and the claws show, but on hard snow the inner toe may occasionally fail to register. The imprint of a front foot is much longer than that of the hind, because of an extra posterior pad, but the widths are about the same. Tracks of the front feet have measured five and three eighths to six and one half inches long, and four to five and one half inches wide; hind-foot imprints, three to four inches long and four to five and one half inches wide. In the same series of tracks there is some variation in length due to sliding and depth of impression, and in width because the spread of the toes increases with the speed of the animal. Anteriorly, the track is broad and rounded, much like a cat track. In loose snow the details are in varying degrees lost and the scuffing enlarges the tracks. But where the details are lost, identification can usually be deduced from the pattern of the four feet.

The wolverine has several gaits, each of which results in a characteristic pattern. For convenience we might list them as walking, trotting, loping (three-track pattern), loping (two-track pattern), galloping on hard surface, galloping in deep snow. In the running gaits the position of the hind feet in respect to the front feet varies. In the two-track lope and the gallop in deep snow the hind feet fall in the front-foot tracks. In the three-track lope the hind feet go farther forward so that only one of them falls in a front foot track; in the gallop on a hard surface, the hind feet may fall far in front of the front feet.

Glimpses of the wolverine are among a naturalist's most notable experiences. The wolverine is a steady boarder at any carcass he discovers, and if one can find one of these there is a good chance to watch him dine. Some carrion freezes solid before it is found; then it is slow work, even for a wolverine, to gnaw off a meal, and he spends considerable time there.

On the morning of March 14, 1950, while driving out [into McKinley Park] in a snow jeep, I observed from a distance a dark object beside a dead moose, and, looking through the field glasses, I recognized a wolverine. He was feeding on the shoulder, changing his position vigorously and frequently, for better gnawing. Once he lay on his side while working down deep in the chest. At short intervals he threw his head up for a look around. After I had watched for some time, I drove to within half a mile of the carcass. When I stopped, I noticed that that wolverine was leaving, but he gave no sign that the snow jeep had scared him. He loped along at a cruising gait without looking my way and traveled up a small tributary just under the bordering snowdrifts. A number of trails leading up and down the creek bottom showed that the wolverine had made many visits to the dead moose. These trails frequently led to lone spruce trees that the wolverine had sometimes climbed. There were claw marks on the bark, and bark fragments were scattered on the snow beneath the trees. One tree having considerable slant and therefore easily climbed had much of the outer bark worn off and was apparently a favorite for climbing. Perhaps the wolverine found this tree useful as a lookout. I surmise that the wolverines use the trees as rubbing posts, for they seem to rub themselves frequently. In many places the animals had rolled in the snow, and in two or three places a shallow hole had been dug and a dropping left and covered over with snow.

On March 28 four inches of new snow lay on the ground, covering the accumulated trails and furnishing a clean surface for fresh ones. As I came opposite the moose carcass, I again saw a dark object on it. I thought it might be the black wolf, as it sometimes was, but it was a wolverine. At first, all feeding on the moose had been done in the region of the shoulder, but now a shaft had been sunk in the hindquarter near the tail. The warm March sun, shining on the dark surface, had softened the tail region a little, and the wolverine or the wolf had worked through the hide. The wolverine, as usual, was working vigorously at the carcass, changing its attack back and forth between the shoulder opening and the tail region. His movements were quick and sudden. At short intervals he stopped feeding to look around, and twice climbed up on the moose for a better view. The object of its watchfulness was probably the wolf. A red fox, curled up on a drift fifty paces away, slept on as though he had not a worry. He was awaiting his turn and making use of the time by sleeping. He probably kept an ear cocked toward the wolverine, and if the wolf showed up, he need not worry about being able to escape him either.

I drove the snow jeep slowly to within a half mile, without frightening anything. The wolverine continued its feeding, and the fox remained asleep in his bed. A raven lit in a willow bush beside the dead moose, giving the wolverine such a start that he galloped fifteen or twenty yards away. But he returned at once, stopping briefly to rub his sides on the snow. The raven remained perched in the willow. After I had watched from this new position for a time, the wolverine departed, alternately walking and loping, using one gait about as much as the other. His short, bushy tail drooped, and his head was held low. He stopped to sprawl and roll, rubbing himself in the snow over an area of a dozen feet across. He also rubbed against some slender willow limbs, causing them to bob up and down and wave in the air. Then he moved a short distance to an open slope and lay down. (His bed proved to be twenty-two inches across and of an irregular shape.) His watchfulness continued, for he rose up occasionally to look around. When I moved forward with the snow jeep, he galloped away, jumping thirty-seven to thirty-eight inches in the soft snow. Tracks showed that, in approaching the dead moose to feed, the wolverine had circled so as to be downwind, probably to learn if anyone was there.

On August 15, while driving in a car [along McKinley Park Road], I came suddenly upon three wolverines in the road. I wanted a picture, but the camera was put away. If I stopped the car, the wolverines would no doubt leave the road and disappear in the rocks and brush, either up or down the steep slope, so I followed slowly. All three galloped down the road ahead of the car, turning their heads on their flexible necks to look at us as they ran. After a short chase I stopped to set up the movie camera. One of them went up the slope, two disappeared around a curve, and I didn't see any of them again. I suspect that these three wolverines consisted of a mother and two offspring.

An interesting observation was made one year on July 21 by Mr. and Mrs. Edwin C. Park along Igloo Creek. For over two hours they watched a mother and two young almost as large as the mother, and observed her nursing twice. The breeding habits of the wolverine are reported to be similar to some of the other mustelids, in that the development of the embryo is arrested at an early stage and remains dormant for several months before development begins again and implantation occurs. The breeding apparently takes place in the summer, but the young are not born until some nine months later. It seems surprising, in the foregoing incident, that such large youngsters should still be nursing, yet perhaps this is less astonishing than grizzly bears nursing into their third summer abroad.

While eating lunch on May 22 George Stiles and I were watching a group of ewes and lambs as they moved downward toward a little creek at the base of some cliffs. After our lunch we stalked them for a movie, gaining a point a little above the creek and just across a draw from them. But they took fright and hurried away without presenting any picture opportunities. We were sitting on the point to catch our breath when up the creek I noticed a dark spot on the snow coming our way. To my surprise, it was a wolverine—bounding along at an easy gallop on the snow-covered creek, coming steadily and purposefully as though to meet some appointment. The gentle slope of the creek bed made travel easier, and he was making good speed, though his gait seemed effortless. At each jump the hind legs were thrown back high and to one side. Coming nearer, he was hidden by the bank, but directly below us he came out of the creek bottom. He glanced toward us but continued on his way through the low bushes without stopping. The incident was so unexpected it seemed like a dream and left us exclaiming in hushed voices.

Tradition says that the wolverine has no fear of other animals. According to Hearn, as quoted by Seton in his *Lives of Game Animals*, a wolverine was known to drive a wolf away from a deer it had just killed. A mountaineer friend of Seton's told of two wolverines driving a black bear from the remains of an elk. R. M. Anderson saw three dogs, "including a famous bear-dog," attack a wolverine; they found it so fierce that they finally gave up and let the quarry go on its way. Fry, as quoted by Seton, reports two black bears giving way to a wolverine at a cow carcass, and three coyotes leaving a dead horse on the approach of a wolverine. The same observer reports that two cougars left deer remains when a wolverine approached. Charles Sheldon writes in *The Wilderness of Denali* of having seen a lynx run from a dead sheep and a wolverine at the same time approach it. Incidents such as these do not necessarily mean that the wolverine could whip these larger animals. More than likely the retreats were made to avoid annoyance rather than from fear of being overcome. Nevertheless, the wolverine appeared to be respected as being able to fight back.

At Mount McKinley National Park tracks revealed on three occasions that a wolf had chased a wolverine. That the wolf gave chase does not mean that he would close in if he overtook the wolverine, for the chase may have been a sporting event. However, a pack of wolves might cause a wolverine some trouble.

The first incident took place on December 2 and was interpreted from the tracks. While a wolverine was loping along a snow-jeep trail at an easy gait, a wolf was moving slowly up from a creek bottom toward the same trail. Their ways met. The wolverine must have scented the approaching wolf, for it halted and then reversed its direction. Upon first turning back, the wolverine was not much alarmed, judging from the slow, loping gait, but after he had traveled on the back track for about twenty yards, he must either have seen the wolf or gotten a warmer scent, for he broke into his fastest gallop. After traveling for 150 yards, he left the road and galloped through the soft snow, sinking deep at every jump. The wolf, on coming to the road, had followed the wolverine at a fast trot, but after a chase of about 350 yards it had apparently lost interest and resumed its lone way. The wolverine had done his best to remove himself from the vicinity of the wolf; and the wolf had not seemed very anxious to overtake this formidable fighter.

Tracks observed on March 29 at the carcass of a moose showed that a lone wolf had rushed toward a wolverine that was lying on a snowdrift beside a leaning spruce. This tree was apparently a refuge, and the wolverine had been resting beside it for that reason. In this emergency, he climbed to safety and peace up through the thick, brushy branches. The litter of loosened bark and broken twigs lying on the snow beneath marked his progress up the tree and showed that he had climbed to the very top. There were scratch marks on the trunk, and a few wolverine hairs clinging to some of the sharp knots. On this occasion I should guess the wolf was motivated by an exuberance of spirit.

On another occasion I was following the trotting tracks of a wolf going over hard, drifted snow near the top of a bench bordering a small tributary of Jenny Creek. He had a good view of the creek bottom, the willow thickets, and the few lone spruces. From his vantage point he had seen a wolverine coming slowly up the creek. Here was another opportunity for the wolf to indulge in a diversion, and he was soon in full gallop. The wolverine had seen the danger and had also broken into a gallop. His course was directly up the creek toward a spruce; the wolf ran almost parallel to the creek but slanted toward the wolverine's line of travel, as though he, too, were headed for the spruce tree. On the hard snow, the wolf's widely spaced tracks showed great speed, but when he reached the soft snow in the bottom, he broke through and his trail was a series of deep holes, where he had wallowed. The quarry could not make speed in this snow either, but he managed to reach the tree ahead of the wolf. The snow around the spruce was marked with many wolf tracks. There were several spots where the wolf had sat on his haunches, probably looking up at the wolverine. The wolf had trotted to the top of a low ridge for a look around then returned to worry the wolverine some more. Eventually, the wolf tired of his sport, and the wolverine was able to continue on his journey.

The cache, typically a miniature cabin on stilts, is characteristic of the north. It is a structure that is both picturesque and useful. When a trapper builds a cabin, he also expects to erect a cache on four poles, because his provisions, even when left in a cabin, are not safe from disturbance. The animal most closely associated with the cache in the minds of many is the wolverine. (It probably should be the bear!) The wolverine is known widely for his habit of misappropriating goods; because of the remarkable ability he has exhibited in breaking into stored provisions, he has been credited with superhuman strength, a reputation at least partially deserved. But his misdemeanors have helped to foster the pleasant architecture of the cache which has such universal appeal. Because of his climbing ability and that of the mice and others, the poles are ornamented with tin or stovepipe, which is wrapped around a section of each pole. The smooth surface presents no hold for the claws and is an effectual block to climbing higher and gaining access to the stores. I like to think of the cache as a gentle way of settling some of the differences between ourselves and the other animals in the hills, so that we can live amicably together.

The wolverine has his own caches to enjoy and worry about. It is not easy to be secretive about them, because of the many sharp eyes and noses in the woods. If a bone or other part of a carcass is carried away, it leaves a give-away scent on every twig and grass stem it touches along the trail. Consequently, when someone like the fox, who follows tracks of all kinds, learns from these scents what the wolverine is up to, he follows the trail and sooner or later finds the cache and appropriates what it contains—unless the wolverine is there. This works both ways, for, the next time, the wolverine may discover one of the secrets of the fox. Thus we find that the caches, regardless of who makes them, tend to serve the community.

A moose carcass north of Six-Mile, quickly dismembered because it was fed upon by wolves and others while still fresh and unfrozen, was frequently attended by a wolverine, who made many trips, carrying away booty. He was providing for the near future, when this food resource would be gone. (The wolverine that fed at the frozen carcass did no caching, because the meat could be only slowly gnawed loose, and no surplus for caching was readily available.)

On one occasion a wolverine stole a frozen section of a moose leg which Ranger Bill Nancarrow and I had hung in a spruce by a rope. I found the drag marks of the leg, and wolverine tracks to one side. The trail led through the woods to the creek bed, where I assumed I would find the cached leg, for across the creek was a steep ridge. The leg weighed perhaps thirty-five or forty pounds, and I marveled that it had been dragged so far. Then, to my further astonishment, I found that the trail led up to a ridge, so steeply that my snowshoes took an occasional slide with me. The wolverine had done much tugging to get it up the slope (some two or three hundred yards), especially in places where the leg had caught in willows. After gaining the top of the ridge, the wolverine had continued over rolling terrain and then gone down into a ravine—where I turned back. A fox had followed the trail ahead of me!

About three weeks later, far up this same ravine, I noted fresh digging in the snow on a steep slope and found a hard-packed platform on which reposed the bones of the moose leg, still articulated but cleaned of all hide and flesh. The end of the humerus had been chewed and hollowed out as though the marrow had been sought. While examining the bone, I thought I heard a sound like the crackling of branches but suspected it was my parka rubbing on twigs. More sounds called my attention to the top of a spruce; there I saw movements and a patch of brown and yellowish fur, and I recognized a wolverine. There was a throaty growl, then several growls. When I maneuvered away from the tree for a picture, the wolverine scrambled down the tree and plunged away through the deep snow, hidden at once by a heavy growth of alders. He probably knew about other cleaned moose bones scattered widely over his domain.

Next winter the wolverine will again leave his snow trails in McKinley Park. On the far hillside there will be a trail with a three-three pattern, and you will know that he has passed that way. You will meet his track in the valley and on the crests of ridges. Here, at least, we may hope that his trails will lead far into the future.

15

The Wolves of Denali

by L. David Mech, Layne G. Adams, Thomas J. Meier,
John W. Burch, and Bruce W. Dale

To those who love wilderness, few things are as exciting as the presence of wolves, whether seen or heard. And nowhere in Alaska do people have a better chance of encountering a wolf, or hearing its howl, than in 6-million-acre Denali National Park and Preserve. Nowadays, nearly everyone seems to recognize the importance of wolves to the Denali ecosystem —and to a more complete Denali experience. But wolves have not always been considered desirable residents of Alaska's oldest parkland.

Back in the 1930s, a broad coalition of groups—including several sportsmen's organizations—pressured the National Park Service to exterminate the wolves in then McKinley National Park, because of reports that wolves were decimating the park's Dall sheep. In response, the government asked Adolph Murie to investigate wolf-sheep interactions. Murie's studies, interpretations, and philosophies—summarized in his book *The Wolves of Mount McKinley*—ultimately led to the park's "ecosystem management" approach that emphasizes the value of *all* species rather than a favored few. Among the many who've lauded Murie's work with wolves is L. David Mech of Minnesota, arguably the preeminent wolf researcher of the past quarter-century. During the mid-1980s, Mech and several other scientists launched a comprehensive study of Denali National Park's wolves on a scale never before attempted. Based on their fieldwork from 1986 through 1994, Mech and several co-authors (listed above) then produced *The Wolves of Denali*, which explores all aspects of a wolf's life, from pack structure to predatory strategies, and competition between packs for food and territories.

Here are just some of their findings: Denali's wolf population is highly dynamic, with a lot of fluctuation. The number of wolves estimated to inhabit the 6-million-acre park and preserve between 1987 and 1994 ranged from a low of 45 to a high of 160. The park's best-known pack, the East Fork, had as few as 6 and as many as 29 members. Territories ranged from 230 to 1700 square miles; the larger areas reflect packs that depend heavily on caribou. Few wolves live beyond age 3; most are killed by other wolves, while some die from starvation, avalanches, drowning, or human hunters and trappers. (A human subsistence harvest is allowed in two-thirds of Denali National Park and Preserve, and some Denali wolves are also killed by humans outside the park boundary.)

The excerpt included here, "Wolves in Perpetuity," is the final chapter of *The Wolves of Denali,* published in 1998 by the University of Minnesota Press.

Almost six decades ago, Adolph Murie stood along the East Fork River deep in the heart of Mount McKinley National Park. High above him the sprawling earthen hues of Polychrome Mountain revealed a geologic history of millions of years. As Murie scanned the hills for sheep or wolves, no satellites whisked across the skies. No busloads of tourists rumbled by. Not even a park ranger intruded on the scene.

Sixty years before that, only Athabascan Indians prowled that area. No park road gave easy access. Only sheep ruts cut diagonally across the mountainsides, and caribou trails meandered miles along the braided rivers, over the tundra, and through the mountains.

But the East Fork River looked the same then as it does now. And Polychrome Pass too. And some miles beyond it, connecting the earth with the clouds and casting its mammoth shadow over the area, stood the massive mountain of rock, snow, and ice that the Indians called Denali, "the High One."

Scattered over the landscape all those many years ago during both periods were the wolves and the moose, the sheep and the caribou, the grizzly bears, the marmots, the eagles, and the ground squirrels. Probably little different from today, they plied their lives with ancient habits peculiar to their kind but profoundly successful.

None of the creatures sported radios in Murie's day or before. Their lives, therefore, were much more of a mystery then than now. Nevertheless, all these unique components of the Denali ecosystem, and all the other parts as well, interact today like they did when the Athabascans hunted among them or Murie watched them. The difference is that today we know much more about those interactions than we did before.

Like everywhere else, the Denali ecosystem is comprised of multitudes of interacting food chains including those involving eagles, lynx, foxes, wolverines, bears, coyotes, and the prey of each as well as many other birds, mammals, and various invertebrates. In Denali, many of these chains interact with the wolf-prey chain in a complex web of life and death.

It is the wolf-prey chain, however, that in a certain sense dominates Denali both in the way human beings perceive the park and also in terms of scale. Wolf prey are the largest creatures of Denali, and the full-time ecological "job" of wolves is to kill them. In doing so, wolves provide food not only for themselves but also for most of the smaller carnivores and scavengers.

Because wolves and their prey are large, it is easier in some ways to study them than to investigate food chains involving smaller creatures. Thus, an understanding of the life of the wolf and its prey in Denali lends insights into the functioning of the rest of the food web. All types of prey depend on plants, which in turn are affected by the basic physical conditions of the soil and climate. All carnivores exist in lower numbers than their prey, and so must circulate about and scan their prey for likely targets. Thus, although the specific workings of the various food chains may vary, they share basic elements.

Denali's wolf-prey system functions today as it did in Murie's day and in the Athabascans' day. Wolves scan every fertile area of the park, avoiding only the sterile ice, rock, and snow of the Mountain.

Picture the park from space: Perhaps it is summer, and individual wolves, some in twos and threes, are trotting up the river bars, along the ridges, across the tundra, fanning out from their dens of pups.

In the East Fork area, a wolf makes its way along the Toklat River, another heads over Sable Pass, and a small group checks out the Wyoming Hills north of the den. To the northwest, Little Bear Pack members spread over the Kantishna Hills, some coursing the barren tops while others pick their way through the tangled willows and alders of their steep valleys. Way off to the southwest, the wolves of the McLeod Lake Pack inspect the myriad ponds reflecting nearby Mount McKinley, head over the eskers, and lope steadily across the flats.

Yard after yard, mile after mile, the wolves cover the area. What they do not see, they hear; what they do not hear, they smell. If they miss some spot today, they may hit it tomorrow, or the next day. Or some fellow pack member may check it out. Although their quest is always food, their other interests include signs of friends and enemies. Thus, as each wolf circulates about the region, it hesitates often, sifting the scents, sounds, and sights for any clue of interest.

Feces and urine yield clues about what other wolves have passed and when. If strange, they may need more investigation and perhaps some scouting about for the maker. Or maybe they require retreat. Signs from packmates may indicate that the area has been hunted recently, or that fresh kill lies nearby.

If a traveling wolf runs into a packmate, the two will usually socialize for a few seconds and travel together for awhile. When they spot an enemy, they may give pursuit, or they may turn tail. Foxes, wolverines, lynx, coyotes, or other competitors are promptly chased. Bears give wolves pause, and unless a meaty carcass is involved, the wolves are usually content to back off. When some difference in motivation besets each of the traveling companions, they will go their separate ways, only to meet again sometime or someday back at the den.

Meanwhile, the moose, the caribou, and the sheep of Denali busy themselves with eating. Bite after bite, they munch their way over or through the vegetation. Each frequents its own type of area and chews its own kind of food. The moose prefers the willows, wrapping its tongue around each fresh shoot, pressing it against the roof of its mouth and stripping off the leaves. Small bands of sheep search the rocky crags for grasses and sedges, and in between, any shrubby willows they can find. Caribou herds frequent the park's high, open slopes, not only to avoid the variety of insects that harass them but also to exploit the hills' profusion of lush grasses, sedges, herbs, willows, and dwarf birches.

As these herbivores feed, they move slowly over the area, picking and choosing their plants but constantly chewing as they go, and only occasionally looking up, unless some troublesome cue alerts them. Thousands of bites are needed to fill their rumens and build their bodies over the summer. When the animals stop grazing or browsing and rest, they bring up their food again in cuds, chew it more thoroughly, and swallow it again, this time for good.

The adult females whose new offspring still survive have an even stronger need to concentrate on feeding during this brief period of plenty. Their nursing young will drain them more of their energy than will anything else. With the breeding season coming again soon, followed by the cold and snow of winter, they must take full advantage of this short opportunity to replenish themselves. Otherwise, they will get no other chance.

These Denali herbivores outnumber the wolves by about 60 to 1. Thus, we can imagine from 70 to 140 wolves (depending on year and season) wandering over the park day after day, one pack here and another there, moving among the moose, sheep, and caribou. Each time a wolf locates prey, it must try to turn the encounter to its own advantage. Many times that is not possible, and the wolf must go on.

During summer, the most opportune types of encounters are usually those involving the young of their prey, especially moose calves. If the winter has been especially snowy, caribou calves may be more profitable. Now and then a wolf may find an old or weak adult ungulate it can kill, or a carcass washed up on a river bar. Beavers, marmots, ground squirrels, hares, and other small prey fill in as wolves come upon them.

Then back to the den or rendezvous site each wolf heads with stomach or jaws full, excitedly approaching the breeding female and her litter of perhaps six pups. They in turn rush the provider frantically and instantly usurp its bounty. Numerous such trips are made, and the pups grow quickly. By about October, they are usually large enough to join the adults in their hunts, and the pack travels as a group.

Bull moose have been fighting for females some weeks already, ignoring food and everything else in a desperate attempt to pass on as many of their genes as possible. They are growing weak, and the wolves will dispatch the older ones. Caribou bulls, too, are trysting and fighting and providing additional food for the wolves. One to 2 months later, Dall sheep rams will fall into the same pattern.

By the end of December, the sun has reached its nadir, light is low, and bitter cold pervades Denali. Snow has covered the park for as many as 3 months already in some years. During others, strong arctic highs hold off the storms, and snow is light. The difference will determine whether or not wolves can depend on female prey during the next few months, especially caribou. If not, they must continue finding moose calves and what miscellaneous older or weaker moose, caribou, and sheep remain.

The number of wolves during the next years may turn on this difference. Caribou herds drift far and wide across Denali's vastness at this time. If snow is light, and food is found in many places, the herds circulate among these areas, warding off the worst ravages of winter scarcity and making discovery by wolves less probable. Windblown ridges expose the lichens, mosses, and remaining grasses and sedges that caribou seek. The less the creatures have to hunt and dig for these dry stands, the more of their precious fat reserves they can shunt to their developing fetuses. The better too the caribou can resist the inevitable attacks by wolves.

Such resistance may then translate into increased dispersal by the wolves' maturing young. As prey become harder to catch, the yearlings and 2-year-old wolves must yield to their parents as they feed the developing pups. One by one, then, the maturing wolves break away from their natal group. A few will visit neighboring packs and somehow work their way into one. Most will head far outside the park toward mates and what could be "greener pastures" but what may end up being their demise.

Even most of the wolves that remain, however, will survive for very limited periods. In 1 year or 2, the pups will be in the same positions their older siblings are and will also depart. The adults will breed again and probably produce pups. However, at any time as they make their way around their territory, they may suddenly be confronted by their neighbors. If so, a fight to the death is probable. One or both breeders may be killed, and some of the younger wolves as well. If the young wolves are not killed, they may languish and die without the adults to provision them.

In any case, some wolves will triumph and survive a while longer. They will continue their travels over their territory, marking it as they go, and howling frequently to warn their neighbors. If the breeders still find food scarce, they may produce only a few pups that spring, or maybe none. The winter weather's fickleness has had a pervasive effect on their life, and they may be lucky to even survive.

On the other hand, if the snow is deep, a different set of effects may cascade through the system. Moose and sheep will find it harder to feed and will weaken sooner. Travel will be harder, more restricted, and more energy-depleting for caribou. The ever-scanning wolves may find the herds sooner, and certainly they can catch and kill the caribou more easily.

The timing is perfect, for the wolves are now fattening up for their own reproduction. A bonanza of vulnerable prey due to deep snows primes the wolves for a productive year. So, too, the lack of competition allows the maturing pack members to remain longer, and the packs build up.

With either scenario, spring brings change. Not only do the sheep and moose in their new freedom from the restricting snows begin to gorge again and immediately start replenishing their lost reserves, but the caribou, too, drift back toward their calving ground in the shadow of the Mountain near the center of the park. The wolves, suspending their own nomadism, begin to dig their dens.

Just as the wolves are whelping, the caribou begin to calve. A sudden burst of easy prey becomes available. How easy and how big a burst depends again on the preceding snows. If light, the calves may provide only a 2-week feast, but if the snows are deep and long, some calves may be available throughout the year. Moose calves come next, and similar workings affect their vulnerability.

So on and on the Denali system churns, year after year, and decade after decade. Winter storms come and go, some more severe, some less. At times herbivore numbers wax, at other times they wane. Wolves respond accordingly and add their effects to the process. They flourish for awhile, and their dispersers probe the outside world. Some find mates and spread Denali genes far and wide; the others perish. Then, when conditions change, Denali wolves wait, their full potential to expand on hold. There will be another day.

In the shadow of the Mountain, there will always be another day.

16

Grizzly Cub: Five Years in the Life of a Bear

by Rick McIntyre

The grizzlies of Denali National Park, similar to others that inhabit Alaska's vast Interior, spend up to one-half year or more in hibernation. During their five- to seven-month waking period, they require vast expanses of wild, undeveloped land to survive; yet they are among Denali's most visible residents, frequently seen near the park's lone road by visitors traveling in large, noisy buses. A couple of facts help to explain this seeming paradox. First, much of the Denali Park Road passes through the tundra habitat preferred by grizzlies—and open tundra makes it easier to spot bears and other wildlife. Second, Denali's grizzlies have grown habituated to vehicle traffic. Busloads of people come and go and the bears simply go about their business, which mostly is the business of eating food.

Back in the mid-1980s, longtime Denali ranger Rick McIntyre had the good fortune to closely follow the life of a male grizzly that often frequented the park road's corridor. A seasonal naturalist based at Eielson Visitor Center, sixty-six road miles into the park, McIntyre in words and photos documented the bear's maturation from a tiny five-month-old cub to a young adult weighing some 300 pounds. "Little Stony," as McIntyre named the bear, quickly earned a reputation as a curious, playful animal, whose roadside antics entertained thousands of visitors. Sadly, after being weaned from his mother during his third summer, Little Stony's innate curiosity led to a series of conflicts with humans. Eventually he got into a garbage dump at a wilderness lodge located near the park road's end. Park rangers decided to tranquilize and relocate the five-year-old bear by helicopter, but Little Stony died during this move. As McIntyre notes, Little Stony's story shows how park developments intended to help people enjoy wildlife and wild lands can sometimes be detrimental to the animals a park is designed to protect.

McIntyre, who describes himself as a bio-historian, left Denali National Park after fifteen summers. He has spent the last six summers at Yellowstone National Park, where he studies wolves reintroduced to the

Yellowstone ecosystem in 1995. A National Park Service employee for a quarter-century, McIntyre is the author of four books, including two on wolves.

The following excerpt, taken from Rick McIntyre's book *Grizzly Cub: Five Years in the Life of a Bear,* was published in 1990 by Alaska Northwest Books. Titled "Year One," it describes McIntyre's first meeting with Little Stony and the cub's first summer of life.

When I first saw him, he was the size of a teddy bear. The tiny grizzly cub stood beside the road and stared at me as I coasted the truck to a stop. He continued to look at me for a few more moments before dashing off to catch up with his mother. The two grizzlies crossed the road, passing within yards of my truck.

I had never been so close to such a young cub. The two bears stayed near the road for the rest of the day, and I spent ten hours watching them.

The cub was only five months old, but already he had a well-developed personality. He played continuously, his play fueled by tireless curiosity about his world.

Everything on the tundra was a potential toy. He picked up a rock that interested him and carried it around in his jaws. Then he attacked a willow bush he came upon, and climbed it until it dumped him on the ground. A second assault got him a little higher, but he soon lost his balance and started to slip. As he fell, he grabbed a branch with his teeth. For several moments he dangled by his jaws from the branch while he struggled furiously to swing himself back up. The branch broke and he tumbled to the ground. Sprawled on his back, he suddenly realized he could turn the broken branch into a toy. The cub juggled the branch, first with his front paws and then with his back feet. When this no longer held his interest, he stood on his hind legs and carried the branch around in his jaws.

But the plaything that best showcased his exuberant curiosity was a snowbank. It took the cub a few tries, but he finally figured out that by sitting down he could slide down the bank—which he did, repeatedly, racing back to the top of the snowbank, sitting on his haunches, and spinning down the snowy slope.

Though the cub's inventiveness enabled him to play for hours with things he found on the tundra, eventually he grew bored and looked for a playmate. Since he had no siblings, his choice was limited to one: his mother. His next problem was how to interest her.

He ran up to her and bit her on the cheek. She ignored the cub and continued to feed. The cub then stood directly in front of her, blocking her path. Without taking any apparent notice, she bowled him over and resumed grazing. She had sent him tumbling down a hillside, but he jumped up and ran back for a second try. This time he slipped beneath her hind legs, walked under her belly, and then pushed his way between his mother's jaws and the food she sought. He rolled on his back, wiggled his four paws in the air, and tried to bite her chin. This also failed to elicit any response. When the sow walked off, he ran after her and fiercely attacked her hind legs. She was oblivious to this assault as well and continued feeding.

Next the cub ran up to her, swatted her in the face, and immediately dashed off. Stopping forty feet away, he looked back to see if his blow had provoked a reaction. If he had done that to another bear cub, it would have sparked a furious game of run-and-chase across the tundra. She was still peacefully feeding, however, paying no attention to him.

The mother bear was determined to eat, while the cub was equally determined to play. All of his schemes and tricks were ignored. The mother seemed too dignified to get involved with something as frivolous as play.

After several hours of this, the sow stopped feeding and yielded to the cub's incessant demands. She sat down and lowered her head to his level. He bit and bashed her face, ears, and neck. She nipped back gently. The cub stood and attacked the fur on her cheeks. He then rolled onto his back and the sow pretended to attack him, which then enabled him to counterattack her face and chest. Sometimes their bites looked fierce; but much the way the family dog romps and mock-bites when playing with children, the two bears seemed to know just how much force to use with each other.

After five minutes of play, the mother rolled onto her back and nursed the cub. A few minutes later, the tired but satisfied cub began a well-deserved nap.

It was not destined to be a peaceful sleep. A few minutes after dozing off, the cub opened an eye and looked for his mother. She was forty-five feet away, chewing on a fresh patch of grass. Afraid of being left behind, he jumped up and ran toward her. Once he was next to her, he lay down again and resumed his nap. Not much later he looked up and found that he had been abandoned again. He rushed to catch up. This time he bedded down right under her stomach. When the sow moved on, she had to lift a hind leg over the cub to avoid stepping on him. Altogether his nap was interrupted three or four more times so that he could keep up with his hungry mother.

When I called it a day at 11 P.M., I was exhausted, but it had been the most absorbing and fascinating day of observing wildlife in my life.

Because the family was usually seen on or near Stony Hill, between the drainages of Big Stony and Little Stony creeks, I began to call the mother bear Big Stony and the cub Little Stony. I learned a lot about bears by watching these two over the next years.

Like all cubs, Little Stony loved to nurse but was often turned down when he asked for milk. As his mother fed, he often sneaked under her belly and tried to nurse. When this happened, she usually walked off, causing him to lose his balance and fall over. Sometimes, if he had a good grip on one of her nipples, he hung on and nursed as he was dragged across the tundra. Occasionally Big Stony swung around and bit him hard enough to make him let go.

As with his persistent attempts to enroll her in play, the cub was not easily deterred from nursing. Again and again he slipped under her stomach and reached up to nurse only to be left behind as she moved off.

When Little Stony got really hungry, he made a whining call that sounded like "waugh." About every two hours, his mother gave Little Stony what he wanted. She chose a spot, sat down, and lay back. He came running, climbed up on her belly, and got busy. As he nursed, he made a buzzing sound. Grizzly sows have six teats, and the little cub went from one teat to another as he drained each. He had to walk back and forth on her belly and chest, and Big Stony often held him in her paws so he wouldn't fall off. Nursing sessions lasted about four minutes. To end them, the sow simply got up and walked away.

Most of the time, the nursing ended before the cub was satisfied, and he pestered her for more. On one occasion, however, Big Stony fell asleep while nursing. For once Little Stony had plenty of time to feed. He made a complete circuit of her teats and drained her dry. Then it was time for a nap. He was so full that he just plopped down on her belly and began snoozing.

One of little Stony's favorite pastimes was willow climbing. As he got better at it, he could work his way ten or fifteen feet up flimsy bushes, using his jaws and front paws to pull himself up. Big Stony seemed to sense the danger in this game and began to pay more attention to his climbing.

One time he was way up in a bush, and she came over and watched him closely. He fell, did a midair flip, and landed at her feet. Immediately, he returned to the willow and climbed back up, even higher than before. He swayed back and forth on a narrow branch near the top, playing to his audience of one. Soon—possibly frightened of the height—he tried to get down. After several false starts and close calls, he finally learned that it was best to reverse directions and climb down headfirst.

In their travels, the family sometimes encountered other tundra residents. The most common other big animal was the caribou. A healthy adult caribou bull or cow can easily outrun a bear and is so confident of its speed that it often walks by bears with little evident concern. Experienced bears ignore these temptations, for they know it's a waste of energy to chase faster animals.

Little Stony had not yet learned that lesson.

He knew instinctively that caribou were safe targets to charge. Often during that first summer, he chased them across the tundra. His enthusiasm was admirable, but the sight of a little ten-pound cub clumsily galloping after a graceful caribou going forty miles per hour was comical. When he tired, he gave up and trotted back to his mother, who had completely ignored the caribou and chase. In some cases, the caribou jogged back to the bears, perhaps curious, wanting to see what the two were doing. This was too much for the cub to resist. He mounted a second campaign and tried to grab the caribou before it got away. He never caught one, but he did his best—and got a good workout.

Caribou were harmless, but other animals on the tundra wanted to eat little cubs: big male grizzlies (also known as boars). Little Stony knew that other bears were to be feared. When he was six months old, an adult bear ambled onto the scene, suddenly noticed the cub, and headed toward him. The cub was only fifty feet from his mother. Instantly he streaked over to her and positioned himself behind her so that her body was between him and the oncoming danger. Then he stood up and looked over his mother's back at the approaching bear.

The sow quickly spotted the strange grizzly. Without hesitation she charged him. The boar stood his ground for a moment and assessed the situation. He outweighed her and almost certainly was stronger. In an all-out fight, he would likely be the winner. On the other hand, the mother bear hurtling toward him was committed to fight to the death to protect her cub. Deciding it wasn't worth the risk, the boar turned tail and fled. Big Stony pursued him a short distance before circling back to Little Stony, who was loudly crying out. A nursing session eased his trauma and quieted him down.

Grizzlies in Denali National Park live on a predominantly vegetarian diet. They would undoubtedly love to catch and eat fish, but the park's glacial streams are mainly devoid of them. Since moose, caribou, and Dall sheep are difficult to kill, most grizzlies learn that Arctic ground squirrels offer them their best chance at a high-protein meal. Adult squirrels contain as many as 2,400 calories, a healthy meal for a bear. A research project found that one Alaskan grizzly sow caught and ate 300 squirrels during the course of a single summer.

Big Stony was a seasoned squirrel catcher, constantly on the alert for them. On seeing one, she immediately rushed it, trying to grab it before it dived into its burrow. If the squirrel reached its home, Big Stony dug after it with relentless persistence, spending as much as thirty minutes excavating a single tunnel.

When his mother caught a squirrel, Little Stony would rush over and demand a piece of it. She never willingly shared a squirrel with him.

When Little Stony was eight months old, Big Stony caught a squirrel and was beginning to eat it. The cub came over and stuck his face inches from her jaws as she chewed. Then he cried out loudly, demanding part of the meal. Ignoring his cry, she turned away and tried to finish the squirrel in peace. He continued to whine and again crowded her as she ate. She dropped the squirrel, growled at the cub, and gave him a good bite on his back. As a result of her punishment, he kept his distance until she finished. After she walked off, he went over and sniffed the inedible parts left behind, mainly the skin and tail. He chewed on them for a while but, except for a little taste, couldn't have gotten much out of them.

As Little Stony got bigger and more experienced, he learned to be more assertive when it came to what he wanted to eat. Just a month after the above incident, mother and cub tried to dig up yet another squirrel. It was late August and an early snowstorm had deposited three inches of snow on the tundra. The sow caught the squirrel after about twenty minutes of work. As always, Little Stony ran over and cried out for his share. She ignored him and continued to eat the delicacy.

Suddenly he lunged for the squirrel, trying to tear it out of her mouth. She retaliated by biting him on the back, but to do so required her to drop the squirrel. For a second, they each stared at the squirrel lying on the ground, then each dived for it simultaneously. Mustering all the force his forty-five-pound body could generate, Little Stony wrestled with his mother over the prize he desperately wanted.

The two bears rolled around in the fresh powder snow, kicking up so much of the stuff it looked like they were in a miniature blizzard. After a half minute of battle, the cub ran off defeated, having been taught his manners by his powerful mother.

Or so it seemed. When Little Stony had gone fifty feet, he stopped to look back. The squirrel dangled from his mouth. Big Stony glared at him in disgust, then walked off. He had taken a big chance for a highly desired snack and won.

The next time I saw the sow catch a squirrel, she quickly looked over at her cub. He was digging at another burrow entrance and had his back turned. Without moving or making much of a sound, she quickly gulped her meal whole, dispensing with the usual chewing that prolonged the delicate taste. Just as she swallowed, the cub looked over and realized something was happening. He charged over and looked first at the wrecked burrow and then at his mother. From his expression, it seemed as though he knew she had caught the occupant, but he couldn't figure out where she had put it. Big Stony turned and walked off, leaving him with his puzzlement.

By September, it was easy to see that Little Stony was becoming increasingly independent. In late spring, when I first saw him, he didn't like to be more than fifty feet from his mother. Now it was nothing for him to lag several hundred yards behind. He demonstrated his independence one day on Stony Hill when he persisted in digging up a promising squirrel burrow, oblivious to the fact that his mother had continued on. When she was 300 yards away from the cub, she stopped and looked around for him. Since he was in a gully, she couldn't spot him. She snorted several times to call him. That did no good so she retraced her steps, back to where he was still digging away at the burrow. She sniffed his back and then walked off, apparently expecting him to follow. Little Stony continued digging for the squirrel that only he believed was in the burrow. When his mother got a good distance away and turned and found that he was still not with her, she went back a second time to get his attention. He only gave up his excavation and followed her when he saw the burrow was empty.

In late September I packed my belongings and prepared to drive to California for my winter job as a ranger in Death Valley National Monument. The last time I saw the two bears that year, they were feeding by Little Stony Creek, concentrating on their eating so intently that they failed to see a wolf moving across the tundra toward them.

A squirrel popped out of a burrow and Big Stony gave chase. Her pursuit took her right toward the wolf. By the time she saw him, she was only 100 yards away. She stopped and looked back and saw that the cub was galloping toward her. He caught up with her and watched the wolf over his mother's shoulder.

Little Stony was still small enough to tempt a wolf. There have been a number of sightings in Denali of wolves stalking cubs. Once a wolf pack separated two yearling cubs from their mother and killed them.

Big Stony stood up and stared at the wolf. She must have presented an intimidating sight, for the wolf quickly left the area.

It had been a great summer for me. I had been able to watch a grizzly family at close range on almost a daily basis. Observing Little Stony and his mother had enabled me to learn more about bears than I had in all my previous summers in Denali. I hoped to return next spring and watch them more. As I left the park that fall I wished them well and hoped that they would enjoy their months in hibernation.

17

Strange Grace

by Sherry Simpson

Sherry Simpson was seven years old when her family moved from Colorado to Alaska's capital city, Juneau. The following year the family moved again (albeit temporarily), when Simpson's father, a civil engineer, was assigned to a summer-long road-paving project—in Denali National Park. Simpson remembers her months in Denali as "probably the best summer of my life as a kid." Living in a tiny trailer at park headquarters, she joined other kids in all manner of outdoor adventures. She regularly played in the boreal forest, visited Denali's sled dog kennels, explored entrance-area trails, walked through tundra, and ran from moose. "A friend and I even had a little cabin alongside Rock Creek (near headquarters)," she says. "In many ways, that summer shaped the person I became."

Thirty years later, now living in Fairbanks, Simpson was invited to spend some time in the field with wildlife biologist Vic Van Ballenberghe, who has studied Denali National Park's moose since 1980. The experience was a revelation. "I fell in love with moose," she says. "They suddenly transformed from slightly goofy animals into a fascinating species." Simpson gives much of the credit for her new perspective to Van Ballenberghe, whom she describes as "not only a rigorous field biologist but a thoughtful person, who wasn't afraid to say that moose were more than just subjects to him."

Simpson began her writing career as a newspaper reporter in Juneau and Fairbanks, with a special interest in science, then joined a master's program in creative nonfiction. She now teaches journalism at the University of Alaska Fairbanks and writes in a way that combines "a reporter's love of facts with an essayist's respect for ideas and language." Science, scientists, and animals remain a special passion, as does Denali, which she continues to explore. In one recent summer, Simpson and friends attempted to retrace the route taken by James Wickersham's party in 1903. "I am interested in all the ways we see that place, whether we're tourists, dreamers, explorers—or all three," she says. "On clear winter days I can see the mountain from the ridge where I live. It is more than a mountain. It's an idea, a mirage, a beacon. I can't wait to go back."

Simpson's essay, "Strange Grace," is based on her experiences with Vic Van Ballenberghe and Denali's moose. An abridged version is taken from *The Way Winter Comes,* a collection of essays published in 1998 by Sasquatch Books.

In Alaska there are rules about what to do if a wild animal charges you. The hard part is not just following the rules, but keeping them straight when it really matters. Wildlife biologist Vic Van Ballenberghe is not the kind of man to lecture a person, but before we entered the woods he reminded me about the moose rules. He wanted me to know what to do if we provoked No. 44, the moose we'd come to see.

"Now if she charges, which is unlikely, run," he said. He pushed his baseball cap back to rub his head and looked at me seriously, sizing me up to see if I was the sort of person who could follow simple directions. "Run if it's a moose, stand if it's a bear," he said. At the moment, it seemed more likely that we would be struck by a speeding car or bus as we stood beside the highway just north of the entrance to Denali National Park and Preserve. People arrive here by the hundreds of thousands each year hoping for a wildlife encounter that doesn't involve bloodshed. Vic enjoys picturing the dilemma of Denali tourists desperately trying to remember which animal requires what reaction.

I do know the difference. I find the prospect of standing firm before a charging bear almost impossible to imagine, but I've always run away from moose with no hesitation at all. The summer I was eight, my family lived in Denali Park, and I bolted from every moose I ever confronted on the trails. It's a simple strategy, really, and doesn't require the kind of mind games and cool-headed calculation that a bear encounter demands. No problem, I told Vic. I'll run.

From the back of his van, Vic pulled out his telemetry gear, a radio receiver smaller than a lunchbox and a gridlike antenna that looked as if it might improve your television reception. He fiddled with the knobs, setting the receiver to pick up the frequency of No. 44's radio collar. She and her newborn calf were hidden somewhere between the road and the Nenana River. We could just barely hear the river thrashing against a bluff in the distance. It was the third week of May, and the leaves were early but the calves were on time. The whine of passing cars and trucks drowned out the receiver's steady chirp. "This is not the most aesthetic spot with the traffic whizzing by," Vic said apologetically.

We skidded down the rocky embankment and into the crowded forest of young aspen and spruce trees. He swung the antenna in wide, flat arcs, and then set out at a steady pace, carrying it like an electronic dowsing rod. He held the receiver close to his ear to judge the moose's direction by listening to the relative volume of the chirps. The sound of big trucks blatting across the bridge receded as we pushed through grasping branches into the darkening forest.

Knowing that I was interested in wildlife, Vic had invited me to tag along during his fieldwork. I think he wanted me to appreciate moose the way he appreciates them. When I mentioned a description I'd read likening a trotting moose to a small boy riding a bicycle, Vic frowned, because this unflattering portrayal implies that moose are awkward creatures, and that's not how he sees them at all. He thinks they are clever and resourceful and really quite gorgeous in the way they fit within the boreal landscape. Maybe all wildlife biologists become enamored of their subjects, but I liked Vic for seeing moose as admirable and lovely, and for wanting me to see it, too.

The more wildlife biologists I meet, the more I believe they tend to resemble their chosen subjects, and it's true that Vic is a tall and rangy fellow, with a longish, melancholy face. When he wears his wire-rimmed spectacles, he resembles the farmer he might have been had he lingered in rural New York on the family farm, instead of taking up wildlife biology and heading to Minnesota and beyond to study moose and wolves. Like a moose, Vic presents a deceptively calm disposition, but he can be riled, as he has been when drawn into the perpetual wolf control controversies that plague Alaska wildlife politics. It is not popular in Alaska to suggest, as Vic does, that exterminating wolves does not guarantee a moose or caribou in every hunter's freezer. Spend twenty years studying prey and predators, and you'll conclude that life and death in the wild form a Möbius strip. It's impossible to trace one side without inexplicably finding yourself on the other.

Vic is the kind of wildlife biologist with blueberry stains on the seat of his jeans. He's spent a lot of time hiking over subalpine tundra, picking his way through trees, sitting on knolls watching moose. Since 1980, he's collared about seventy-five moose in Denali National Park. In a field where three years is a long-term study, his work is a Boston Marathon of research. Each spring he finds his collared cows (nineteen this year) and counts their calves. Then he keeps counting as most of them disappear into the empty bellies of bears. Only ten or fifteen percent of Denali calves survive their first year. Each fall, Vic returns for another six weeks to observe the rutting season. He is a disciple of the old school of wildlife science, which prefers to learn about an animal by following it around, watching what it does, and trying to figure out why. It's true he dabbles in the blasphemy of radio collars to find particular moose, but without this kind of modern sorcery he would not be able to explain in excruciating detail, for example, the way Moose No. 47 evaded bears for three years and successfully raised a set of twins and two single calves by making a fourteen-mile circuit between the park hotel and the Savage River every two weeks. Partisans of the new school of wildlife science rely on computers to model ecosystems and to program population dynamics. But the new school doesn't know much about the ordinary lives of moose. The new school doesn't know, for example, that moose will fall to their knees and gobble up every mushroom in the forest, they love them so much.

Deep in the young forest, we heard a rushing sound that was either wind through the new leaves or the river we were approaching. After a long Fairbanks winter, I felt my pores absorbing the luscious color of green. I tried to imagine how moose feel about the unfurling vegetation after months of eating twigs and bark. It must be something like relief, and gladness.

After a few minutes of walking, Vic stopped and lowered the antenna. He bent his knees and pointed into a thick copse at the flicker of a pair of large ears pointed toward us. I never would have seen her. In the shaky days of their calf's new life, cows hide in forests like this. They lie still and quiet at the approach of predators, even dropping their heads to the ground, hoping enemies will pass by.

"Look right through there where the aspen is peeled. A lot of times at a place like this they eat the aspen bark," Vic said in an ordinary tone, pointing out the skinned trunks. His voice startled me. I expected the cow to jump up and charge us or to take off, but her ears merely radared toward us as we circled her, crackling through branches and last fall's leaves. There's no point in stealthiness, Vic said. A moose either tolerates you or it doesn't, and stage whispers and sneaky moves won't much matter.

When we stopped, the mother unfolded like a creature fashioned from origami. She rose first on her front legs, and then hoisted herself up. Her looming bulk appeared, then her dark underbelly, and then, finally, we saw the impossibly tiny calf that barely reached halfway up her legs. Afternoon light sifted through the trees, illuminating the calf's chestnut hide. For long minutes, we all looked at each other. The cow didn't seem alarmed or annoyed, just appraising. Some biologists say they'd rather face an irritated bear than a moose with a calf, but I came to see that Vic's quiet confidence soothes moose. When he comes upon them, he stands still, hands in pocket, and just looks. He moves easily in their presence. Seeing how he was, I made myself still, trying not to jerk my hands around or bob my head and advertise my excitement and nervousness.

Slowly, elegantly, the female stepped away from us, followed by the smudge of color and uncertain motion that was her calf. They dissolved among the trees, returning to their hidden lives. I stopped holding my breath.

Back at the road, back in ordinary time, the current of cars rolled on along the Parks Highway, carrying people unaware of all that lay just beyond their view. Even in Alaska, where wilderness is not so far from any door, animal encounters are usually as unexpected and ephemeral as a lightning flash. Those moments are so brief, we forget that every moment, wild animals are all around us, living complicated, unknown lives.

Until I saw No. 44 and her calf concealed in the forest, I thought I knew almost everything worth knowing about moose. In Interior Alaska, there's not much mysterious or engaging about a creature that always seems to be loitering by the road, poaching from summer gardens, or parceled into neat white packages labeled "ribs," "rump roast," and "burger." A moose is a traffic hazard, a big brown ottoman of an animal, a piece of mobile scenery that looks quite nice posed on a postcard. More than any other animal save the raven, moose breach that invisible membrane between settled Alaska and wilderness, wandering back and forth as they please.

But still, I could not explain exactly what moose eat and why, could not picture them sleeping, mating, birthing, dying, could not say a single true thing about moose despite having seen them a hundred times or more. I had never really looked, and so I knew nothing about the strange grace of moose.

People are often tempted into investing animals with personalities, but individual moose behave so differently that it's wrong to think of them as mere biological automatons. Once Vic and I spotted a big moose across a bog, and the bull took one look at us, wheeled around, and galloped away. But others allowed us to approach within forty or fifty feet. To Vic, some are "spooky," or afraid of humans. Some have such mild dispositions that they are "supertame," meaning that they don't worry much about people. Some are smarter than others. Some seem just plain nice. "To me they have personalities," he said, thinking it over. "I'm not sure that's a good term, but I think they do." Then he added, "I think the number of facets in their personality is probably limited." This is true of some people as well, I mentioned. He said I had a point.

Though moose are not especially social animals, they do sometimes form strong attachments to each other. No. 49 Jr. is so named because she remained with her mother, No. 49, for more than two years, a remarkably long time considering that most cows drive away yearlings in the spring. "They were tight," Vic said. "I saw the mother groom her and lick her. They would bed down together."

Once, as he watched a yearling and a mature bull loitering near a crowd of cows, one of the cows started vocalizing. The yearling dashed over and started nursing. "He got down on his knees. I just could not believe it. He had antlers and had to be careful not to poke her," Vic said. "Surely she had a new calf and lost it." To my question about whether cows can count calves, Vic said he's seen them run from a bear or wolf, try to collect the calves, and, realizing one was missing, turn back to find it.

If moose have personalities, then the moose with personality-plus is the World's Tamest Moose. That's what Vic calls her, anyway, although her official name is 83/2. We looked for her one afternoon in the park, hiking through the roomy forest and across bogs, squishing last year's cranberries beneath our feet.

I almost collided with Vic when he suddenly stopped in an aspen grove, swung his antenna around, and then remarked, "There she is." The moose craned her head around and regarded us mildly over her shoulder. Vic always saw moose before I did, even those that stood nearby looking at us. Something about their irregular shape helps them fade into the landscape. Vic closed his receiver and propped the antenna against a tree, then stood for a moment regarding the moose. She reached out with fleshy lips and stripped leaves from a branch. She chewed. She shook herself ponderously, and long hairs flew off in a cloud. She snorted. I had never seen a moose this close that wasn't running from me or at me. Vic thinks she recognizes him from his smell and from the sound of the beeping receiver. "When she hears the radio, she realizes, 'It's the pest,' " he said.

She shifted toward us, and Vic motioned me back a bit. Then she eased herself down into the moss. "You know they trust you if they do that," Vic said. She raised twins one year that were not afraid of him, either, and one of them ventured so close that he almost reached out to stroke it. Another time a bull fell asleep right in front of him. A red squirrel jumped on the dozing moose, mistaking it for a big brown log. Eventually the squirrel realized its mistake and scrammed. The moose never stirred.

The World's Tamest Moose chewed her cud so loudly we could hear her over the rustling trees. I looked at the whorls of fur, the bristly mane, the gently flared ears. I was sure I knew what a moose looked like until she stood before me. A moose is not brown. A moose is the shade of walnuts, October grass, sable, deep earth. A moose's underbelly is dark, the rear haunches creamy.

193

Like brown bears, who are also not brown, some moose are blond, some nearly black.

People say moose are homely and awkward and somewhat absurd, the product of some misalliance between cow and camel that contrived that hump, that hero sandwich of a nose, that vaguely ridiculous bell dangling from the throat. In likening the parts of a moose to those of other animals, we miss the functional beauty of the whole, the biological rejoinders to an environment that produces every kind of hardship: short summers, terrible winters, not enough food, and a couple of the world's most earnest predators. Bears snooze away winters tucked in cozy dens; wolves enjoy the companionship of their own kind. But moose, they tough it out, eating bark and twigs, wading through snowdrifts, burning up their own flesh through the long dark nights. "Moose are so perfectly adapted to the environment, and people are so poorly adapted to it. Moose don't have anything. They just get by on senses and smarts," Vic said.

People don't really know moose, and some would argue that we can't possibly understand a moose (or any other animal) since we're always seeing through the caul of human perception. But because Vic spends so much time with them, he understands things. He knows plenty of biological minutiae, such as how much the average female moose eats on a summer day (twenty-seven pounds of leaves). He's measured moose droppings and tested fat and counted bites of leaves. He ponders moose mysteries such as the odd light-colored rump patch, the timing of the rut, and the higher purpose of antler development.

More than that, he knows individual moose. "Their stories are all pretty interesting: the successes and failures during their lives, close escapes from predators," he said. To explain something about the narrative curve of a moose's life, he showed me the lower jaw of No. 52, one of the first group of eleven moose he collared in 1980. As he talked, I ran my fingers over the eroded ridges of her teeth, fitted the camber of the bone's curve against my palm. When she died in the winter of 1994, she was about twenty-one, at the distant end of a moose's life. In all the years Vic followed her, out of all the young she birthed, she raised only one calf.

These are things you learn by following moose around and paying attention, something hardly anyone ever does. One day a woman idled her car up to Vic's van to find out what we were looking at. "What do you see, a moose?" she asked, and then, spotting the cow off in the brush, said, "Oh, yes. Thank you." She started to pull out onto the road. "She's got two babies," Vic offered. "Oooh," the woman said, looking bored, as she rolled up her window and left.

This indifference is understandable, in a way. Wildlife documentaries show animals doing something, not just being. The close-ups are irresistible, the narrator's somber tone helpful. People aren't particularly interested in natural history; they want natural drama.

"It's not in our culture to have more than a superficial look at wildlife," Vic said. "People's comments about moose are 'Wow! It's as big as a horse.' Or, 'Isn't it ugly?' Or something very, very shallow. They come, they look, they snap a picture, and they take off."

Eventually, by spending time with Vic, I learned better how to watch moose, not by knowing what a moose looks like, but by knowing what part of a moose looks like. A ruddy island turns out to be a cow's back. Two trembling points resolve into ears. A bristly motion is not wind through the trees but a bull on the move. After a while, I learned to see moose all around us.

Seeing a moose and understanding a moose's world are not the same thing, though. In the half-light of midnight in May, I watched a moose and her calf just off the Parks Highway. In the past few days, this particular cow had birthed the calf, repeatedly chased off her bewildered yearling, and lingered by this picture-perfect pond. Photographers and gawkers lined the road in the day-time, making these the most photographed moose in North America, Vic joked.

In the still air, the water reflected the reclining cow, the calf curled by her side. After a bit, the calf yawned, Disney-adorable, and then licked and nuzzled at its mother's flanks. Then it began chewing on leaves within its reach. Now that I knew something about a moose's life, I knew its probable fate. I like bears and wolves, and I would not begrudge them the hot, bloody satisfaction of feeding themselves and their own young. But at that moment I wished I could lay a curse on all bears, obliging them to eat only roots and berries, and perhaps the occasional ground squirrel. Ditto for wolves.

For maybe half an hour, I watched before I began silently urging the calf to rise so I could see it better. I couldn't help it. "Move! Cavort! Frolic!" I whispered impatiently. It's so hard to witness nature on its own terms.

Writer Barry Lopez advances the notion that at the moment of encounter, wolves and their prey engage in a "conversation of death," in which the preda-tor "asks" for the moose or caribou's life, and the prey submits. Vic Van Ballenberghe says this is bullshit. There may be a moment of calculation, judg-ment, decision, yes, but there is no mutual agreement, no surrender. There is only hunger, fear, struggle, pain. Vic studies death because he wants to under-stand how moose detect and evade predators: "I'm sure around predators they make decisions all the time: Should I run? Should I fight? When should I run? What are the predator's intentions?"

One day, we watched a bull moose wander toward a cow on a distant slope. Something happened, something we couldn't see. The bull moose began running, blasting through the brush at an alarming speed. The cow started running, too, and she ran so fast that she caught up to the bull and passed him. On parallel courses, they charged toward the road, and then they veered into the trees. They were afraid of something, something we couldn't see, and that made me nervous, because I could suddenly feel the landscape as a place that concealed predators but could not mask the constant intent of death.

That sensation intensified when we went looking for one of Vic's collared moose. Photographers and bus drivers had seen an injured calf staggering along the road near Savage River the previous night. Vic wondered if the calf was one of the twins belonging to No. 49 Jr.; the family had narrowly escaped a bear a few days before by fleeing down the middle of the road for a couple of miles before venturing back into the brush. But the gully they entered was the same place a bear had killed calves last year. "It's hard to avoid them. It really is," Vic said. One summer, a single bear harvested calves like it was gathering berries, killing three sets of twins within twenty-four hours. Often a moose can successfully hold off wolves from stealing a calf; but bears, with their power and implacable hunger, are more difficult to escape.

To see whether No. 49 Jr. had escaped her pursuer, we hiked up a rocky draw, crossed a clear stream by hopping from stone to stone, then pushed through willow thickets. Vic spotted the tips of 49 Jr.'s ears long before I did. He circled closer to her, leaving me to be plagued by a few dozen mosquitoes and thoughts of how death sounds so ennobling when it applies to wild animals and so distasteful when it applies to me. The willows stood higher than my head, and the breeze riffled them just enough to confuse sounds and disguise the motion of anything big. I felt a preternatural awareness of where my flesh ended and wilderness began. Suddenly it seemed obvious how a heightened and constant sense of alertness might be useful to a moose. I was relieved when Vic parted the brush and joined me. Both calves were still alive, he said. The fate of the injured calf was no mystery at all, really; certainly it was out there somewhere, dead or dying even then.

Over the years Vic has hunted and killed perhaps fourteen or fifteen moose, but once he started studying Denali moose it just didn't seem right anymore. That doesn't prevent him from reminiscing about especially delicious moose steaks from dinners past, even while standing in the presence of living moose he admires. I asked him if he secretly roots for the moose when they're confronted by bears and wolves.

"You've got to maintain that scientific objectivity," he said, with a small, wry smile. Moose calves are important food for bears and they're a valuable part of the energy cycle, he said in his best scientist's voice. Then he added, "You hate to see them die. You really do. Many biologists would deny they have emotional ties to their animals. I don't deny it. You get attached to animals. That moose we were looking at this morning, the World's Tamest Moose? I'd like to run up and kiss her on the mouth. I really like her. She has allowed me to see a lot of neat things over the years, and I really like her."

There are many ways for moose to die: deflated by a hunter's bullet, clawed down by a bear, hamstrung by wolves, smashed by a car. In Southeast Alaska, someone once saw a pod of orcas kill a moose swimming across a strait. Bull moose die slowly from rutting injuries. Cow moose die in birthing. Hard winters waste them away. And for all her evasive tactics, later in the summer No. 49 Jr. lost one of her calves.

I've seen moose carcasses before, but most were carved up for meat or lying by the roads where cars struck them. None of them had histories, and certainly none had names, unlike the remains of the bull moose lying hidden in the woods near the park entrance. "Poor old Chip the Moose," Vic said, squatting by the bones and hide. "Chip" (so christened by one of Vic's more sentimental graduate students) had died the previous November of some unknown cause—perhaps from rutting injuries, perhaps from some deep weakness that made him vulnerable to winter. Shucked of flesh and hide, the bones were cast like runes upon the moss. The spine was as thick as my forearm, knee joints bulkier than two fists together. Vic kicked at a horny hoof and said, "Think how many miles his feet walked during his lifetime." Foxes, ravens, and magpies had gnawed the ribs ragged. Chalky coyote scat littered the ground, and scrape marks beneath a spruce tree showed where a bear had clawed earth over some chunk of meat this spring. Tiny blue iridescent beetles crawled through the spine's Gothic architecture. "When they die, there's a whole fleet of things that eat them up," Vic said. Most everything out there wants a piece of moose, including the person who took the antlers and skull that Vic had dragged into the woods earlier in the spring.

The technical term for animals like moose is "keystone species," which means that without moose to feed the North, the world would not get along nearly so well. Moose don't simply wander across the land like a grocery store on legs, though; they change it. Vic's research extends beyond the living creature itself, and so he knows how the very landscape responds to moose. Moderate browsing stimulates plant growth, creating better habitats that, in turn, encourage

197

foraging. Urine and droppings enrich the soil, feeding the fungi that speed up decomposition and improve the turnover of nutrients. Willow leaves from browsed plants decompose more quickly than leaves from uneaten plants, causing nutrients to cycle more quickly. When moose strip aspen bark too heavily, a common practice when better forage isn't available, the trees that die are replaced by spruce trees, shifting the forest's character. Even a decaying moose changes the very earth beneath it. The ripened soil favors different plants, and slowly a new pattern of vegetation appears wherever a moose dies.

Moose influence the way carnivores behave, too. In the winter, bulls head for deep, shadowed river valleys; the willow thickets provide food and the lack of direct sun protects the soft snowdrifts that hinder wolves. Cows follow their own strategies against predators. In spring, they spread out to bear their young in aspen-spruce forests, and there they remain for weeks, shrouded in solitude, because the only thing that can save a moose calf is time, time enough to grow into its legs so that it can run like hell when a bear or wolf catches its scent. Some moose then stick around one place, while others roam a circuit. In Denali, some like to hang out with their calves near the park hotel and headquarters, as if the presence of people might deter predators, while others literally head for the hills. But bears and wolves know a few tricks, too. They return to old killing grounds, remembering what worked for them and what didn't, trying out new tactics that moose then react to. Vic's work shows that in the past few decades at Denali, it is bears that have become the major predator of moose calves—not wolves, as everyone thought—and this is a shift from the way things used to be here. Prey and predator are always tracing that Möbius strip of life and death.

And moose bind people to their own traditions. When the hills ignite into maroon and gold during August and early September, hunters from villages and towns travel up rivers and across flats and into the woods, searching for moose. How differently we behave in the woods and in our own provinces because of moose. Moose make us watchful, nervous, grateful. All winter, people eat their kills, sharing good fortune, hard work, the taste of something feral and strong. When I eat a moose steak or a fragrant stew, I'm also eating willow leaves, aspen bark, mushrooms. I'm eating the earth.

Here is a story about Moose, then. Raven created the world. Bear claims the world. Wolf circles the world. But Moose shapes the world.

More than once, Vic mentioned a fall day when he watched twenty-two cows and twelve bulls gather for the rut. The animals roamed around him, coming and going, engaged in their mysterious interchanges as he watched and watched. Vic still thinks about that occasion, because he wonders whether humans can ever shed their own perceptions and see the world as animals do. On that day, he came closest. "Sometimes it's almost possible to slip into something else, you know," he said.

Naming that "something else" is difficult, but one of Vic's favorite writers, scientist Loren Eiseley, recognized the sensation, too. He described it as seeing the world from an "inverted angle," from outside normal perspective, and he believed that occasionally animals sense this strangeness, too. "The time has to be right; one has to be, by chance or intention, upon the border of two worlds," Eiseley wrote. "And sometimes these two borders may shift or interpenetrate and one sees the miraculous."

At the end of summer, Vic took a friend and me to see Moose No. 44 and her calf. It was after Labor Day and the park had closed. A cloudy sky muted fall's slow burn. We parked at an empty campground and walked for fifteen minutes, slipping through aspen and spruce trees. We scuffed through piles of moose droppings, walked through suburbs of mushrooms, and crunched across a sheath of fallen leaves that seemed to light the forest with a saffron glow. The astringent smell of crushed Labrador tea surrounded us.

We came upon the pair bedded down in the secret heart of a forest, just as we had seen them in the spring near the Nenana River. They heard us coming and stood, unfolding like creatures made of origami. Vic pointed out the antler nubbins on the calf, who now weighed about 300 pounds. After a few thoughtful moments, the cow looked away, and the calf kneeled and began yanking at her udder so hard his ears flapped. The mother yawned. When the young moose finished nursing, he turned and gazed boldly at us. Vic said yes, he probably was curious.

No. 44 lay down to chew her cud, and the calf nibbled at shrubs, occasionally glancing over as if just remembering we were there. Sometimes he kneeled to reach some delicacy. He drew closer. Golden leaves rained down on all of us. I could hear the whispery rasp as they landed against each other.

If such a thing as animal fear exists, this primal calm must be its converse. A strange comfort emerges from learning the fate of individual animals, knowing that sometimes evasion and luck and proper decisions work for a moose like No. 44. But I knew this was a momentary peace. Soon snow would fall. Darkness would fill the basins and valleys and seep across the plains of Interior Alaska. The hungriest season approached.

I sat on the forest floor and looked at the moose, trying to absorb not only the shades of their fur, the shape of their bodies, the way they looked at us, but the motion, the comportment, the character of moose. Later I wondered if this was the feeling Vic and Eiseley meant, a dreamier layer of awareness and recognition possible only at the border of two worlds. At that moment, though, I surrendered all thought. I believed I could lie back and sink into the tangle of moss and rotting leaves and black crowberries, and the moose would simply step around me in their deliberate way, as if I were no more troublesome than a tree.

After a while we left them. It was growing cool and dim there in the forest, and it seemed as if winter waited among the shadows. "Don't you ever just want to stay?" I asked Vic, but I knew his answer already. I turned after a few steps to look again. The moose were gone, as if they had been slabs of loamy dark earth animated for a time by blood and bone and muscle, and now they were reclaimed by a landscape that yields nothing easily.

18

Denali Journal

by Tom Walker

Best known for his photographs of Alaska's wildlife, Tom Walker is also an accomplished natural history writer and the author of several books, including *Denali Journal: A Thoughtful Look at Wildlife in Alaska's Majestic National Park*. Now in his mid-fifties, Walker's interest in the Denali region was initially sparked in his teens by the writings of Charles Sheldon and Adolph Murie and later fueled by the stories and photos of a friend who worked in then Mount McKinley National Park in the early 1960s. "Even now," Walker writes, "I recall his picture of a person sitting within feet of a magnificent Dall ram. To a budding wildlife photographer, the image was gasoline on the fire."

Walker traveled to McKinley Park in 1969. "Despite rain and snow, lack of time, money, and proper equipment, despite a suffering companion and a dilapidated, untrustworthy vehicle," he discovered a place and experience that for once exceeded his wildest imaginings. On his initial forays, he camped along the Denali Park Road; but it wasn't long before he began taking extended trips into remote wilderness. Deeply moved by the landscape, its wildlife, and what Murie would call its "wilderness spirit," Walker built a cabin near the park's southeastern boundary. More recently, he's made his home in the Alaska Range, not far from Denali National Park's entrance area.

Over the past three decades, Walker has explored the Denali region by car, shuttle bus, airplane, ski, and snowshoe; but his favorite and most satisfying way remains by foot, while carrying a pack. Along the way, he's come to know Denali's wilderness and wildlife as few others of his contemporaries have—and he has kept detailed notes of his journeys, adventures, wildlife encounters, and natural history observations. Those writings are the basis for *Denali Journal*. Published in 1992 by Stackpole Books, the book focuses on wildlife, weather, and habitats along the ninety-mile-long park road. Besides his own notes, Walker uses government reports, interviews, and historical information to "flesh out" his own observations. Organized by season, the book mixes journal entries from the early 1970s through 1990.

Over the years, much has been written about Denali's wildlife and land-scape during the summer season. So, while Walker emphasizes the months of May through September in *Denali Journal*, I have included here abridged chapters that tell of the "off season," beginning with his section on "Autumn," and following with "Into Winter," and "Out of Darkness."

■

FROM "AUTUMN"
September 2, 1981.

What a wonderful year for cranberries and blueberries! This afternoon, while waiting for two bull caribou to finish their rest, I sat amid scarlet bearberry plants and munched both the blueberries and tart crowberries within arm's reach. There were enough left over to fill a plastic bag for tomorrow's breakfast.

Although the caribou did little more than ruminate, I enjoyed watching them. Like moose and sheep, caribou graze or browse for an hour or so, then lie down to chew their cuds. Their ruminations are often punctuated by naps—but they allow their alertness to flag only for short periods. These two caribou, for instance, took turns dozing. While one stayed awake, the other would lay its head on the ground and sleep for five or ten minutes, then jolt awake with a quick look about. They seemed incapable of what humans call relaxation. Justifiably so. If an animal were to sprawl on the tundra and fall fast asleep for an hour or two, it might waken to the bite of a mortal enemy.

Despite threatening morning skies and a blustery wind, I spent the entire day on the slope with the caribou, hiking back to the road in bright, late-afternoon sun. When I got off the bus at Igloo Campground at eight-forty-five, an amber light was sneaking onto the peaks and shoulders of Cathedral Mountain, while the wind shook the last daylight from the treetops. By nine-fifteen I was the only one still cooking dinner in the quiet campground. A few people sat by warming fires; one stood watching the alpenglow. While eating, I heard the murmur of voices from within small tents. A pleasant serenity settled on the dusky scene. Life without TV.

September 8, 1974.

Everyone looks for bears, moose, or caribou. The more common animals don't get much notice. For example, the ubiquitous marsh hawk, now called the northern harrier, seldom attracts attention. Gray jays flit from tree to tree. Arctic ground squirrels, called parka squirrels by Alaskans, sit beside the road or on open slopes. Red squirrels chirr from forest limbs, and at this time of year spruce grouse often sit along the road edge. Coveys of ptarmigan are also common. Sharp-eyed folks can often see soaring golden eagles. The few times a bus does stop for a look at a ptarmigan or a squirrel, there's always the voice in the back of the bus: "What is it? What do you see? Is it a bear? No? Let's go."

On the return bus trip, someone comments that animals are cruel. A fox had killed a squirrel right by the bus; we watched as the fox tore the squirrel apart and ate it. Someone else said that animals have harsh existences and die terrible deaths. I suspect that these interesting opinions are commonly held and that behind them is a belief that humans are neither cruel nor susceptible to terrible deaths. But I wonder which is worse, to be a squirrel torn limb from limb by a fox and die within two or three minutes, or to be a human fighting cancer for months or even years, undergoing all sorts of horrific treatments before succumbing? Ironically, as more people come to appreciate nature, they are often horrified by its reality. It's hard for me to think of natural predation or natural animal mortality as *cruel* because the term implies *intent*. I've never seen animals inflict pain for pleasure. On the other hand, torturous human deaths and deprivations have stemmed from prejudice, religion, and politics. I'm sure Holocaust survivors could tell us much about cruelty, but could a ground squirrel?

September 10, 1978.

Clear and windy at Igloo. Thirty-four degrees. A few short miles away at Teklanika this morning it was eighteen degrees with a heavy frost. If June 15 is roughly the average date for the last spring freeze, then the growing season here is only a little more than seventy to eighty days.

Autumnal colors have peaked and faded in the park's higher elevations. This year the peak was about September 3. Some years it's as late as the second week of September or as early as the fourth week of August. How long the colors persist depends partly on precipitation, wind, and frost. Wind and heavy rain or snow pull the leaves from the plants. Sometimes the tundra and taiga seem ablaze one day, drab the next. Other years, the colors linger and fade as the leaves drop one by one.

September 13, 1979.

This afternoon, right behind the Wonder Lake ranger station, I watched a grizzly swim to the beaver lodge in the middle of the pond. After shaking itself, the bear sniffed at the lodge, then tore into it, flinging sticks left and right as if digging out a squirrel. It dug and pulled at the sticks and mud until it had torn an opening big enough to gain access to the beaver's sleeping chamber. Although I haven't seen a beaver in this pond for a while, no doubt the lingering aroma of castor excited the bear.

Its rump wiggling at the sky, the grizzly delved into the mysteries of the lodge's interior for quite some time. Then it backed out of the hole and stood blinking in the bright sun. A twenty- to fifty-pound beaver would make a good meal, but there were none to be taken from this lodge. After a few more desultory explorations, the bear belly-flopped into the pond and swam west toward the road. A passing road grader spooked the bear as it emerged from the water. It bolted across the road, over the tundra, and disappeared into the timber along the lakeshore.

In early evening near Wonder Lake's outlet, I watched the same bear as it fed on blueberries. Since the bear had been soaking wet earlier, its color indeterminate, I based my judgement on size and general appearance. It was a prime, mature animal with jet black legs, a golden head, and a fully furred body that all but glowed in the afternoon backlight. A bear of this color is often referred to here as a Toklat grizzly, as if it were a distinct species. Neither Adolph Murie nor Charles Sheldon ever wrote about Toklat grizzlies, although each made note of the great color variation of Denali bears. But Dr. C. Hart Merriam, a taxonomist, concluded from one of the specimens provided by Sheldon that indeed the region's bears were a distinct species. Merriam labeled them *Ursus toklat*. Early taxonomists tended to identify dozens of bear species and subspecies based on minor variations in skull and bone measurements, hair color, and body size. Modern taxonomists tend to lump animals together, recognizing fewer species and subspecies. Grizzlies do vary in color from black to almost white. This bear's entire hindquarters are stained with crushed blueberries. Using the fruit bush's botanical name, would the early scientists have classified it as *Ursus vaccinius*?

September 20, 1990.

This morning, just inside the park's south entrance, not far from Triple Lakes, eight Canada geese and seven trumpeter swans fed and rested on a small pond, taking a break in their southward migration. These are not the only migrants visible just now. Numerous sharp-shinned hawks, as well as other sky hunters, are common on the ridges above the Nenana [River]. Cranes can still be heard morning and evening. Wings dust the treetops and peaks as the birds move south. Some years, especially when early snow mantles the summits, I, too, wish I could take wing and join the clamorous flights on their journey toward the sun.

September 22, 1990.

[Autumnal equinox]. All this week I've been observing a group of cow moose and two bulls in the timber a few miles west of park Headquarters. Each day, Monday through Wednesday, I could find them in one copse or another in the same little drainage. Yesterday I could find only one moose, the smaller bull, a forked horn.

Today the other bull may be dead. Late in the afternoon, a large gray wolf emerged from the drainage. He was rather slow and lethargic, unconcerned with the two cars that stopped to watch him. His stomach was distended. After a bit he went back into the brush.

An hour later the wind shifted and carried the smell of death to the road. The twilight timber was calm and still. I cupped my hands and howled once. A moment passed. Then from the ridge across the creek, one, two, perhaps three, adults answered. The yapping of pups joined in. Then silence. By the kill, a deep howl lifted through the trees. The pack answered. The song went back and forth before a final silence. Soon shapes ghosted through the timber. An adult, then three pups, stopped to stare toward the road. Then they were gone, and ebony night enfolded the silent forest.

September 30, 1985.

The road is closed again in early morning because of ice, then is reopened by midday. In the afternoon, a grizzly with heavy, silver-tipped coat wanders across the road near Sanctuary. His thick pelage creates the illusion of great size. I watch him meander up the snowy slope and through the brush flanking Mount Wright. He wanders slowly, pausing to dig some berries from beneath the snow and once to tear open a rotten log. Then he rears to his hind legs and scratches his back against a dead spruce. His facial expression is almost human. *Ah! What a relief.*

Soon only the old males will be active; the females and cubs will be in their dens. Within two weeks, even the males will be in hibernation. This sighting makes an exciting end to this year's stay in Denali.

Before the bear moves out of sight, he looks back at me . . . and yawns.

FROM "INTO WINTER"
October 8, 1988.

Plus thirty and snowing big, heavy flakes that quickly melt, soaking the seven moose almost as rain would. Only the snow on the bull's antlers stays frozen. The moose seem not to notice the snowfall as they browse through the laden willows. Apparently the rut has waned; the bull feeds as intently as the cows. It is not uncommon for large bulls, which may weigh fourteen hundred pounds or more prior to the rut, to lose three hundred pounds over the winter.

I wonder how many of these moose will survive the winter. The bull and the calf probably face the severest challenges—the bull because his strength has been sapped by the rut and the calf because it, like all calves, has little stored fat. Much of the calf's energy must go into growth. It cannot, moreover, reach the higher browse available to mature animals and will have to share the taller plants its mother breaks down.

Even in a mild winter, diet is often insufficient to maintain a moose. So, in large measure, survival hangs on stored fat. But once the usable fat reserves are depleted, the body begins burning muscle for energy. Since muscle has less than half the energy of fat, an accelerating downward slide begins. Once the stored energy is used up, the animal will die. As one scientist has put it, "With wintering wildlife, there is no deficit spending."

Winter 1988–89 turned out to be one of the coldest on record. . . . In the park, January averaged twelve degrees colder than usual. The first three months were without precipitation, clear and cold. At park Headquarters, the coldest temperature recorded in January was minus fifty-one, in February, minus thirty-one, and in March, minus thirty-three. . . . other areas within the park, especially at lower elevations, probably experienced colder temperatures. Relatively low snowfall, however, lessened somewhat the impact on wildlife.

October 17, 1981.

Most ponds and small lakes are frozen; a few inches of snow cover the ice. Shelf ice expands along the rivers; slush runs in midchannel. It is foolhardy to attempt to walk on the ice now. Fox, wolf, and coyote tracks cross some ponds, but they are a sucker's lure. Thin ice and open water are hidden by the snow. I resist all temptation to cross the inviting flat surfaces.

A large cache protrudes above the snow in front of a beaver lodge. The ice is likely to be thin there, too, because of the movement of beaver beneath it. Unless it thaws (there's still the chance of a chinook), it is winter for the beaver. Either they are prepared and have stored enough feed in their cache, or they will perish in their ice-locked lodges. In years of light snowfall and continuous cold, even a well-prepared colony may know shortage or starvation if thick pond ice seals off their cache or the pond freezes to the bottom. Twice I have seen starving beaver that have gnawed their way out of the lodge because of food scarcity. They were killed by predators.

November 21, 1977.

Plus ten and clearing when I awoke. Although it is one month until winter solstice, the shortest day of the year, there is little light before 10 A.M. After several cups of tea and a leisurely breakfast (if you can call shivering in a cold tent "leisure"), I hiked toward the distant ridge and the rutting sheep.

Where two days ago I'd encountered the small herd, today I counted sixty-five sheep. Ten were rams, perhaps another ten were four- or five-year-olds. Even at a distance, I could see the heavy-horned rams protecting individual ewes and the turmoil as rams chased ewes, rams chased rams, and lambs did their best to stay out of the way. Although I know conception must take place now so the lambs will be born at the optimum time, the timing of the rut still seems odd to me. The sheep have been coping with winter for more than a month. Perhaps some of them are already weakened by cold and poor diet. Now through mid-December they must face the dual test of the onslaught of the worst weather and the rigors of the rut.

Long plumes of wind-driven snow boiled from the peaks to the south. Above me, a ground blizzard began to swirl around the sheep. Once close to the sheep, I huddled in the lee of some rocks for protection while I donned all my clothing. I'd hoped to be able to use color film to record some of the rutting behavior, but that didn't look possible. Not only was I hampered by limited daylight, but the sheep had moved onto a north-facing slope where the sun would not shine. The cold combined with the wind—always the wind—was a real limitation; I had to handle all my gear and film while wearing gloves.

I managed a few rolls of black-and-white film but didn't shoot anything extraordinary—young rams courting disinterested ewes, older rams guarding estrus ewes. Then above the band I saw two mature, evenly matched rams approaching each other in threat display.

One ram turned and moved some yards away, where it stopped to paw at the snow and nibble some grass. His rival, head held high in classic pose, stood motionless where the two had met. The ram scratched at the snow, then pivoted. Both reared to their hind legs and bipedally charged. Still some yards apart, they dropped to all fours. Following a brief pause, both lowered their heads and pawed the snow. Once again they charged, the final hop turning into a powerful lunge that ended in a head-cracking butt. For some minutes, they stood eye-to-eye, studying each other. Then both turned and separated. They pawed at the snow and seemed to feed. Then they whirled again and collided in a butt as loud as two boulders clacking together. In the aftermath, the larger ram lashed his opponent with several hard foreleg kicks. When the pummeled ram tried to turn away, a head butt to his shoulder initiated a chase across the slope.

Soon most of the herd, as well as the two rams, had moved onto a slope too precipitous for me to follow. I watched the chase until it ended. The dominant ram became interested in a ewe at one edge of the scattered herd just as the light began to fail and the wind picked up. Despite my heavy clothing, I could not stop shivering. I headed down, happy to have witnessed the classic battle for dominance: two mature animals fighting for the right to breed, ensuring that only the strongest ram would pass his heritage on to future generations.

December 21, 1990.

Winter solstice. As the sun slides along just below the southern horizon, only briefly peeking above the lower summits and through mountain passes, its tantalizing glow rekindles the quiet agony of longing for solar warmth and sparkling light.

In these mountains at 63 degrees north latitude, "sunrise" occurs at nine-twenty-eight A.M. and "sunset" at two-nineteen P.M., providing a total of less than five hours of dim light. Today we lose one minute of daylight, tomorrow none, and the next day we will gain one minute. Although it's imperceptible, the Northern Hemisphere will begin to receive more sun. By March we will be gaining six minutes of daylight during each twenty-four hour period. I toast the incredible earth.

I am already planning summer trips: hikes into mountain basins, treks along coastal streams. Sojourns to watch migrating birds, mountain sheep, and lumbering bears. I wonder what the spring and summer will hold. Will the weather be kind, a mixture of sun and rain, or will we have clouds and rain. (A depressing thought on this particular day.) And I wonder what the year will mean to the park, its wildlife, and people.

The wildlife experience in Denali today has changed little in twenty years. I cannot see into the future, but I hope the same will be true twenty years from now. Rams will climb the crags, bears will grub the Toklat soapberry patch, and caribou bulls will spar on the ridges above Wonder Lake. I toast this day, the winter solstice, as I look forward to increasing light—not only on the surface of the earth but in the minds of men and women.

FROM "OUT OF DARKNESS"

March 19, 1990.

In the darkness, at the hour of false dawn, silhouettes of distant mountain peaks separate from the night as the faint dawn light snuffs out the stars and recaptures the sky. Blue washes the horizon, revealing a landscape of snow-drowned thickets, forest, muskeg, and meandering river surrounded by crenellated summits.

From the cabin window I can look across the Nenana River and into the park. Soon the light will be strong enough for me to see through the spotting scope the herd of caribou wandering the ridge above Triple Lakes, their many trails spreading through the snow like fissures on ice.

What strikes me most about late winter, now that the worst days of cold and darkness are behind us, is the *color*. On a clear morning like this one, night surrenders in pastel hues of claret, ruby, gold, even jade. The peaks and ridges to the west will awaken in a crimson wash of alpenglow, of sherbet colors you can almost taste. Each evening the process is reversed, but the colors are no less intense.

Midday on the tundra, the sun blasts off the ice and snow with an intensity that can blind. Except for the trees and brush that rise above the snow, the land indeed suffocates under a white blanket. Earlier in winter, there seemed little hope of ever seeing the sun again or feeling its warmth; now the strengthening solar heat is almost shocking. Soon the snow will fade and disappear under lengthening daylight. For animals and humans alike, it is none too soon.

April 1, 1974.

Minus twenty-two degrees. The cold snap continues, but the sun is returning. Solar heating has brought the temperature up to zero the last two days, yet it is hard to be patient. I want summer. I want to see jaegers coursing over the tundra, to hear the whistle of wings over the ponds and the cry of loons. It's the absence of birds—their variety, their abundance, their songs and calls—I miss most in winter. (Each species has only one song but several calls to announce arrival, territory, feeding, and breeding, and to summon the flock or young.) How many bird species migrate north every year—150? 160? In early summer the taiga is alive with avian melodies, but winter brings a deafening silence. What have I seen or heard recently? A horned owl. Gray jays. Boreal and black-capped chickadees. Some redpolls, crossbills, grosbeaks, woodpeckers. And the ubiquitous ravens. That's it.

Spring arrives soon—by air express, I hope.

April 6, 1980.

Awoke early this morning to a terrific caterwauling coming from the slope behind the cabin—a sound like that of a child in pain. Once my mind cleared, I recognized it as the wailing of a lynx.

I leaped out of bed, got dressed in everything handy, and went out. The new-moon darkness was complete. A light breeze soughed through the spruce. Motionless, I tracked the lynx by sound as it moved along the ridge parallel to the cabin. Then its yowling, although much amplified, sounded like that of a housecat in heat. Knowing that lynx are sometimes called by hunters, I tried imitating its call. Silence. Then a loud wail startled me. I remained silent as the lynx continued. After a while the sounds died away and I slipped back inside, uncertain whether I was shivering from the cold or from the preternatural night cry.

April 24, 1975.

Plus twenty-eight and snowing. Winter again. It's difficult to accept this wind-driven snow blasting through the trees, these whiteouts on the tundra. No wonder the worst cabin fever comes this time of year. A taste of spring and summer, days of sunshine and solar heating, then a midwinter storm. Terribly confining in the cabin. I spend the morning splitting wood and shoveling snow that I know will melt in a few days, perhaps even tomorrow. Anything to be outside. I almost ache with anticipation. *Will this winter never end?*

April 27, 1978.

Overcast. Horned owl songs ringing through the woods each night this past week. The snow has melted enough to permit limited travel in the timber now that the snow shadows under the trees have expanded and joined. But the underlying soil is so thoroughly frozen that the water stays on the surface and does not soak in. Even small rivulets are in flood. Many voles and shrews, which spend their lives beneath the snow or under the grass and in the soil, are forced out. Boreal and great horned owls are not the only ones to take advantage. Yesterday I saw a gray jay pounce on a shrew as it scurried across the snow.

Today, despite yesterday's snowfall, from the timber came the sweet song of the ruby-crowned kinglet, its rich melody another harbinger of summer.

Part V

Modern Adventures

19

The Alaskan Mile
by Daryl Miller

While sailing through Cook Inlet on May 6, 1794, British explorer
Captain George Vancouver spotted "distant stupendous mountains covered with snow, and apparently detached from one another." Historians
now generally accept Vancouver's description as the first written reference to the two highest mountains in the Alaska Range: 20,320-foot
Denali and its companion peak, 17,400-foot Mount Foraker (also known
by the Native names Sultana, "The Woman," or Menlale, "Denali's
Bride"). Nearly 110 years after Vancouver's reported sighting, expeditions led by Judge James Wickersham and Dr. Frederick Cook would
make the first and second attempts to reach Denali's summit. Each party
fell far short of its climbing goal; but in the course of their approach
from Cook Inlet and eventual retreat to the coast, the members of Cook's
party completed a remarkable, if unintended, circumnavigation of the
Denali-Foraker massifs.

In the nine decades following Cook's 1903 expedition, more than
8,000 people reached the top of North America and hundreds more
walked upon Sultana's slopes. During that same period, three expeditions encircled Denali and another party circumnavigated Denali's Bride.
But no one even attempted to repeat Cook's amazing journey. Then along
came Daryl Miller and Mark Stasik.

Miller, who is now Denali National Park's chief mountaineering
ranger, first attempted to climb Denali in 1981. He later guided on the
mountain one season before joining the park's mountaineering staff in
1991. By the end of 1999, Miller had participated in more than a dozen
Denali expeditions along three different routes; stood on the summit
three times; and assisted in more than thirty rescues.

In 1986 Miller met Stasik, a timber framer and mountaineer who had
made his own first trip to Denali a year earlier. Settled in Talkeetna, a small

end-of-the-road town at the southern fringes of the Denali region, Miller and Stasik soon became good friends. In 1989 they joined in an ascent of Denali's West Rib, a technically difficult route with several thousand feet of steep ice and snow. At other times, they teamed up on Denali back-country patrols and explored both the Alaska Range and its surrounding lowlands. The Denali landscape became their wilderness backyard, a place they grew to know year-round. In 1995 the fifty-one-year-old Miller and thirty-one-year-old Stasik agreed to attempt the second Denali-Foraker circumnavigation ever—this time in the depths of winter.

Accounts of the Miller-Stasik expedition appeared in the 1996 *American Alpine Journal* and also in the April 14, 1996, edition of the *Anchorage Daily News* Sunday magazine, "We Alaskans." This version is taken from "We Alaskans," though the title of Miller's *American Alpine Journal* article is used.

S ince breaking camp five hours ago, Mark and I have been traveling in darkness. The winter days are very short and very cold now. Eighty miles and seven days from the warmth of Talkeetna, we've settled into the discomfort that's bound to accompany a 350-mile winter ski trip around the wild perimeter of Mount McKinley and Mount Foraker. Winds off the frozen Chulitna River scour our exposed skin. We struggle with our packs and snow pigs—the heavy sleds that carry our assortment of gear.

I hate my pig for revealing my lack of training for this trip. The pain is bearable, but there are 270 miles of wilderness left, with a broad array of obstacles to overcome.

Today is nice. The wind has relented some. I can feel my nose for the first time in a week. Mark's tiny, clip-on thermometer indicates a relatively balmy 15 degrees below zero as we enter the river's first major canyon complex.

Red and yellow granite walls climb to block the sun, creating a strange world of shadow. The snow is deeper and softer. Trail breaking becomes slow and laborious. How different this is from standing in the Talkeetna ranger station sliding a finger along frozen rivers on the big wall map or flying over the route in an airplane.

But my daydream ends with the loud crack beneath my skis and the heaving of unstable shelf ice. As our route approaches a narrow section of river channel, I notice several deep, open leads. Rushing water can be heard echoing violently against towering cliff walls.

Gliding out across snow-covered ice at midriver with the reluctant pig in

213

tow, I glance back to see Mark several hundred yards behind, a lone speck in the white wilderness.

Then, the worst happens. A snowy trapdoor gives way beneath my skis, and I plunge into the river. The current sucks my skis and legs downstream beneath the ice.

Panic fills my chest.

I struggle to hook my arms over the wafer-thin edge of ice circling the black hole. The swift, chest-deep current keeps knocking me off balance. The pig teeters on the edge, ready to fall.

If the sled goes in, the extra drag will surely pull me under. It will be all over. I yell for Mark, not sure if he can hear me—or see me. My eyes are just above the ice, but the snow blocks my view. My breathing turns ragged in the freezing water.

Finally, I hear Mark answer, but I can't understand the words. Then I see him about 25 feet away. He pulls a throw bag from his sled. He tosses it to me—but I can't reach it. The tangled, frozen wad of rope falls 10 feet short. Mark pulls it back and throws again. This time it hits me. I clutch the rope—and safety—as Mark quickly pulls me from the hole.

Immediately, my concern focuses on the danger of freezing to death. Mark pulls out a camera and takes a picture. It would be a shame, he says, to avoid documenting this event.

A giant bonfire would be great, but there's no wood. I shed my wet clothes, slip into dry polypropylene and down a Thermos of hot tea. Mark shakes the ice out of my frozen but still functional wind suit. I dump the water out of my bunny boots and pull them back on over dry socks. And then we're off again.

For the next three or four days, our problems with water will continue. After resupplying at a cache on Honolulu Creek, we turn onto the West Fork of the Chulitna for an icy version of Russian roulette. Precarious ice bridges span open braids of water. Cautious now, we belay each other across. It's time-consuming, but a lot safer. At least psychologically.

Where the water is shallow, we simply ford the river, wading knee-deep. Our gaitor leggings freeze as soon as we reach shore, but in general things go well. That changes as we approach the West Fork Glacier, where I rip the bindings out of my new, foam-core Karhu cross-country skis. There is no way to make repairs. I'll be on the back-up snowshoes for the next 250 miles, and my snowshoeing technique will need to improve if I hope to keep up with Mark, who quickly labels me the "Nomad Shuffler."

Still, the glacier is a welcome sight. We are on familiar ground now. We climb over Anderson Pass following fresh wolf tracks, then head west up the massive Wall Street (Muldrow) Glacier, dodging immense and seemingly bottomless crevasses.

By Day 17, we are approaching "Gunsight Pass," where we decide to rope up. Some of the crevasse bridges in the lower icefall appear questionable. The pass looks climbable, but with heavy packs, bunny boots and the pigs, it's almost certain to be an exercise in anxiety.

Unable to locate any place on the headwall to place ice screws or pickets for protection, we decide to unrope and climb alone. This way, if one of us should fall, he won't pull the other down with him.

Being the slowest, I go first. The pig tries to pull me down. My single ice ax and bunny boots strapped into flexible crampons offer only minimal security on black ice, but after several hours I reach the top.

Sitting on the pig, I watch Mark work a different route that starts easily enough but grows steeper. He's nearing the crux when he stops, attempting to rest. Then, in a concentrated frenzy of effort, he flails his way up, reaching the top. We're over.

The desperate climbing on steep ice behind us, we descend onto Peter's Glacier, only to wallow in old, waist-deep snow. It takes us three days to reach our second cache at the head of the Muddy River on the vast piedmont plateau north of the Alaska Range. Trekking west, we watch several hundred head of the Denali caribou herd grazing on the rolling slopes above Iron Creek. Over the next couple of days, we'll regularly see their tracks mixed with those of wolves. We'll hear wolves at night, and we'll howl back. And I will be fortunate to spot a pack of seven on the Foraker River, trotting at a pace that looks easy and deceptively slow until you realize how little time it takes them to disappear over the horizon.

As we move west below the Foraker and Herron glaciers, several red foxes are spotted hunting, and fresh wolverine tracks dot the snow. Our route takes us through thick timber and wide river valleys as we work toward the Swift Fork of the Kuskokwim River and the next cache.

Nearly a month into the trip, Mark has begun having unpleasant conversations with his snow pig. He seems very touchy when asked about these exchanges. After witnessing several heated discussions, I notice how he sometimes grabs the pig by the throat and stands it up for better eye contact. These episodes become more passionate as we endure endless sidehilling—sidehelling?—or entanglements in thick stands of alder.

In the evenings, Mark spends a lot of time writing in his diary by the light of a candle stub. He's keeping a very detailed, descriptive account of each day.

Mine is less so. After a few minutes of writing, my fingers always stiffen from the minus-30 degree cold.

At night now, I find it difficult to sleep even with a hot-water bottle stuffed in the sleeping bag. I lie in one position, trying hard to keep my body from rolling onto the frozen socks and gloves I try to dry during the night. And then there's the bagels. Every night, we take turns sleeping with several frozen bagels. It's the only way to thaw them enough to render them chewable in the morning. We also leave the tent doors partially open to cut down on the condensation from our breath.

Moist air is freezing sleeping-bag zippers shut, creating modified straight-jackets. This prevents an easy exit for late-night potty calls. I eventually give up all hope of sleeping comfortably and accept the reality that the only time I'll be warm is while moving during the day.

I come to look forward to that, along with a morning cup of hot java and our dream critiques. Mark is sleeping easily. He envisions wild and feverish encounters with women, South Pacific Islands, and death by overindulging in chocolate. My dreams focus on various forms of suffering, especially freezing to death, mixed with occasional fantasies of cheese on fresh bagels. (Mark is lactose intolerant, so we have no cheese.)

Nearing dark on the coldest day of the trip—Mark's thermometer falls to minus-40 degrees (though we're certain we're far below that)—we approach our third food cache at "Little Siberia," 140 miles from the Chulitna swim. This cache has been left under a single-flagged spruce tree.

Looking across the vast taiga near the Swift Fork, we notice with dismay that all the spruce trees look alike. So do the desolate hills and barren ice lakes. I argue for a lone spruce tree a quarter mile away, but Mark holds out for a tree three miles away.

As a full moon rises over Foraker, we trudge through the extreme cold to the tree, then struggle to pitch the tent, which froze into a cylinder of ice after we splashed through overflow on Somber Creek. It's a stiff and icy shrine when we get it up. Brewing hot soup, we collapse in our lumpy, frozen sleeping bags.

The whiteout that greets us the next morning is a welcome change. It forces the first real break in 29 days of travel—nearly all of it through weather that keeps most animals huddled warmly in their dens. Weathered in, we decide to celebrate with a pint of rum, a new supply of Drum tobacco and some vacuum-sealed, precooked steaks of moose and caribou.

I fire up the stove inside the tent to thaw the rum, which had frozen solid. As usual on this trip, we cook inside to heat the dome.

Suddenly, we're trying to cope with the flash fire from hell. As I pump more pressure into the fuel bottle attached to the already flaming MSR XGK-stove, fuel begins spraying everywhere. Instinctively, I turn off the stove, cover the spray with my hands and yell at Mark: "I think we have a big problem here!"

Meanwhile, the XGK—which burns for a good minute after it's turned off—continues to flame. A breath after my warning to Mark, a "whoosh" shoots through the tent. Flames engulf my head, gloved hands and everything around me. There's fire on my chest. The smells of singed hair and melting nylon permeate the tent.

"Get out!" Mark shouts. "Get out of the tent!"

He's on fire, too, and fighting his way out of his sleeping bag. He throws flaming gear at me in an effort to clear the tent. If it burns, we'll be in serious trouble.

I dive into the vestibule and roll in snow. I try to grab the flaming gear flying out of the door and smother the flames. Mark shoots out like a wild terrorist with tangled, Rastafarian hair in flames, rolls in the snow and sits up.

"Hey, Daryl, are you OK?" he asks.

"Yeah, sure," I say, smoke still rolling off my parka. "Are you OK?"

"Yeah, yeah," Mark says. "I'm OK. . . . Damn! That's the best tent fire I've ever been in!"

Minutes later, we're hurrying to get back inside the tent to avoid freezing. Repairing the faulty pump, we gingerly restart the stove and heat some rum before surveying the damage: one fuel-soaked bagel, a number of new vent holes in my clothes, faddish punk hair, molten beards, missing eyebrows and eyelashes, and several new holes in my already flat and frozen Thermo-Rest pad. Mark insists the latter is for the better: Sleeping on a cold, hard surface will be good for my back and prevent overheating.

Early the next morning, we leave the wildfire camp in the direction of the ridge separating us from the Chedotlothna Glacier. We have our eye on a spot we dub "Nomad Pass," where we can cross back to the south side of the Alaska Range.

McKinley authority Bradford Washburn, upon seeing a photograph of this pass, will later assure me: "Daryl, that is not a pass; it's just a place where you guys crossed the Alaska Range."

As it turns out, he's right. We have badly underestimated the distance and the 4,000-foot climb to the gap. What was expected to be an easy two-day approach turns into a long, four-day climb of a jagged and broken glacier. Moving along the medial moraine on the east flank, we run into herds of wintering Dall sheep, which seemed shocked to find humans wandering here.

Some 14 miles from wildfire camp, we reach the base of a steep and crevassed headwall, one that had looked moderately easy when we flew over it earlier in a plane. Climbing to the lip of a huge crevasse, we decide to make it our camp for the night. The weather is the usual cold, this time with a gusty, nasty wind blowing snow out of the north. We down-climb several rope lengths into the crevasse to the edge of a 30-foot-deep snow bridge. We probe it for stability, then chip a platform for the tent, thinking we'd fare better in an avalanche here than on the exposed, unstable snows above.

Next morning, Mark leads out of the crevasse and up a bergschrund, chopping belay platforms as he goes. Our plan is for Mark to climb a rope length on belay, then for me to climb, leaving our sleds tied to the end. Together, we pull the pigs up to each belay platform. The headwall is a constant 50 degrees, sometimes increasing to 60 degrees. We try to stay near a rock band along one side because of fears of being swept off by avalanche.

Mark chops 13 platforms in the course of the day. At each, we labor to haul up the 150-pound pigs. The tiny thermometer says it's minus 30. Estimated upslope winds of 30 mph push the wind chill to 100 degrees below zero. Staying warm in my burnt parka is hopeless. Saving my feet from frostbite is a matter of moving enough to ensure circulation. Many times this day, I wish to be back in Talkeetna.

By dark, we top out in worsening weather. Options now are few. The wind is blowing so hard it's difficult to breathe. We can't survive this for long. There's no choice but to rappel toward the Yentna Glacier.

Hacking through ice, we prepare a rock to hold the rope for the descent. It's set so we can pull it down at the end. We hope it won't hang up. The rappel into the unknown darkness is slow and punishing in the screaming wind. Finally, we locate an ice ledge and chop a place for the tent. We tie it with rope to hold it in place.

Sitting inside, bracing the tent sides against the wind, we're happy just to be alive. We tell ourselves we've completed the hardest part of the journey. After the painfully cold three hours spent chopping and digging the tent in, Mark lights a warming candle, but I can barely see him in the ice fog from our breath. With his icy beard and chiseled face, he looks like some sort of crazed Viking warrior from some earlier age.

The short, cold night passes with little sleep. Morning light pushes us on. The wind-whipped snow is a howling blizzard. Visibility is zero. Traveling unknown ground with no landmarks, we descend by compass toward the Yentna through a crevassed maze, blindly feeling for solid footing in hurricane-force winds that smash us to the ground again and again and again.

Six days from the wildfire camp, we still have a long way to go to our next cache at Spruce Creek. The wind chill is so severe, we have to keep moving to survive. We're blown down constantly. We estimate winds on our backs at a constant 80 mph, gusting to 100 mph. On several occasions, our bodies are lifted off the ice only to be yanked back by the weight of our sleds or the pull of the rope. Unable to see Mark up ahead, I sometimes feel like a human kite flapping on a long line in a wild and raging winter nightmare.

When we decide to stop, we encounter a big surprise: It's almost impossible to walk sideways across the glacier, perpendicular to the wind. Repeatedly knocked down, we resort to crawling to a huge boulder that provides the only possible shelter.

Working feverishly into the early morning, we chop another tent platform. Ice screws and carabiners try to hold down the tent. The climbing rope is tied over it like a giant fish net, in hopes it'll keep the nylon structure from ripping apart.

By morning, we just want off the glacier. Packing frozen sleeping bags into the packs, we begin a six-mile trek downslope to the "Trench," a deep, glacial river laced with crevasses near the juncture of the Yentna and LaCuna glaciers.

At first glance, a crossing appears rather easy. But it takes two full days of miserable and tedious travel to cover the next two miles. Many times, we cross broken sections of ice laced with huge seracs. The pigs sometimes hang eagerly below us, inviting a quick trip down. On Day 39, we spend a cold night at the bottom of the trench, shivering after eating the last cup of instant mashed potatoes and smoking the last Drum. We've been traveling on 10 days' food now for 12 days, and still we're 20 tough miles from the next cache.

The next day, we climb out of the trench, over the Ramparts Range and, at last, begin the descent of the familiar Kahiltna Glacier. Moving slowly through heavy crevasses, we suffer the pangs of hunger. Mark tries to put the best face on it he can. Starvation, he says, stimulates erotic dreams and interesting hallucinations. And going without food eliminates the bothersome chores of cooking and eating, saving us about three hours a day.

By Day 42, after a difficult 16 miles the day before, we find ourselves lying in the tent not wanting to move. We drink lots of water in the morning and eat snow most of the day, and while that keeps us well hydrated, it does nothing to provide energy.

Mark is right about the hallucinations, though. I envision a huge, warm bonfire consuming my pig, which has taken to grabbing onto every brush and tree limb now that we are off the glacier. Our progress, however, has slowed dramatically.

We only move a mile at a time before falling in the snow to sleep or rest. We walk past each other, staring with hollow and distant eyes, saying nothing but understanding each other completely.

Our last push has taken us up Cache Creek, only a few miles short of our precious cache on Spruce Creek. Languishing in the tent, dreaming of food, we hear snowmobiles far in the distance. We look at each other, knowing that for the first time in more than a month contact with other humans appears imminent.

We sit in the tent until we hear voices, then crawl out, wobbling over to a couple standing by the machines. They are obviously homesteader types, pulling a sled behind their snowmobiles with snowshoes and gas cans attached. They seem to know where they're going.

The man takes one glance at us and says, "You boys look a little hungry."

They insist we take some food and a pack of smokes. I try to stuff an entire Baby Ruth candy bar into my mouth. Small pieces break off and fall to the ground. I notice that Mark is on his hands and knees in the snow, carefully picking up each crumb of chocolate and eating it.

I stuff several slices of bread in my mouth, and our conversation with the snowmobilers hits a lull. The couple watch us eat for several minutes then decide to leave us a little more food before driving away. We thank them as best we can in between swallows. A can of tuna fish and the rest of the bread make several sandwiches. Which disappear in a blink.

Several hours later, rested on full stomachs, we reach our last cache. There, we eat ourselves into a deep sleep, our stomachs bulging.

Snowmobiles become more common now. We run into friends from Talkeetna who loan us money so we can stop for a night at The Forks Roadhouse for real food and showers.

Two days and 30 miles later, we recross the not-so-frozen Chulitna and walk down Talkeetna's main street, returning to our homes. We'd been on the trail for 45 days, traveling 350 miles. I'd lost 25 pounds. Most surprisingly, we'd returned as better friends than when we left.

The rest of our experience—the solitude and the fear, the joy and the agony, the hardships and the pleasures—is all but impossible to explain. We'll cherish them forever.

20

Riding the Wild Side of Denali

by Miki and Julie Collins

After coming north in 1942 to work on the Alaska Highway, Richard Collins got a job in Alaska with the Federal Aviation Administration (FAA). The FAA assigned him to a tiny bush community on Lake Minchumina, some forty miles northwest of what was then McKinley National Park. There, in 1956, Richard met Florence Rucker, a geologist and pilot. The two married and in 1959 Florence gave birth to twins: Julie and Miki. Now in their early 40s, the sisters have resided their entire lives in the immense, roadless wilderness of Alaska's Interior, except for nine "unhappy" winters spent in Fairbanks, while attending high school and college.

In their book *Trapline Twins,* Miki and Julie describe an early childhood much like that of other children: They played on swing sets, rode bikes, and watched movies imported by the FAA. But they also found "youthful bliss" in the forest and lake, and on mud flats across the bay.

As his daughters got older, Richard Collins taught them important homesteading skills: how to pilot a plane, drive motorboats and snowmachines, work a chain saw and diesel generator. Meanwhile their brother Ray (older by a year and a half) taught Julie and Miki how to shoot, ice skate, set traps, track wildlife, and gut animals killed for food. While Ray was in many ways their mentor, the sisters say, Swedish trapper Slim Carlson was their idol. A longtime resident of the Denali region, "He lived off the land, traveling by dog team along hundreds of miles of trails he cleared himself, back in the days when there was wilderness enough for everyone." Before dying at age eighty-nine, Carlson left his eighty-mile trapline to Richard Collins, who in quick order handed it over to his daughters.

After graduating from the University of Alaska Fairbanks, the twins returned to their Lake Minchumina home just outside the expanded borders of Denali National Park and Preserve and resumed the traditional rural subsistence lifestyle, which includes trapping, hunting, gardening, berry picking, fur sewing, gill-net fishing, and mushing. The Collins sisters also manage a kennel of ten to fifteen dogs and own several horses.

This excerpt, "The Journey Home," is an abridged version of the first chapter of *Riding the Wild Side of Denali: Alaska Adventures with Horses and Huskies,* published in 1998 by Epicenter Press. In this book, as in their earlier book *Trapline Twins,* the sisters took turns writing chapters. Miki wrote this one.

The grizzly stood elbow-deep in blueberry bushes, his tawny shoulders rippling darkly as he browsed along the treeless flanks of the Alaska Range. I watched him warily from across a brushy draw, my little horse alert by my side, her blue-flecked eyes growing big and round as she stared at the unsuspecting bear. Lilja didn't look scared, exactly, but she did look terribly impressed. Comet and Streak, my two big pack dogs, waited eagerly, ready to dash after the bear the instant I might suggest it.

Earlier in the day we had left the end of the dirt road behind as horse, huskies, and I struck out across a sixty-five-mile stretch of uninhabited wilderness to reach our home. My twin sister, Julie, waited there with our parents, busy caring for our team of sled dogs and doing other September chores, leaving to me and the two staunch dogs the job of getting Lilja to her new home.

Our journey had only just begun, and already I was getting into trouble. Typical.

If I went forward, I'd drop down into that brushy draw where I couldn't see the bear when he first heard or smelled me. If he approached, he'd be right on top of me before I saw him. My best bet was to get his attention while a couple hundred yards still separated us, to see what his reaction to us might be.

"Hey—ho!" I sang loudly.

His massive head jerked up. The instant the grizzly caught sight of us, he wheeled toward us, coming at a swift, fluid, yet lumbering stride through the knee-high dwarf birch, not running but walking awfully darn fast.

A .45 Ruger Blackhawk revolver hung from the saddle. I snatched it from its holster, glancing at Lilja. The little horse had never been exposed to gunfire, but I decided I'd rather chase a horse bolting from a shot than a horse bolting from a charging grizzly. Gripping her lead rope tightly, I squeezed off a shot into the air.

Lilja hardly twitched as the pistol boomed, bucking in my hand. The grizzly snapped to a halt, springing up on his hind legs for a better look. I fired again, and this time he spun away, loping rapidly down the shoulder of the mountain.

I reloaded the pistol and slipped it back into the holster. Then the dogs, horse, and I picked our way cautiously on around the mountainside.

As children, my twin sister, Julie, and I, like so many girls, craved horses. Roaming the overgrown silt bars of the Old Channel, a shallow slough flowing near our home where wildlife abounded, sometimes we would find moose tracks and pretend they had been made by wild horses. They weren't, of course, but it was fun to dream. But as we grew up in Alaska's isolated Bush country, a land without roads, pastures, or even much wild grass, we set aside those unrealistic dreams. We could have moved to warmer climes, or even just to the road system within Alaska, but we belonged to the wilderness. Our parents lived here before we were born, and except for a few winters away getting a higher education, this vast subarctic land had always been our home.

For twenty-six years we had trapped and mushed and adventured in the remote spruce-covered lowlands north of the Alaska Range. Between running sled dogs on an eighty-mile trapline in the winter, raising a large garden and fishing for dog food during the short summers, and harvesting our year's meat and berries every fall, with an occasional thousand-mile dog sled trip for excitement, our lives were already full. Our love for horses was not forgotten, but Life marched on without them.

That is, until 1986, when we first heard about Icelandic horses and their amazing ability to forage off the land and survive the harshest winters. A scant five months later, I was traveling across Interior Alaska with a short, thick-maned palomino pinto mare.

After trucking Lilja (pronounced in the Icelandic way: *Lil-yah*) north from a farm in Canada, Julie and I had learned—sort of—how to ride and handle our thirteen-hand (fifty-two-inch) mount during a summer in Fairbanks. Now I had to get her home, and that meant a long, hazardous journey on foot across a wild land.

I'd been through this pristine area once before by dog team, and had no difficulty finding my way over the 3,500-foot bald mountain, a mere foothill of the Alaska Range. Below us a large glacial river roared through a low-walled canyon, and just a few miles to the south Denali towered to over 20,000 feet, its lower flanks already showing the white snows of September. Everything I needed for the forty-five mile, three-day leg of my journey to the Birch Cabin on our winter trapline was either on those dogs or lashed onto Lilja's stock saddle; once we were on the trapline, Julie could resupply me by floatplane.

Of the more than 100 pounds of supplies we were transporting, most was animal feed. Comet and Streak shouldered thirty-pound packs for the first several miles, but soon I dismounted Lilja, tying their packs to her saddle and leading the horse while the dogs ran unencumbered up the mountainside.

Under our feet lay a carpet of tundra shrubs, dwarfed blueberries, crowberries, cranberries, mosses, lichens, and scrubby grasses, all turning vivid hues of red and gold, gray and ochre in response to the chilly fall nights. An occasional caribou paused to stare at our unlikely entourage as we crossed the high country, and by nightfall we had descended to treeline on the far side of the mountain.

The following afternoon found us down on flatter country, nearing the river crossing where the current, shallower but still racing fast, braided through a mile-wide plain of gravel bars. The water ran high for September, sweeping in standing waves over the granite cobbles. Anything over knee-deep might knock me down, but this was the best place to find a way to the far side.

Moving slowly, I used a poke stick to feel my way across one rushing channel after another, watching the ripples for dangerous spots. Lilja and the dogs followed unquestioningly.

Then my prodding stick missed a drop-off. Without warning I plunged into chest-deep water, and the current dashed me off my feet, spinning me downstream as I started to swim. Lilja stopped, standing firm as the lead rope jerked tight in my hand. Swinging me around at the end of the rope, the current washed me back against the shallow bar. I stumbled to my feet, dripping with icy water.

"Good girl," I said, shivering. "Let's try that again!" The dogs backed off and I picked my way upstream, eventually locating a safer crossing.

We camped that evening on a slough we call the Twelve-Mile, a beautiful creek lower down but here just a dry, willow-lined wash cutting through a vast plain of scrub spruce. Lilja, finished with her evening meal of sweet feed, grazed on sparse yellowing grass and bright green horsetails growing in the sand. Occasionally she poked her slender white nose under the tarp which served as my tent, making sure I hadn't slipped out on her. The dogs curled up peacefully on their nests of spruce boughs, and I slept warm and cozy on the thick saddle blanket.

One more exhausting day brought us to the Birch Cabin, right on schedule. We were down on the flats now, threading our way around countless shallow lakes and bogs, in an endless sea of scattered fifteen-foot-high scrub spruce growing from layers of deep, wet, spongy moss. Twice Lilja had sunk belly-deep in soggy, moss-covered drainages. Both times she surged forward, leaping onto firm ground, dirty water streaming down her white legs.

The homey sight of our little cabin on the bank of a wide creek revived my spirits after twelve hours of riding and walking. This was one of our main trapping camps, with a nice fourteen-by-eighteen-foot log cabin, a small cache for food storage, and a few spruce-pole dog houses scattered around the overgrown yard. Our first overnight stop on the trapline during the winter, it acted as a base for camps farther out the trail. For now, it was a comfortingly familiar shelter. I picketed Lilja where she could graze on the thick, coarse bluejoint grass growing around the cabin, and after slapping up plastic windows and lighting a fire in the stove, I took a swim in the icy creek, washing off the swamp muck that rose to my waist.

Running back to the cabin, I stopped short at the sight of Lilja grazing placidly around the cabin door. A horse! A real, live horse, right here at our Birch Cabin! A rhinoceros could hardly have seemed more out of place. Affectionately I brushed the mud from her white-and-gold coat, picking short-needled spruce twigs from the exceedingly thick topknot she wore as a forelock, a trademark of the Icelandic breed. When temperatures dipped to fifty below next winter, that thick thatch of hair nearly covering her little ears would protect them from the cold.

We spent a day of rest at the cabin, Lilja happily mowing down yellowing grass while I picked a couple gallons of cranberries to cache for the approaching winter. Julie flew our brother's Super Cub floatplane out with a resupply of feed, landing on the closest lake four miles away and hiking in to spend the night before I headed on with my little crew.

The first forty-five miles had taken us three days. But now we were heading into unfamiliar country, leaving our trapline trail to pick our way across nine miles of marsh and muskeg to hit the Old Channel seven miles from home. The winter trail followed a boggy creek system most of the way, and I decided to cut across country to the river to stay on higher ground. The nine-mile portage would be the most challenging part of the trip. With no landmarks, I depended upon a compass to find my way, and I worried about crossing creeks and bogs with Lilja. I knew I did not have enough experience to judge what was safe for a horse and what was not. I was used to traveling with dogs, who can walk across quicksand with impunity, dash through the deepest bogs, and scramble up the steepest banks. But horses aren't like dogs.

I would soon learn that horses and bogs don't mix—or rather, they mix so well as to become inseparable. Many of our bogs have a thick layer of yellow-green moss camouflaging deep, mucky water. Once a horse's sharp hooves and long, slender legs break through the spongy, overlying surface, its great weight prevents it from climbing out again, with potentially fatal results. Sometimes a horse can scurry across soft ground, but soft, safe ground is unfortunately hard to distinguish from the soft, horse-eating variety.

We struck out bravely, marching across muskeg and marsh, bog and slough. Lilja followed with a blind trust as I walked ahead, slogging through watery moss and once tiptoeing across a twisted, overgrown beaver dam. Occasionally we marched swiftly along low ridges, prehistoric sand dunes, their tops dry and firm with a game trail inevitably running along the crest. Usually, though, my feet sank several inches down into spongy moss and tussocks as we wound our way through the stunted black spruce.

Then, crossing an innocuous-appearing moss-covered drainage, Lilja fell in. Her hindquarters broke through a layer of floating moss into deep, dirty water, sinking until her belly rested in the deep red muck. This time she was too tired to struggle out.

For ten minutes I coaxed, prodded, and pulled. Finally in desperation I slapped her hard across the flank with the snap end of the heavy lead rope. With a grunt she jerked away, heaving herself upright, and several more blows drove her back to safe ground.

Trembling, I calmed her as the dogs stood by quietly. When we started again, I traveled more cautiously, seeking the firmest route in that land of moss and mire. Instead of reaching the Old Channel by evening, we camped only half-way there.

During the first part of the trip I had always been aware of Comet and Streak, of where they were and what they were thinking about. Now I was so intent on Lilja that I ignored the dogs. Yet they were always there, buoyant and cheerful when we moved along, or standing aside worriedly when things went wrong. They shouldered heavy burdens so I could save every bit of Lilja's strength, even though the weight of their packs wore them out and the horse carried little more than her saddle as I walked ahead. I counted on those two 110-pound dogs, with their laughing faces and striking black-and-white malamute masks, and they unfailingly came through for me.

The muskeg stretched on and on. Sometimes we walked "quickly" through deep, dry lichen or humpy-bumpy tussocks. Other times we trekked a half-mile out of our way, pushing through tight, stickery brush, to find safe crossings over drainages. Yet for all our caution, we had progressed only a short distance the following morning when suddenly Lilja sank again, her legs disappearing into reddish watery moss, just two feet away from solid ground.

This time I knew she wasn't going to make it out on her own. Something in her eyes told me she wasn't even going to try; something in the way her hindquarters sank to the stifle, and her forelegs were disappearing nearly to her quivering shoulders, told me we were in deep trouble.

"Get up, Lilja," I snapped. Needing to turn her resignation into fear, I struck her rump with the lead rope. She made a brief, futile effort and then lay still, shivering with cold and distress. I knew then she couldn't do it, and no amount of wishing, shouting, or prodding could help her. Groaning, Lilja shut her pink-rimmed eyes as if to say, *I'm going to die now, and there's no use making a fuss over it.*

With trembling hands I hitched her picket line to the rigging of her saddle, driving my arms elbow-deep in cold, dirty water to work it down to the heavy D ring where the cinch attached to it. Now at least I had something to pull on if she sank in deeper.

I leaped away again, dropping to my knees by the small bundle I'd snatched from her saddlebags the moment she went down. Inside, carefully wrapped in plastic and foam, lay my only lifeline to The World: a two-meter amateur radio, the size of a walkie-talkie but more powerful. At home, Julie answered my first call.

"Lilya's in a bog and I need a comealong to get her out," I said.

"Right," Julie answered, her voice tightening. "I have to gas up the plane, and then we'll be right out."

"You'd better hurry," I warned.

Julie could air-drop me a hand winch, but she'd have to find me first. In that trail-less tangle of bog and moss, taiga and marsh, Lilja and I were specks against a mottled, September-brown background.

I returned to the little horse. She had rolled onto her side and the swamp crept up to the top of her right hip, bog water turning her white coat a reddish brown. Her left shoulder lay partially exposed but her right side had disappeared, and her neck sank until the water nearly closed over it. Worst of all, her head slid back and sidewise into the water. One eye and an ear sank out of sight and as her tiring neck muscles sagged, her nostrils slipped momentarily underwater. She jerked her head up again, eyes rolling wildly.

"Lilja, Lilja!" I cried, catching her head up and lightly slapping her muzzle. "Hang on, girl. I'll get you out."

227

A twig of a spruce tree twisted from the nearby bank, and I tied the reins of her hackamore up to it, holding her head clear of the water. Then I tried to build a Spanish windlass, anchoring it to a nearby black spruce. Leonard Menke, a longtime trapper, had told me how years ago. But the biggest trees around were under two inches in diameter and rooted only in shallow moss overlying the frozen permafrost below. I didn't have enough rope, and I couldn't remember exactly how to make it anyway. Nothing worked.

Then I heard the familiar rattling buzz of the Super Cub. I snatched up my radio as the little plane came into sight, angling south of me.

"I am on your left," I said into the mike.

"Negative copy." The roar of the 150-horsepower engine reverberating in Julie's radio nearly drowned out her voice.

My battery was failing. I switched to my tiny reserve. "TURN LEFT!" I shouted.

"Roger."

Lilja groaned softly. I stood quivering. In the distance, Julie banked her small plane in my direction.

"Hang on, sweetheart," I urged my little horse. As Julie headed too far north, I pulled out my compass. "Take a heading of 160 degrees," I ordered.

"Roger. You're very scratchy."

Fear gripped me anew. The spare battery was failing. Julie passed by a half-mile away. "Turn left!" I cried into the radio.

"Negative copy."

"Left!"

She didn't answer. My radio was dead.

I knew she would have only taken time to dump in five gallons of gas, which that powerful engine drinks up every half-hour. And half an hour just wasn't long enough. Helplessly, I watched her circling a short distance off until at last she banked toward home.

She'd be back, but I didn't know if she'd find us in time. Horses cannot withstand being down for long, and Lilja was suffering from the cold as well. Desperately, I hurried back to work on the windlass but that proved hopeless. The trees were too spindly and the only rope I had was Lilja's fifty-foot picket, made of one-inch nylon webbing. When Julie returned, I waited until she flew abreast of me and then roared "LEFT!" into the tiny radio.

That was the last word for my radio, and put my sister practically on top of me, circling and circling. I slopped to the middle of the open bog, spread out my bright green tarp, and then stood shin-deep in the cold, mucky water, flagging with a red shirt, confident that either Julie or Daddy, in the passenger seat, would spot me. If I wasn't so sure that they would spot me any minute, I would have taken the time to build a fire, and the smoke would have pinpointed me immediately. As it was, they couldn't pick me out of the dappled background for over an hour.

Then one wing dipped and the plane swung down, circling low. At last! After one pass I saw Julie line up on the bog to make the drop. Throttle back. Set up the approach. Full flaps. The narrow red plane coasted down, down, coming straight toward me. The door opened and Daddy, in the back seat, leaned out. As they passed fifty feet above me, he hurled out two packages. One held a spare radio battery. The other contained two comealongs and about a hundred miles of rope.

"Okay, Lilja, things are going to start popping now!" I sputtered, scrambling back up the low bank that separated the bog from stable ground. I swiftly fastened the rope onto the harness I'd rigged on her, and then tied off one of the winches to three of the stunted trees, hoping they would not uproot under the strain. Grimly, I started to crank.

The rope grew taut, and then she budged. When she felt the movement, Lilja struggled briefly, lifting herself up before lying still again. I cranked some more, and every few inches she heaved herself forward and upward. Then the comealong jammed.

I snatched up the other one. This winch had a faulty release. I could only use it once, and if that didn't do the trick by the time the cable wound in, I'd have to waste precious time fiddling with the darn thing.

"Lilja, get up!" I ordered. The rope tightened. Her body slid upward, all 650 pounds of it, and she lurched forward. Her front hooves clawed at the mossy bank. The cable shortened. I had only a few inches left. "Come on, girl!"

She jerked up, straining, and as I cranked in the last eight inches, sliding her forward, her hind legs came free and she staggered up the bank. She had been soaking in that cold bog for three hours, and appeared mildly relieved to have escaped with her life.

A light drizzle misted down as I dropped the comealong and hurried to the little mare, praising her as I squeezed the dirty water from her trembling body. I didn't linger long. We started walking again, more to warm Lilja up than to get anywhere, and we camped in the early afternoon as soon as she seemed somewhat recovered from the chill.

By then, damp from rain and my exertions in the bog, I worried about the possibility of hypothermia in myself as well as in the shivering horse. Splitting some dead standing spruce to expose the dry wood inside, I built a small but hot fire and covered the wet, chilly mare with everything I had: two burlap sacks, a sweater, a wool shirt, the saddle blanket, a large plastic bag, rain coat, rain pants, dog packs . . . she looked like a cancerous patchwork coat, but she finally warmed up. I kept back only my sleeping bag for my own safety.

I stood her by the fire, rubbing swamp dirt from her drying fur and heating water in my one-quart cook pot to soak her feed in for a hot meal. I had to make about six pans of soaked food, alternating with more pans of warmed water, each of which she swallowed in two or three mouthfuls. We were all reduced to drinking bog water, and I picked squiggly inch-long bugs and stray bits of grain out of the pan when I finally cooked my own dinner. Julie returned that evening, guided to me with the help of the spare radio battery and the smoke of my fire, to airdrop a resupply of food.

It took us four days to cross that terrible stretch. I had strayed too far west, down from the drier ground I'd been aiming for. Two or three times a day Julie buzzed out, giving me directions on how to get around the worst areas. Each evening she dropped me feed so we never had much to pack. Most precious of all were the little sketched maps she drew, detailing the terrain and labeling trouble ahead. I trekked around "Lots of Small Slu's," I backtracked down "Long Slu" to cross "Big Tamarack Marsh," and almost lost Lilja again when I had to cross a chest-deep, vertical-banked "Creek." Once in the water Lilja couldn't climb out on the far side. Eventually she solved the problem herself, rushing off downstream and locating a better spot to haul out. Then I ran into "Big Swamp" and had to double back again, finding my way around it and tip-toeing across the last two "Slu's."

We hit the Old Channel right on track and just three days late. I laughed and cried and called Julie on the radio. We planned to celebrate our twenty-seventh birthday when I reached home, even though it wasn't the right day.

"Kill that chicken and bake that cake, I'm on the Old Channel!" I sang into the radio.

Comet and Streak, ever present, scented the familiar waters of their river. Knowing home was not far away, they threw open the doors of their boundless capacity for exuberant joy.

"*Oh-dee-oh-dee-oh!*" Streak shouted.

"*Eee-dee-eee-dee-eee!*" Comet shrieked, and together they hurtled their powerful bodies down onto the muddy silt bank for a good roll followed by a vigorous romp, shouting and shrieking all the while. Lilja picked up on their high spirits, lifting her head to test the air, and then dropping to her knees, plopping down to roll on the damp silt, to the detriment of her saddle and pack.

Those two devoted huskies, the pick of our "pack" for summer work, stabilized my emotions on that memorable trip. Always reliable, always strong and familiar next to the vast mysteries of the Horse, they readily shouldered heavy burdens to spare the little mare. They would have liked to chase that grizzly to Kingdom Come (or so they thought from a safe distance), but at a word from me they stayed right by my side. Oddly enough, every time I left Lilja to scout out a safe route, one dog invariably stayed with her while the other came with me—and they seemed to take turns. Now that they saw that the purpose behind our mad travels was to get home, they whole-heartedly endorsed my every move.

We still had seven miles of brush and quicksand to contend with, but this was my country now, my childhood playground, and I knew every bend, every dangerous spot. Julie and Daddy paddled up the shallow river to meet us, and we camped together that night at our annual moose camp before Daddy headed home in the canoe, leaving Julie with me to head confidently down the riverbank with our little horse and two very happy dogs.

It didn't take long to figure out that even this part was going to be hairy. Recent flooding had left quicksand all along the willow-lined banks, with nothing but endless swamps farther inland. There was no way around this stretch, yet if the horse fell in we could never pull her out with only waist-high willows to anchor a comealong to.

Lilja tiptoed swiftly over the softer spots, delicate white nostrils flaring. Suddenly one hoof penetrated the silty surface into quicksand below. Instantly the little horse collapsed in a heap. Her weight spread out, she stopped sinking, and after resting calmly for a moment she regained her strength, sprang to her feet and, wresting her leg free, scampered on downriver.

Several more times Lilja sank into the treacherous mud, and each time she saved herself by throwing herself to the ground to stop sinking until she could catch her breath and go on. Finally we reached the spot where we had to cross the river. From the far side we'd be on firm ground the rest of the way.

Julie and I swam the narrow stream first, teeth chattering in the cold, to check out the far bank. I looked it over skeptically; even though we felt this was the best spot, I wasn't sure Lilja wouldn't sink into the soft mud as she climbed out.

Julie led the horse into the water. I grabbed the mare's long, flowing white tail as she plunged in and started to swim, towing me behind. Moments later

Lilja heaved herself out on the far side and stepped onto solid ground. We made it!

In triumph we marched the last mile and a half home through the golden birch forest, Comet and Streak surging excitedly ahead as Lilja strode regally behind, a raggedy blanket thrown over her wet body. As we walked into our dog yard, our chained huskies—some of whom had never seen a horse before—burst into an astonished cacophony of greeting, alarm, and incredulous exclamations. Their wild antics didn't faze Lilja. She surveyed her surroundings with a domineering eye and then placidly fell to munching chickweed as if content to live here for the rest of her life. She knew right where she was: home.

21

Way Out Here:
Modern Life in Ice-Age Alaska

by Richard Leo

Three years out of college, settled into his first "real" job in corporate America and immersed in the materialistic wealth of New York City, Richard Leo could not shake the question that had troubled him much of his still-young life: "Is this all there is?" A short hitchhiking vacation to Alaska in 1980 unsettled Leo even more. Here was a place of huge mountains, vast open spaces, and wilderness stretching from horizon to horizon. A place far different than any he'd known, it increased his hunger for a different path. Alaska might be an answer to his personal riddle. It might also be the "better world" he desired for the children he would some day father. So, in early 1981, Leo abandoned the center of twentieth century civilization and, with $900 and his girlfriend, headed north to the nation's Last Frontier.

Leo's still-forming vision demanded that he become a wilderness homesteader, though nothing had prepared him for that lifestyle. Born in the Midwest, he had spent his first twenty-nine years in urban and suburban settings. It did not matter; he would get on-the-job training while building his homestead. Hitchhiking from Anchorage to Fairbanks to inquire about federal parcels in the state's outer reaches, Leo met a local who told him about some state-owned lands that had opened up out Petersville Road, south of Denali National Park. Following a hunch, Leo caught a ride to one of the remote Petersville sites. There, in the Upper Susitna Valley, he found a home. Instead of high rises, health clubs, and crowded subways, his new neighborhood included the continent's highest mountain, lush forests, glacial rivers, grizzlies—and few people. Though he could barely imagine the life ahead, Leo was certain it would be a "wild, wonderful adventure." The dream, the possibilities, were enough.

The reality, Leo says, has exceeded his wildest imaginings. In the midst of wilderness, he has found a world based in family and land, a home where "beauty, faith, and community" can flourish—and where his sense of community has expanded to include the nonhuman world. Unable to adapt, Leo's girlfriend returned east, but he found another woman to share his life. Together Richard and Lucia have raised three boys (the oldest is now in college) and a kennel of sled dogs.

Richard Leo recounted his move to Alaska and first years as a homesteader in the 1991 book *Edges of the Earth*. The excerpts reprinted here are abridged versions of two chapters taken from his second book, *Way Out Here: Modern Life in Ice-Age Alaska*, published in 1996 by Sasquatch Books.

WHAT'S HERE

Is the real question
Who am I? Or
When am I here?

HO-SAN

In winter, Alaska's Susitna Valley records some of the most severe weather on earth: blizzards approaching 100 degrees below zero [wind chill] near the surrounding glaciated mountains, as much as twenty-five feet of snow on the valley floor.

The twelve feet of snow we average per winter at our homestead requires that we dig a trench to reach the doorway. Winds pack the snow like cement against the north side of the house. Our five-year-old son will commonly wear a face mask and ski goggles to play outside when the windchill bites.

But in summer the same valley is a temperate rain forest. As in any rain forest, the amount of life is staggering. There are constant echoing bird calls, huge dew-slick ferns, swarming bugs, spawning salmon, and wolves. Underbrush is so dense a machete is standard equipment for travel through the overhanging woods.

Nowhere else on earth does such an icescape transform into a humid jungle, seasonally.

Winter's aurora borealis and silverpoint starfields fade behind the constant daylight of subarctic summers. For three months bracketing the summer solstice the sky grows no dimmer than a pastel of orange radiance during the "night."

The U-shaped valley is enormous. It contains 4,000 square miles of spruce and birch streaked by long open tundra meadows studded with shallow lakes.

Few people live amidst its wilds. The great parabola of snow mountains that contains the valley is surmounted by Denali, the continent's tallest peak and [one of the highest vertical rises] on earth.

Hundreds of creeks like veins descend through canyons creasing those mountains. They all flow into the Susitna River, which lies in the center of the valley. The Big Su drains America's fifth-largest volume of water relative to its length. Only the Mississippi, the Ohio, the Columbia, and the Yukon are bigger.

Not long ago an ice sheet thousands of feet thick once filled the entire valley. It flowed unimpeded 150 miles south from the valley's top into the Pacific Ocean. That ice remained for most of the 35,000 years during which human beings gradually populated the Western Hemisphere after crossing the wide Bering Land Bridge from Asia. Those original Americans curved around the valley's insurmountable arc of snow peaks to follow ice-free grasslands into the rest of the truly New World.

Then as now the land beyond the concealed valley was too dry to build glaciers; moisture blown up from the Pacific was caught by the range and dropped inside the valley walls. While Inuit and Clovis and Mayan and Aztec and Inca cultures gradually evolved, this valley was completely hidden from *Homo sapiens*.

Not until as recently as 500 years after Christ did the first people crest the passes between the lowest mountains to gaze down into the valley.

What those fur-clad Athabascan Indians saw must have been staggering.

If the season was early summer—which I assume was the case, because game trails leading into the passes are evident before the explosion of greenery, and because freedom from snow slog makes wandering joyous—and if the skies were clear, which they commonly are at that time of year, the expanse below probably made them weep at its beauty or laugh abruptly at the unexpected marvel or whoop-'n'-holler with the discovery or simply stand in silent communion with something profound and powerful. An entirely different ecosystem than that from which they'd come stretched before them, the newest arable land on earth.

What they saw was this: an ocean of gold-green birch canopies budding into leaf commingled with the darker green of spruce rising to foothills covered by russet alpine tundra, above which stood white mountains of such height and mass the horizon bent. Curtains of breeding swans and geese rose and fell in the tributary canyons lush with willow and alder and marsh grasses fed by the melting blue ice of the still-withdrawing glaciers.

Even the scent was different from the sparser, more arid land north of the range—richer, more floral, *bigger*. Everything would have seemed bigger. The fecundity was and is unparalleled two latitude degrees below the Arctic Circle.

Now horticulturists in the lower part of the valley grow cabbages the size of sports cars, beets like basketballs, anaconda-thick zucchini. The upper valley grows some of the world's largest salmon and trout, moose and bear.

Anchorage, with 275,000 people, Alaska's largest city, sits on the Pacific coast twenty miles from the tidal delta of the Susitna River, yet is isolated from the valley by a flanking range of coastal mountains, the Chugach. Two hundred-twenty miles from Anchorage by the only road up through the valley, the route to the valley winds over the winnowing end of the Denali massif into the rest of Alaska.

That two-lane blacktop road wasn't completed until the 1970s. Until then access to the reaches of the upper valley, where we live, was as limited as to the roadless areas of Nepal.

Even before the advent of Caucasian exploration and inadvertently introduced disease, the aboriginal population of the valley was not much more than a thousand at its highest. Athabascan seasonally nomadic hunter-gatherer technologies were not conducive to empire building. The land remained impervious to easy travel or permanent settlement: deep snow by winter, dense underbrush by summer.

Real wild land accepts habitation on its own terms.

In 1896, the first American to leave record followed a fever into the valley. He was drawn not by wanderlust nor pilgrimage nor vision quest, but by gold. Explorer and prospector William Dickey—an Easterner by way of Seattle—stood on an alpine tundra pass to look up, and up, at the world's most abrupt mountain. He wrote a dispatch when he returned to "civilization" that the New York *Sun* printed ballyhooing the "discovery" of "Mount McKinley," named for an Ohio politician who championed the gold standard.

The discovery of gold in the foothills of the mountain that the Athabascans called Denali had a much greater impact.

By 1905 the foothills on either side of the valley were being prospected. The miners ventured into the land by boat, dogsled, snowshoe, and donkey. Their numbers peaked at perhaps 3,000 when the Alaska Railroad from the Gulf of Alaska was completed in 1923. Fairbanks, across the range, was the destination and terminus of the railroad, because of the far more extensive gold rush in the Territory of Alaska's interior, north of the Susitna Valley. More than *40,000* people flooded that country.

The railroad also created a small village near the center of the upper valley at the confluence of the Susitna with its largest secondary rivers. Talkeetna boomed as a railroad construction camp (a clapboard bar-and-inn, a general store, a score of cabins on platted house sites along the mud "Main Street") and then busted when the gold finds didn't amount to anything like those in the Klondike or Nome or Fairbanks.

By the mid-1930s some miners remained in the upper valley, along with the last of Talkeetna's shopkeepers, a few trappers, and the dwindling Athabascan population.

The cumulative effect of this second wave of human incursion into the valley was the same as the original aboriginal migration: the profundity of the wilderness was little affected.

Bears avoided the scattered log cabins of the few remaining placer miners toughing it out in the foothills. Ravens flew over trackless forests to cross the blip of Talkeetna amidst the trees. New growth covered trails. Winter buried the land for most of the year.

The valley remained one of the least explored, mapped, and known areas on the planet.

World War II brought a flurry of activity to the Alaska Territory. An army base in the coastal town of Anchorage doubled the population to 10,000. Statehood in 1959 brought another influx of federal money. Still, little in the valley changed. Talkeetna's population remained at a few hundred. Few of the peaks walling the valley had been climbed, most not even named. The railroad ran just a few trains a week on through to Fairbanks, mostly freight. Finally, in 1974 when the Trans-Alaska Oil Pipeline started construction—the next Alaskan boom—change began to reach into the valley. The town of Wasilla, on an arm of the Pacific just twenty air miles north of Anchorage, was incorporated that year, soon becoming the fastest-growing community in America. Wasilla is now the hub of the lower valley, grown to 4,400 industrious people, with a central business strip lined by a McDonald's, a Wendy's, a Burger King, a Taco Bell, a Pizza Hut, two 7-11s, three shopping malls, a mutable number of banks that go boom and bust, and a hundred other small businesses ranging from dogsled supply stores to hairdressing salons. About one-third of Wasilla's work force commutes to Anchorage.

North of Wasilla, signs of economic development are increasingly widely spaced along the single road up through the valley: Ivan's Bait and Tackle ("Live Worms"), Goble's Gamble Ar-Vee Dumpsite, Wolf Safari ("You Getta Pettum"). Telephone and powerlines that follow the road stop halfway between Wasilla and the pass out of the valley.

Two of Denali's glaciers, the thirty-six-mile-long Ruth and the thirty-mile-long Eldridge, come to within four miles of the blacktop. The smaller and more distant Peters surged five miles in 1985, 200-foot ice towers toppling in its path.

Official wilderness areas of Denali National Park include most of the high country that defines the north and west arc of the upper valley. Denali State Park is contiguous, extending across the lowland forests to the eastern foothills. All that parkland, too, is wild: almost wholly trailless and uninhabited.

The entire population of the upper valley, by the most recent census, is 920. Half that number is in the riverbank village of Talkeetna. People come and go, build cabins in the woods and then flee the isolation, collect welfare in the village while waiting for a real job elsewhere, buy into a small business and then sell out.

Most of us who remain do so because of what we see in the land. The power and beauty of this place is as necessary to those of us who have chosen it as the Tibetan highlands are to those who originally found sustenance there.

One major difference, however, between historic Tibet and this equivalently remote and mountain-dominated world is that here there are no monks, no people who don't try to fix or improve their economic world. This is, after all, America's Alaska, the culmination of Manifest Destiny where the pioneers are determined to make a "better" life than that which they've left.

The valley remains new to human habitation. Immigrants bring their culture with them. Only in time do they adapt to what is pervasive in the land.

The Susitna Valley is unique not just for its extremes of climate, its contrasts in culture (true wilderness accessible within a three-hour drive of fast food), or its *terra incognita* status in human history. This valley is *familiar*, paradoxically; it resonates deeply in our collective unconscious. Human beings took their last evolutionary step into that which we are today amidst a Pleistocene environment duplicated here: conifer forests rising to game-rich tundra rising to glacial canyons within which cave bears den. Long severe winters and short intense summers. Proximate perennial ice.

When Ice Age glacial sheets covered much of North America, Europe, and Asia, this landscape and climate was what we knew. Our genetic dispositions have a basis here—dispositions to dominate and to herd together for the sake of survival, to wander alone in hope of revelation, instinctively to seek *more* in order to allay fear of scarcity, and to stand silently, if only for a moment, in humility and awe at all that exists beyond ourselves.

A few years ago I spent an afternoon with the (now former) Superintendent of Denali National Park, discussing the parklands within the Susitna Valley. His belief was that the human proclivity to expand our domain ultimately cannot be denied nor contained, nor should it necessarily be. "Because when we've come to the ends of the earth there will still be the stars!"

I tend to believe that the manner in which the earth is reaching the end of its capacity to sustain our proclivities bodes poorly for the stars. The universe may be infinite but our desires are redundant, and "more" is a limited philosophy of life. "Further" will inevitably bring us back to just where we are.

This valley now is a stage on which to see much of human history recapitulated. Here's a lab to study the nature of our nature, perhaps the last and best place for maintaining a connection between what we've been and what we've become, where we have deepest roots and where we've just arrived, that which has always been fundamental and that which seems necessary at the moment.

Last spring I went up to Alder Point, a 4,000-foot foothill flanking the terminus of the Ruth Glacier. It was March, the traveling conditions were good (firm snow, lengthening daylight), the sky was clear, and the hike up the peak was easy after securing the dog team at its base. The view was so expansive I idled through the dusk. The great mountains above were silhouetted against the last lingering light.

Then with a start I realized the entire valley below me was dark. There was no visible point of light anywhere—no house light, no streetlight, no campfire, no nothing.

As more and more stars came out the forested valley floor became blacker and blacker. I knew that fifty miles away was the beacon of the Talkeetna air strip, but it was lost in the expanse.

I saw streaking meteors and the outline of the peaks against the starscape. That was all.

I began to worry that I wouldn't be able to find my camp. The valley, I understood once again, was that vast. I yelled for the dogs but my voice had no echo.

Then, eerily, the dogs far below began to sing with the wavering howl of wolves. When I'd fixed my direction, I started down.

An hour later I stumbled into camp. The dogs wagged their tails.

It was all familiar. It was all unearthly.

FROM "AROUND THE HOMESTEAD"

Our homestead is not so much the center of our world as it is the base, the jumping-off point. For millennia Western civilization thought of Earth as the center of the universe. The cosmos was considered to be rather like what we knew as home, just bigger. It seems so much more true to see what sustains us as a very small place from which to investigate the endless and utterly unfamiliar Everything Else.

Near the foothills of Denali, far removed from any road, the homestead's main log house, "guest" cabin (read: "place to store stuff"), sauna, root cellar, woodshed, and garden are together smaller than a nice suburban ranch house. But The Ridgeline (as we've come to call our twenty forested acres in the grand manner of baronial estates and trailer parks) feels expansive. Our three boys have to use a whiffle ball to play baseball because any ball more solid will be hit beyond the small clearing and lost in brush. And yet the area in which we bat seems plenty big, like a carless street would seem for city stickball.

Fifteen years ago, not long arrived from New York City, the seventy-five spruce I felled from various corners of the land for cabin logs seemed like plunder to me, an excessive impact on the landscape. Now, however, each season we have to whack berry bushes and vines and saplings from the 50-by-25-foot "backyard" just to keep it clear of the continuously encroaching forest.

The spring from which we dip water into buckets for drinking is fifty yards down the ridge; the creek where we fish in summer or ice skate in winter is fifty yards beyond that; the swimming lake is a quarter mile away out on the open tundra. These distances require stepping away from the cleared area into the forest where in truth a grizzly could be passing coincidentally, to grim possibilities. But the sense of connection between those nearby places and the psychological safety of the homestead structures has become intuitive; there's no separation between the uncertain "there" and the secure "here."

From that beginning the wider circles of connection expand. By dogsled in good conditions we're about an hour from the mountains; they've moved closer in our conception of what's "part" of the homestead and what isn't. By foot in summer the gravel road where we leave our truck is two hours away, but the trail has become so familiar it's hard to retain the original mind-set of being "isolated" in the woods.

This awareness of being connected to more of the world than a glimpse of the tiny clearing amidst the trees would indicate means that there's an absence of the feeling of alienation. Anxiety isn't a part of the general mood of daily life. Not anymore. At first, though, there were times of raw terror, waking up suddenly in the middle of the night, heart pounding, to stare through the bedside window and think, "What is *out* there?" Now the land's benign. It's all home.

There are still dangers, of course, and we're a long way from a hospital. My wife's a skilled midwife, with both Western medical training and a practical wisdom about traditional healing arts. But having an in-house doctor doesn't remove the risks inherent in living remote.

Those risks, however, are familiar now, not frightening. It's a practice in attention to deal with good ol' dangers like felling trees or loading a gun or just walking the trail.

And so we can concentrate on what else there is to see.

REACHING HOME

After having been anywhere in the wider human world—the post office (a full day's trip there and back) or our closest neighbor's house (across two ridges and a creek)—getting home requires a trek.

In the winter it's a cruise by dogsled. Except during or just after a heavy snow when the dogs have to swim like porpoises (dive, paddle, surface, breathe, dive, paddle, surface, breathe . . .), the run is fun. It's like downhill skiing on level ground: Knees bent! Keep your balance! *Zoom.*

The few others who live in the roadless part of the valley use a snowmachine to reach their cabins, or cross-country skis.

But in summer there lurks the possibility that the long, unavoidable walk will become an unwelcome chore, a slow, soggy, annoying commute. A backpack (to carry supplies) is as requisite as rubber rain boots, so there's no chance for a smart jog. The trail can get so overgrown with brush that the ground itself is an assumption; a step can be an act of faith.

It's the summer trail, though, that provides necessary perspective, in part because it *isn't* luge-chute adrenalin-amped swift. The length of the hike and the variation in terrain usually forces anything being carried internally to be dropped. All the stuff from having been out in the social world—petty angers, imagined slights, flattering comments—gets chucked to decrease weight, but not right away.

First comes the recapitulation. The beginning of our trail lends itself to an overview of Life, because it's hard. Sloughs cut channels that need to be leaped, grunting. The creek yearly washes out parts of the path, requiring a stomp through new brush. The fertile flood-deposited soil grows head-high grasses, tangles of willow. Those first few hundred yards create the opportunity to consider what I *really* should have said on the pay phone to the credit collection company, to kick at the brush in my guilt for having been abrupt with a friend who would have liked a patient ear. I stumble across the sloughs and flail at the grasses.

Then the trail crosses a giant cottonwood with a three-foot-thick trunk that for fifteen years has spanned the creek, an absolutely necessary bridge still withstanding flood and rot. It fell, of its own, exactly at the point and during the time when a way was needed across the water. A cottonwood is one of

241

the rare trees that existed during the time of the dinosaurs. I see miracle every time I balance my way over it. Life is suffering, sure, but there is also a whole lot else going on.

For the next few miles the trail meanders through forest, high ground. Walking becomes easier. Sunlight filters through the treetops. Kinder memories surface. Those carried from the road begin to drop away.

Right beneath this spruce we once found a bird's nest with six small chicks in it. Just over there was where we scared a black bear from a moose carcass. Here is the spot where we discovered a trail-side spring behind the ferns and brought a cup to leave beside it. Mingled with the memories are new perceptions of the day: moose prints, fresh, cow and very young calf; pink blueberry flowers opening a week or two earlier than usual, maybe from the winter's light snowfall, warmer soil; the song of lots of Swainson's thrushes, good, the loveliest melody of all the valley's migratory birds; whoa! that bear scat wasn't there last week. Time to sing my own songs, *loud,* to announce my presence.

"My feet are my only carriage / so I got to push on through . . ."

Within the hour the trail opens onto a long, narrow stretch of tundra, a moist fairway of ankle-high flowers and grasses. The mountains rise on the revealed horizon. Even if it's cloudy I know they're there, above the stratus.

The walking's harder, though, squishing along. The tundra is a dense mat of vegetation atop ground water. This is where lingering hindsight (. . . maybe I should have waited for the day's mail to come in, just in case . . .) becomes foresight: anticipating the end of the trek, hollering hello to the kids, bringing news to my wife, sharing what I've packed in to eat or read. If the dogs are barking, their voices waft in and out on breezes.

Sandhill cranes occasionally feed on the tundra. Once a black bear trailing four (count 'em) cubs crossed the trail on the far side of the biggest lake. That sure provides a quick shift of perspective.

Something always happens, though, even as simple as having a dragonfly light on my shoulder. Everything that occurs takes my attention. It's difficult to remain involved with myself.

Those couple of hours just to get home from anywhere are as essential to this life as the bridge across the creek. Rushing to get *there* misses *here.* Each slow step reveals something new. There is always more than what we first see. Otherwise what we know is all there is, which is terminal.

SPRING

There are still two feet of snow on the ground though the stars have already been burned from the midnight sky by unending daylight. The snow pack has

settled so firmly that it's like greased concrete, making the whole world a highway for sled travel. The birch are beginning to bud and the first of the songbirds have returned.

There are no bugs. Nothing to swat at, wave away, suffer.

Brilliant sun by day. Cold and luminous by night. Mushing in a tee-shirt.
Skiing in shorts. And no bugs.

I am goofy with happiness at how perfect this all is. There's no flood and
no mud, no slog and no sweat. This is the brief season with the very best of
both summer and winter. Fish are biting in the open creek and any animal
can be tracked casually by its prints in the snow.

This morning was below freezing, solidifying the snow cover. Two trumpeter swans flew overhead. Suntan time in a few hours on the back porch.

What more from a world could be asked?

This could be asked: is a short period of primo excellence worth months
and months of blizzard and drizzle and slop and struggle and bugs?

Christianity has the concept of epiphany: "a sudden appearance or mani-
festation of God in his glory." Zen calls the same thing *kensho*: a moment,
without time reference, in which the divine is present everywhere, ecstati-
cally. Modern psychology, in its endearingly bumbling way, offers terms such
as "self-actualization" and "peak experience." The idea is all the same. After
travail, *yes*.

Often I find myself complaining about the weather, and then it changes,
and I complain about that, and then it changes, and I find something not quite
right again until I'm exhausted trying to get the climate to fit my needs.

So here it is: just what I want. Day after day of it, unexpectedly.

When climbers attempt Denali they suffer through weeks of grueling slog
until, maybe, they stand on the summit in sun for a few minutes. Is it worth
the struggle? Ho!

When serious anglers gear up for the salmon season they can wait to hook
into one for what seems like forever, cast after cast, hope after hope after nibble.
Then when a big fish finally strikes and the line whizzes out singing, does it
eradicate the frustration of having stood inert in the rain?

What about monks endlessly practicing prayers or prostrations in aching
expectation of revelation: when the white light and tears descend, has a lifetime been absolved?

There is a whole lot of light on this world now, summit bright. Does it
make up for the forty below and the brown fall floods and the bugs? Why,
even a single day of this spring idyll is enough to—

Damn. A mosquito just bit me.

The birds are back. Sandpipers and phalaropes on the tundra. Thrushes and swallows and sparrows and warblers in the woods. The great geese overhead.

The boreal forest is once again wired for sound. Whales and dolphins "see" with their ears deep in the ocean. Their world becomes three-dimensional not with binocular vision but with chirps and trills and songs. Standing in this deep green forest at dawn or dusk is like snorkeling into a humpback whale migration: the sound comes from everywhere.

But now that the birds are back, what are they going to eat? There is still snow general over all the land. The creeks are open, but the lakes remain frozen. How will the flocks survive? This is not bird-feeders-in-every-backyard country, mainly because there are so few backyards.

Once, after a winter hunt, we cut open the gullet of a spruce hen—a grouse, a wild chicken—to see what it ate in January. We found a hundred spruce needles, nothing else. Its intestines smelled like spruce. We stared across the forest at the sea of spruce. Talk about heaven on earth for the right kind of bird.

The black-capped and boreal chickadees that live here through the winter eat the twig ends of birch where the seeds remain. There are almost as many birch as spruce in this part of the forest. What a rich land. If you have the right kind of stomach.

For 140 million years this part of the world was a tropical swamp where dinosaurs had it as easy as spruce grouse and chickadees do now. The large ostrich ferns that will be the first green shoots after the snow melts off were even larger then. But what are the migratory birds going to do for the next few weeks waiting for the ground to thaw or the continents to shift again?

Maybe the geese and swans that are spiraling back to their breeding grounds have some way to feed that isn't apparent to me. Certainly the light radiant on the snow is beautiful, but is spiritual nourishment sufficient to keep them healthy?

I've learned that just a few open leads in otherwise frozen creeks can allow aquatic birds to feed. Old vegetation swirling beneath the current is better than no vegetation. That doesn't seem to answer the needs of 10,000 birds, however. It also fails to address the needs of perching birds and songbirds and robins who won't find worms for weeks.

But here they all are, plainly aware of something that I'm not. From a bird's view the land is already greened to the south. Summer's happening down along the coast near Anchorage while this upper valley remains another season. Still, the birds here don't commute a couple of hundred miles daily. They're *here,* chirping and trilling and singing.

We made a bird feeder this year since the snow is lingering. It's big enough to serve all the new arrivals. We found a fifty-pound bag of Alaska barley that I've been storing for probably ten years ("Hey, what's this old bag in the corner under the pile of junk?"). It didn't look bad at all, but we had fresher supplies, so I brought it out for the birds. I dumped the bag in the front of the house, atop the snow.

Within hours ravens ripped the bag apart probably hoping it was the carcass of something. That left grain scattered widely.

Gray jays took over from there. They tossed grain around like Midas flinging gold. But the jays, like ravens, are year-round residents who know the lay of the land. The jays ignored the barley to clean the dog food bucket after I fed the dogs, their normal hand-out meal.

That left the migratory birds alone with all the seed. And they didn't flock to it. They continued to sit in the trees announcing their pleasure. They're *everywhere,* except in the front of the house.

They don't need my largesse. I don't know how they all manage in a spring like this one. But here they are.

This morning was another hard snow crust after a freezing night. And the birds didn't stop singing.

22

Denali State Park:
In the Shadow of The High One

by Bill Sherwonit

When people speak (or write) of "Denali," they usually mean either the mountain itself or the national park in which The High One is located. To Alaskans, however, Denali can also refer to an entire region of the state, one that stretches from the far northern reaches of Denali National Park and Preserve to the foothills and lowlands immediately south of the Alaska Range. Known as South Denali, the landscape south of the range is divided into private, town, borough, Native corporation, state, and federal lands. Here, among this complex quilt-work of ownerships, is a parkland little known to those who live outside Alaska and frequently overlooked or ignored by many residents: Denali State Park.

Sometimes called "Little Denali" in deference to its larger federal neighbor, this 325,000-acre unit is among Alaska's oldest state parks. Since it was formed in 1970, politicians, business interests, and tourism boosters have wished to make Denali State Park a major visitor destination—one that would alleviate the pressures on the nearby national park. Past schemes have failed, but development and economic pressures continue to build, especially as large-scale "industrial" tourism increases its demands for new destinations and visitor attractions. For now, most use remains concentrated along the George Parks Highway corridor, where visitors stop at roadside pullouts to view Denali and other Alaska Range peaks. But backcountry wild lands beckon an adventurous mix of hikers, backpackers, wildlife watchers, berry pickers, hunters, skiers, mushers, and snowmobilers.

My own relationship with Little Denali began in the late 1980s. For years I bypassed the park while headed north from my Anchorage home to "grander adventures." But, in time, I gradually introduced myself to the state park's natural wonders. During the past decade I have explored Denali State Park's alpine ridge tops; shared its forest trails with black bears, moose, and chickadees; camped beside a lake filled with spawning salmon; and spent days in quiet solitude while immersed in a wild landscape of wooded lowlands, tundra-topped hills, glacially fed streams, and distant towering mountains that rise in mesmerizing fashion, to the top of the continent. Once or twice a year (and sometimes more), I also return to a lakeside public-use cabin, a place of peaceful yet invigorating retreat.

The following excerpt, from *Alaska's Accessible Wilderness: A Traveler's Guide to Alaska's State Parks,* was published in 1996 by Alaska Northwest Books.

T here it is, that big thing in the middle."

"Show me again. Where is it?"

"Where's what?"

"Mount McKinley. It's disappeared behind the clouds right now, but we could see its summit clearly just a few minutes ago."

So the conversation goes at Milepost 135.2 of Alaska's George Parks Highway, on a partly overcast June day. There's enough blue sky to raise people's hopes of seeing McKinley and enough cloud cover to mostly hide the mountain that's also commonly known by its Athabascan name, Denali.

Only 42 miles from the highway turnout, North America's highest peak looms 18,000 feet above the surrounding tundra and river valleys, a vertical rise that's among the highest on earth. Denali's height, combined with its subarctic location, also makes it one of the coldest mountains on earth, if not *the* coldest. Even in June, nighttime temperatures on its upper slopes may reach -40°F. Denali is so massive that it creates its own weather systems, occasionally producing storms with winds above 150 mph. The mountain is also frequently battered by storms born in the North Pacific; and because of its northerly location, scientists estimate the available oxygen on Denali's summit is equal to that of Himalayan peaks 2,000 to 3,000 feet higher. For all these reasons, Alaska's "great ice mountain" has earned a reputation as the ultimate challenge in North American mountaineering.

Yet for every person who attempts to climb Denali—about a thousand a year—hundreds more appreciate its grandiosity from afar. All that most visitors want is to see the giant granite monolith; one good look and maybe a few pictures are enough. But even that can be a challenge. Most years, it's clearly visible only one in three days from Memorial Day through Labor Day, the prime tourist season. Visitors on tight schedules, as many are, can't afford to be picky. If Denali comes out, it makes sense to stop at the nearest pullout and catch a glimpse. Though it's best known as the centerpiece of Denali National Park and Preserve, the mountain is often more easily seen from the George Parks Highway, the principal road linking Anchorage and Fairbanks. And among the highway's most popular "Denali viewpoints" is the paved turnout at Milepost 135.2, a convenient, scenic rest stop in Denali State Park, "Little Denali."

Back in late 1960s, some visionary Alaskans imagined a state park that would capitalize on both the new Parks Highway (completed in 1972) and Denali's tremendous tourist appeal. Less than a 3-hour drive from Anchorage, this park would relieve some of the growing visitor pressure at what was then Mount McKinley National Park. More important to state interests, it would become a major year-round destination, complete with luxurious hotel, visitor center, snowmobile trails, and scenic ridge-top drive.

All of the grandiose schemes promoted in the late sixties and later years have so far failed. Among the most accessible of all Alaskan parklands—it's bisected by the Parks Highway and bordered on its eastern edge by the Alaska Railroad—325,460-acre Denali State Park remains one of the least known. What politicians have been unable to do, however, the tourism industry may accomplish. Princess Tours has built a luxurious "wilderness lodge" along the Parks Highway, on private land just inside Denali State Park's border. In just a few short years, this newest of Alaska's Princess Hotels has already begun to make the park more of a destination.

Leaving the road-side crowd of Denali viewers, I travel north 12 miles to Byers Lake Campground. Less than half its campsites are taken at midday, and I leisurely drive through spruce-birch forest to find one that appeals. Like most highway travelers, I hurried past Byers Lake for years. Then, one September, after a particularly hectic visit to Big Denali, I stopped on my return to Anchorage and found bliss: numerous vacant campsites—and no clouds of dust, crowds, RV caravans, or rush of people. Instead, a rich autumnal serenity. Birch leaves floated softly from trees to earth, the sweet-sour fragrance of ripening high-bush cranberries filled the air, and somewhere out on the nearby lake, a loon wailed loudly in its haunting, mournful way.

Now, in June, leaves are opening, not falling, and the cranberries that survived winter have lost their pungency. But the campground is again subdued. The only sounds are the gentle swish of wind through needles and leaves, the occasional chatter of red squirrels, and the whistles and chirps of chickadees, warblers, and thrushes. Out on Byers Lake, two anglers sit in a raft, waiting patiently for a fish to bite, while on shore a family of four picnics beside the lake, an older couple walks arm in arm through the campground, and two bearded backpackers enter the forest. And the rest of the highway's travelers keep passing by.

Fourth of July weekend. After too many summers of saying "next year," I'm camped on Kesugi Ridge. My day began 9 hours ago in Anchorage, under dark, drizzly skies. Now, at 3:30 P.M., I lounge beside a mountain pond, beneath brilliant heavens. But the promise of sunshine and 70° warmth isn't what drew me here; it could just as easily be foggy or raining. I've come to loll on luscious moss carpets, nap among purple monkshood and fuchsia shooting stars, and walk in the footsteps of grizzlies and black bears. I'm here to watch eagles ride thermals until they become black dots on an infinite blue canvas and to follow rocky ridges wherever they will take me. But mostly I'm here because I'm curious about this place called Kesugi Ridge.

Built from a mixture of volcanics, sediments, and granite, Kesugi is a 4- to 6-mile-wide, northeast-trending spine of rock that parallels the Parks Highway for 25 miles. The ridge lies just east of the highway and is easy to spot, but most road-bound travelers overlook it because eyes are inevitably drawn to the west, where Denali and its satellite peaks leap into the sky.

Quite ordinary in comparison, Kesugi and neighboring Curry Ridge barely edge past 4,500 feet, and instead of jagged spires or enormous rock walls, the tundra-topped ridges have a gently rolling nature. Considered the upland "backbone" of Denali State Park, they're more plateau than mountain.

Kesugi—a Tanaina Indian word meaning "The Ancient One"—is nonetheless considered among Southcentral Alaska's premier backpacking routes. One reason is the view. The Alaska Range dominates the western horizon, a remote mountain kingdom of knife-edged ridges and granite walls larger than Yosemite's. And rising above it all, the snow- and ice-capped throne of Denali. Many of the same great peaks can be seen from the highway, but the ridge top shows the full panoramic sweep of mountains, glaciers, tundra-covered foothills, wooded lowlands, and glacial rivers.

Kesugi also offers hikers and backpackers easy access to pristine alpine backcountry less than 5 miles from the highway. All it takes is a few hours of uphill grunt work, thanks to a 36-mile trail network pioneered in the mid-1970s by state park ranger Dave Johnston and Young Conservation Corps members. The best place to get above treeline quickly is Little Coal Creek, where it's only $1\frac{1}{2}$ miles and 715 feet vertical gain from trailhead to tundra.

It's at this trailhead that I've joined seven other backpackers on a 3-day, 16.7-mile holiday "tour" of Kesugi Ridge.

We start out among spruce and birch trees, chased by mosquitoes and serenaded by thrushes. From the forest we emerge into the subalpine zone, where a series of switchbacks takes us past alders, willows, geraniums, bluebells, and cow parsnips. Then, finally, alpine tundra. Above treeline, the hiking is ideal. The dirt path we follow is narrow and occasionally disappears, but the route is well marked by rock cairns. It would be difficult to get lost here, though not impossible when fog or low clouds roll in.

After setting up camp beside a tundra pond, I climb a gentle ridge above our lake and sit among volcanic boulders that have grown thick lichen beards. Far below, the Parks Highway is a narrow gray ribbon winding through lowland forests and paralleling the glacially fed Chulitna River. I scan the landscape with binoculars, but find no other signs of human development. It's hard to imagine that government bureaucrats once planned to build a scenic road and 300-room hotel along this ridge. Nothing got built, but that '60s tourism scheme led, in a round-about way, to Denali State Park's birth two years later. The developers' dream didn't die, though. In 1989, state parks officials again proposed a visitor center and lodge complex for Kesugi's northern flanks. The plan sparked a lawsuit, filed by several individuals and conservation groups, and it eventually died in court.

Below me, another group of backpackers is crossing the tundra, and two new tents have sprouted on the grassy bench. Wishing to be alone with Kesugi a while longer, I climb higher, to the ridge's eastern edge. Several thousand feet below is the Susitna River, one of the region's largest glacial streams. Beyond it are green rolling hills and broad forested plateaus that seem to stretch forever. Dark clouds drop scattered showers on distant hills, and returning to camp I wonder how long our good luck with the weather will last.

Not long, it turns out. By morning, Kesugi Ridge is also in the clouds, and where the Alaska Range stood yesterday, there's only a flat wall of gray. The day becomes a blur of fog and clouds, of rolling tundra and creek crossings. We see lots of wildflowers and birds, a red fox and ground squirrels. No bears, but lots of grizzly conversation, inspired by bear scat and holes where they've been digging. Kesugi's Troublesome Creek Trailhead is routinely closed from mid-July through September 1 because of the potential for bear-human conflicts, and a few years earlier, on an end-to-end Kesugi trip, a friend saw nine black bears in four days.

At 5:30 P.M. we reach our campsite, a grassy meadow beside a sparkling clear and deliciously cold mountain brook. We've only traversed a third of the ridge route, but tomorrow we'll be leaving Kesugi. The others retire to their tents early, but I stay out among the tundra flowers and songbirds. At 10 P.M., the sky opens just enough for one short burst of intense orange light, and the landscape takes on a surrealistic glow. A parting gift from The Ancient One.

Labor Day weekend. Summer's end, and another backpacking trip into Denali State Park's alpine backcountry. This time I'm alone, camped at 3,400 feet on a gentle ridge in the Peters Hills, 16 miles west of the Parks Highway and 5 miles south of Big Denali. If, looking at a map, you imagine the state park to be an oddly shaped, west-facing boot, I'm next to the boot's toes. Five miles from the nearest road, I'm also a mile away from Long Point, where, it is said, Alaskan landscape artist Sydney Laurence gained much of the inspiration for his famous paintings of Denali. Both the man and the mountain have, in a sense, led me here.

The Peters Hills, I've been told, offer even more fantastic views of Denali than Kesugi Ridge—maybe the best views anywhere, if you also want to see the other two members of Alaska's most famous mountain family: 17,400-foot Sultana and 14,570-foot Begguya. Officially named Mount Foraker in 1899—after Ohio Senator Joseph Benson Foraker, who eventually retired from politics in disgrace—the Alaska Range's second-highest peak also has two Tanana Indian names. The better known one is *Sultana,* "The Woman"; the other is *Menlale,* or "Denali's Wife." Seen from Anchorage, Sultana and Denali appear as twin mountain giants, nearly identical in height; but from the Peters Hills, it's clear that the shorter Sultana sits to the left of her imposing spouse. Between the couple is the range's third-highest peak. Like the other two, it stands grandly above the mountain crowd. It would follow then, that this third giant is "Denali's Child." Or so Alaska's Interior Natives believed, calling the mountain *Begguya.* English-speaking mapmakers decided otherwise and named it Mount Hunter, after an easterner—Anna Falconett Hunter—who never saw the peak.

My first morning in the hills, the Alaska Range is shrouded in clouds, so instead of Denali gazing, I take a leisurely walk up to Long Point. It's only the beginning of September, but already alpine bearberry leaves are crimson, blueberrry leaves are purplish red, willow leaves are yellow. But not all of the tundra's summer verdancy has been lost; grasses have yet to turn, and the shiny leaves of the evergreen mountain cranberry won't change at all.

In contrast with these autumnal reds and golds, temperatures are positively summerlike—the weekend's high will approach 60° F—and swarms of insects fill the air. Most aren't interested in human flesh or blood, but there are enough mosquitoes and biting flies to be an annoyance. White sox, small black flies with white-tipped legs, swarm when the wind dies down, so I hope for steady breezes. Another, more pleasant summer remnant are the wildflowers. Most have already gone to seed, but a few hardy late bloomers are scattered among the berries: ground-hugging mountain harebells, their sky-blue petals perched on inch-high stems; pink mats of moss campion; and, in protected creek swales, fuchsia fireweed spikes.

Even before reaching 3,929-foot Long Point, I can imagine why painter Sydney Laurence might have come here. The higher I climb, the more the world opens up in every direction. When there's nowhere higher to go, I pick out familiar landmarks. To the east and northeast are the glacially muddied Chulitna River, the dirty snout of the Ruth Glacier, and several places I've visited this summer: the Parks Highway, Byers Lake, Kesugi Ridge. Due south are vast lowlands that stretch to Cook Inlet, 100 miles away, while to the southwest are the Yenlo Hills, and beyond them, Mount Susitna, a gentle hill I'm more used to seeing from Anchorage as the legendary "Sleeping Lady." Immediately to the southwest and west are the Peters and Dutch Hills, then several waves of unnamed hills and valleys, and finally, the Alaska Range.

Following the range's sweep from west to north, I come full circle to the glaciers, valleys, and mountains that form Denali's frontispiece. With its heights hidden by clouds, the northern landscape's most eye-catching element is the Tokositna Glacier. Fed by dozens of pale-blue fingers, it cuts through steep-sided peaks, then snakes between dark green forested foothills. The glacier, in turn, feeds the Tokositna River, a braided, silt-laden stream that bends around the base of the Peters Hills. Born in the national park, much of the Tokositna River meanders through Little Denali and is one of the state park's few floatable waterways.

Shortly after noon, the thick overcast begins to rupture and Denali's upper reaches poke above the clouds. This partial unveiling starts me thinking about Sydney Laurence. Widely regarded as Alaska's preeminent landscape artist, Laurence is best known for his early 20th-century paintings of what art historian Kesler Woodward calls "a romantic and unspoiled Alaska." Born in Brooklyn in 1868, he learned to paint in New York and Europe, then abandoned a promising career in 1904 to prospect for Alaskan gold.

Once in Alaska, Laurence hardly touched a paintbrush or canvas until 1912.

A year later, given a grubstake and outfitted with a sled dog team, he headed north in the dead of winter to paint Denali's portrait. The 400-mile trip took March, April, and May to complete (the journey made more difficult by the fact that Laurence was still on crutches from a shipwreck accident). Once there, he was forced to return to Seward to pick up art supplies, on order from Seattle, before starting work. By fall, Laurence had completed 43 studies of the mountain. The final painting, a 6-by-12-foot oil on canvas titled "Mt. McKinley" and now owned by the Anchorage Museum of History and Art, is regarded as one of his crowning achievements.

There would be other trips, other McKinley paintings. Whether they were inspired by the view at Long Point is debatable. None of the perspectives, or the description of his camp, seems to fit. No matter. Whether he stood here, or five miles away, Laurence's spirit and connection to Denali touch these hills.

The Peters Hills, like Kesugi Ridge, are not much to look at from a distance. Fifteen miles long and 4 miles wide, these gently rounded, tundra-topped knobs and ridgelines barely reach 4,000 feet. Both they and the nearby Dutch Hills are dissected by dozens of small, clear-water streams. That, in itself, is not unusual. What's special about these creeks is that so many are named. There's Coal, Slate, Divide, Bunco, and Poorman Creeks, and Lunch, Fox, Davies, and Pioneer Gulches. Look closely enough at maps of the area, and you'll also find symbols for buildings, landing strips, and mines. There's even a road—and a mostly deserted nearby community—named Petersville. Nearly all the construction, and the naming, was done in the early 1900s by gold miners. Once ranked among Alaska's major placer gold districts, the Petersville region now yields little ore. Instead of gold, recreation brings people to the area: hiking and backpacking in summer, hunting in fall, mushing and snowmobiling in winter. And, of course, there's the view of Denali.

Only the northeastern corner of the Peters Hills, maybe 10 square miles, lies within Denali State Park. It was added in 1976, part of a 42,000-acre expansion. And once again, tourism played a role. The Peters Hills, many bureaucrats and politicians felt, would be the perfect place to put a visitor center. By making a portion of the hills parkland, the state could protect the area from conflicting development.

The first person to target the Peters Hills was neither an Alaskan nor a politician, but a visionary New Englander whose name is intimately tied to Denali: Bradford Washburn. A highly successful mountaineer, photographer, author, cartographer, and scientist, Washburn is widely considered the world's leading authority on Mount McKinley; since the mid-1930s, he's devoted much of his life to its study and exploration. In the early 1950s, and again in the late 1960s and mid-1970s, Washburn proposed Long Point as the site of a simply built visitor center and lodge that would "not be an intrusion into the wilderness . . . [but] would give large numbers of people an opportunity to see real wilderness."

But simplicity wasn't what Alaska Senator Mike Gravel had in mind when he visited the Peters Hills in the late 1970s. Standing at Long Point, Gravel envisioned "Denali City," a huge Teflon-domed structure just above the Tokositna River. Within the climate-controlled dome would be hotels, shopping centers, condominiums, and golf courses, plus a cultural and international trade center. Next to the city, there'd be a downhill ski resort. And an aerial tramway would take passengers across the Tokositna to a restaurant and observation deck in the Tokosha Mountains.

As strange as it sounds now, Gravel's proposal was taken seriously in some political quarters. Reflecting the anything-is-possible attitudes inspired by Prudhoe Bay and the Trans-Alaska Pipeline, the state senate in 1980 appropriated $1 million for an in-depth look at Gravel's "recreational community," minus the dome. Washburn wasn't nearly as thrilled: "McKinley needs something more," he told a reporter. "But the things Mike is talking about are not the things that I am. . . . I just hope I haven't lighted a campfire that is going to burn down the forest." Washburn needn't have worried. Neither his, nor Gravel's, vision has so far led to any development in the Peters Hills.

Still, the idea of a South Denali visitor complex simply won't die. On the same day that I hike into the Peters Hills—15 years after Mike Gravel proposed his grand vision—the *Anchorage Daily News* publishes a story headlined "New angle on Denali proposed." The gist of the story: a task force studying Denali National Park issues has recommended that a "modest" visitor center with hiking trails, campground, and public-use cabins be built in the Tokositna River Valley below the Peters Hills. For it to work, the Petersville Road would have to be upgraded and extended several miles.

Pat Pourchot, a former state senator and task force member, says the Tokositna facility will boost tourism and give Alaskans easier access to Denali National Park. The funny thing is, though, that the group's preferred site is within Denali *State* Park, less than 3 miles from Long Point. Another task force member emphasizes: "We are talking about the area where Sydney Laurence painted his paintings. It's such an incredible place."

I agree. It's incredible. Not only the scenery, but also the wildness, the solitude, the primeval essence of the place. Except for some abandoned weather-station clutter at Long Point and occasional rock cairns, this northern end of the Peters Hills remains free of human sign. And few people travel the 4 to 5 miles—much of it uphill, across untrailed tundra and through dense willow thickets—that it takes to reach the state park. In three days, I will see only two other people here.

By some strange twist of circumstances, I've brought the September 1, 1994, edition of the *Daily News* with me into the Peters Hills, and open to the South Denali story as I'm sitting down to dinner. I'm shocked, angered, storming to myself: *No. Not here. Go build your tourist mecca somewhere else. Why should the wilderness of Denali State Park be sacrificed to solve the national park's visitor dilemmas?*

Oddly enough, signs of human presence already exist in the valley below. A primitive road and beyond that, an ATV trail, wind along the base of the neighboring Dutch Hills. With binoculars I can see some shacks and a pickup. And 4 miles west of camp is a placer gold operation with several trailers, machinery, and mine tailings. Somehow none of that bothers me as much as the proposed visitor center. The miners were here long before the park; they built Petersville Road and opened this land to hunters and hikers and backpackers. There's been no large or hideous scarring of the landscape, and the miners aren't encroaching on protected parkland. Besides, they tell stories of the region's past, not its future. Large-scale "industrial" tourism, not mining, is the looming shadow here.

Sunday morning, my last in the Peters Hills, brings subfreezing temperatures: water left in a pot overnight is glazed with ice and both tent and tundra are heavily frosted. It also brings clear skies and the Alaska Range panorama I've been hoping to see. The mountains are still in predawn shadow when I emerge from the tent at 6:30 A.M. I get the stove going to boil water for coffee, then grab camera gear and a granola bar and rush back to find a place among the lichen-covered rocks above camp. There's no need to walk to Long Point for this morning's show.

Day's first light touches Denali shortly before 7 A.M. It suffuses the mountaintop with a pale pink glow, then gently washes across the range, giving definition and depth to what had been a flat gray silhouette. It's a familiar view, not far different from the one we have in Anchorage. But here in the Peters Hills, I have a front-row seat, one that offers infinitely more detail. The monolithic wall of mountains seen from town now becomes a granitic sea of serrated ridges, spiked towers, and immense rock faces. And behind the first dark waves of mountains stand the three ice giants, looming above the rest. The color and intensity of light rapidly changes, with rose turning to yellow, then eventually to white under the sun's glare. I scan Denali's ridges and walls with binoculars; they look so forbidding, unassailable. It seems a lifetime ago that I stood upon that mountain.

Touched by a presence that's inspired painters, poets, and climbers, I realize it's true: there may be no better place to see Denali and his family. And I wonder: can Denali possibly cast such a spell on someone who's watching from a hectic, crowded visitor center? Perhaps there's a way to make the South Denali project work, without losing the wild essence of these hills. I can't imagine how.

Mid-September, Byers Lake. A cold drizzle falls as I walk to the lakeshore campground, 2 miles from the road. Sockeye have again returned to spawn and die, and many decomposing bodies already float lifelessly along the shore or lie along the lake bottom. Others, just now arriving, have crimson bodies and olive-green heads. Near the campground, two trumpeter swans swim serenely offshore, occasionally dunking their heads to feed on lake-bottom plants. Summer residents of Byers Lake, they'll soon depart for coastal wintering grounds. Later, more than 30 mergansers will dabble in shallow waters nearby. Fish-eating diving ducks, they too are local summer residents who'll soon fly south. As though in training for their flight, several adolescent mergansers vigorously flap their wings.

The campground is deserted, and I have the pick of six sites. I pitch my tent, then go down to the lake. Three dozen sockeye salmon swim offshore and several male-female pairs guard nest sites, where muck and other debris have been cleared away to reveal a white, sandy lake bottom. The salmon circle relentlessly, in a sort of mating dance, and aggressively attack any fish that intrude upon their space. Soon eggs will be laid and fertilized and the salmon will die, adding nutrients to the lake system. A final gift to their offspring.

By 7:30 P.M. the drizzle becomes a steady downpour. There'll be no one else staying here tonight. And no views of Denali. Within a week or two the rain will be replaced by snow, and soon after that, the campgrounds will close for winter. Lulled to sleep by tapping rain, I spend my last night in Denali State Park dreaming of swans and great ice mountains. In the morning, I too will be headed south for winter.

23

In Denali

by Kim Heacox

Following in the path and spirit of Charles Sheldon, Adolph Murie, and other Denali activists, Kim Heacox is a naturalist and author who has worked to preserve the landscape's wildness and wilderness spirit. A full-time freelance writer and photographer since the mid-1980s, Heacox spent nine years (1977–85) as a seasonal employee with the National Park Service, including one "truncated" season as a Denali National Park ranger in 1981. He also lived near Denali's entrance area from 1991 to 1995, while his wife, Melanie, worked as a park naturalist.

Now a resident of Gustavus, near Glacier Bay National Park in Southeast Alaska, Heacox finds it harder to return to Denali—not only because of the distance, but also because of the changes he has seen. "I miss Denali terribly," he says. "Sometimes you find a place and it takes hold of you and won't let go. But at the same time, that place changes in a way that saddens you."

Having learned firsthand the power of Denali's wildness, Heacox considers it essential that the park continues to inspire people's lives. But he fears that Denali, like too many other wildlands, may fall victim to its own mystique—and to economic forces determined to capitalize on the park's popularity. Because it is Alaska's most famous parkland and one of its most accessible wilderness areas, Denali faces enormous tourism and development pressures. "The park is constantly under assault," Heacox says. "Tourism demands just keep growing and the technology, the gadgetry keeps improving. And all of that endangers the park's wild essence."

Since his first visit in 1981, Heacox has witnessed a degradation of Denali's wildness and the visitor experience. If unchecked, he warns of "a slow, insidious strangulation of its wilderness integrity." He considers it his purpose and responsibility to "sing a requiem; a long, sad song of goodbye," to the Denali he knows—and passionately loves. But Heacox's words (and certainly his photographs) are as much a celebration of Denali's wildness as they are a mournful dirge. He seeks, in both story and pictures, to capture the wondrous nature of this place and to remind those who love Denali—or any wilderness—that they must remain vigilant in their work to protect its wild essence.

The three essays reprinted here are excerpted from Kim Heacox's book *In Denali: A Photographic Essay of Denali National Park & Preserve, Alaska,* published in 1992 by Companion Press.

THE RIVER

Shallow at its edges, deep in the middle; a tireless agent of erosion and deposition, it runs turbid and tumbling toward the sea, as it has for 10,000 years and more. Here a riffle forms, there an eddy, elsewhere rapids rise and fall like a dragon's back, throwing droplets through the air.

I remove my boots. Am I really going to cross this river? I remove my socks. Of course I am. I roll up my pant legs. Should I reconsider this? I put on an old pair of tennis shoes brought along for crossing rivers. No, there's really nothing to reconsider. I tie my boots to my pack. Perhaps I should wait until morning. Nonsense, it's only a river. I hoist my pack onto my back and look for a place to cross.

Like most rivers in Denali, this one runs in channels that diverge, converge, and diverge again, braiding across great beds of gravel, sand, cobbles, and rocks. All kinds of rocks: granite, gabbro, and gneiss; limestone, sandstone, and schist; chert, argillite, and tuff; a veritable palette of earthtones and tectonics, the handiwork of aeons forged from the geologically complex Alaska Range, excavated by glaciers and moved and smoothed by the river.

I walk on, looking for a spot where the channels are numerous and the water shallow. Unlike the river, the channels themselves are temporary; sooner or later—this year, next year, ten or one hundred years from now—a dam of sediment or ice will form, the water will flood around it, and a new channel will be born.

This spot looks good. I plunge in. Five steps later I'm flooded to my knees, my legs are half-numb, and I'm less than one-third the way across the first channel. The current is strong and hypnotizing. My footing shifts; I stumble and nearly fall. Every passing second I stand in mid-current, the odds stack against me. Should I continue? Yes, I think.

I look up to catch my bearings, and to my surprise I am not alone. Staring at me from the opposite side of the farthest channel is a red fox.

Most foxes I have seen are on the move, hunting, heading out, heading home, often with a ptarmigan or arctic ground squirrel in its jaws, but this one sits on its haunches and stares at me with amber, cat-like eyes. My legs go completely numb, and it occurs to me that I must look as peculiar to the fox, standing thigh-deep in the river, as the fox looks to me, sitting stone-still on the bank.

Certainly no fox would cross this river, not here at this time of year. Farther upstream, maybe. In winter when things are frozen, probably. But here and now, in this turbid, roaring, subarctic, glacial meltwater river? Never. Foxes know their limitations; they have their boundaries. They survive.

I turn around. The cold is more than uncomfortable; it is painful. Five steps from the bank and I'm biting my lip. Rocks tumble against my ankles. Four steps; my head is pounding. Three steps; the river goes shallow. Two steps. One. I stumble ashore and fall on the bank, gasping. My legs are red, my ankles bruised.

Pain, joy, water, rock, sun, wind; I lie next to the river and catch my breath. Sitting up, I look for the fox, but it has gone as quietly as it came; a hunter fleet-of-foot. I, too, must go. So listening to the river, learning from the fox, and feeling alive in a way only the wilderness can impart, I hoist my pack and turn upstream toward the mountains.

THE MOUNTAINS

It takes four hours of steady uphill hiking to reach the top of the ridge. Not many people go there, but I do at least once a year, mostly to see Dall sheep, the only species of wild white sheep in the world. A band of about thirty live up there, mostly rams with sweeping horns and penetrating golden-brown eyes. The ewes have shorter horns and keep a close watch over their lambs that gambol over the tundra on legs as light as wings.

Storms that send me scurrying for cover hardly faze them. They graze on green, summer slopes, always within close reach of rocky cliffs for protection from wolves. Every so often a golden eagle will dive on them, hitting a lamb hard enough to kill it, or knocking an adult off a rocky ledge where it falls to its death. Survival is a daily chore.

Whenever I think I know all about them, they do something new; a twitch, a posture, a nuzzle, a challenge. Once I witnessed a ram walk a ledge that narrowed until there was no room to turn around. Undaunted, he simply planted his front hooves and rotated his hind legs up the rocky wall behind him, over his head until he faced the opposite direction and walked back to find another route.

Feeling smug, I like to think these sheep have grown comfortable with me. Several times they have bedded down right outside my tent, once so close that a ram blocked the entrance and I couldn't get out. I quietly zipped open the door and he was ten feet away, staring at me in a transcendental moment, species to species.

I could no more shoot one than I could strangle a child. Yes, if I were starving it would be different. And yes, hunting is part of our human ancestry, like cave dwelling. But since the Age of Enlightenment and its contemporary counterpart—the Age of Environmentalism—the game has ended, the sport has soured. And speciesism, like racism and sexism, has been labeled a particularly human blend of arrogance and ignorance. Perhaps only when we stop shooting wild animals will we stop shooting each other. "A man is rich in proportion to the number of things he can afford to let alone," wrote Henry David Thoreau. Do wild landscapes tell us anything of true wealth?

Denali National Park is a Walden Pond; a place to practice humility and respect.

In Autumn the tundra turns from green to gold to red. The snow falls. The last time I see the sheep, the rams are charging and butting heads in the autumn air, and the lambs are close to their mothers' sides.

Winter sets down as cold as steel, and I retreat to my home just a few miles from the park entrance, thinking about the sheep in the darkness of winter at forty below, day after day, month after month. They are up on that mountain, huddled together, watching for wolves, scraping for food, surviving. A few die each year from predation, starvation, rock slides, and avalanches. But the band survives. And climbing back up there and seeing them the next spring is, for me, a sight filled with miracle and promise.

THE RIDDLE

Among the riddles of the ancient Chinese is one about a man who discovers the most beautiful place in the world. The riddle is a conundrum: a puzzle without a solution, because the man shares his discovery, and people flock there in such great numbers that the place is changed forever, and is beautiful no more.

It is the pioneer's paradox, the process of people destroying, or at least eroding, the very thing they love, often the natural environment, and it exists not only in ancient China but throughout the entire modern world. Though national parks should be exempt from this, they are not.

And Denali? Will the same mistakes made elsewhere be made here? Or will people learn that to truly save a place they must close doors in front of them, rather than behind them? Hopefully, Alaska will escape the Manifest

Destiny mentality that fenced, paved, and tamed the lower forty-eight states, and we who can alter any landscape in the world will have the wisdom to leave this one alone.

It is vital, of course, that people come here; that lives are touched and inspired, that wilderness values are affirmed, and anxieties are washed away. Yet it is equally vital, in a world of greed, and conundrums, that visitors not be herded into mediocrity, that the park experience—and the park itself—not be impaired in any way, or even jeopardized.

At six million acres, Denali National Park and Preserve is about the same size as Massachusetts, nearly three times the size of Yellowstone. Running through it are icy mountains that break their backs in the Alaska Range, their summits reaching to 14,000 feet, 17,000 feet, and finally to 20,320-foot Mt. McKinley, more properly called *Denali*—the native name meaning The High One—the highest mountain in North America.

From the mountains, the land sweeps to every horizon in striking patterns of tundra and spruce forest, kettle ponds and braided rivers, wildflowers and willow thickets. More than 600 species of trees, shrubs, and herbs live here, some growing profusely in protected valleys, others hugging windswept ridges in button, mat, and rosette shapes.

Every summer, from eastern Siberia, the Pacific, Latin and North America, birds arrive to raise their young. Shorebirds nest on the tundra, raptors on the cliffs; more than 150 species occur here. But Denali's most sought-after residents are the large mammals: grizzlies, wolves, caribou, moose, Dall sheep, red foxes, lynx, and others—38 species of mammals in all. Nothing stimulates the heart more than the sudden appearance of a bear, a wolf, or a caribou moving over the land with wild, ancient poetry. Like the birds and plants, they fit into the landscape as an integral part of a greater whole, manifesting laws of survival and diversity, embodying what has been called "the greatest subarctic sanctuary in the world."

This, then, is what Charles Sheldon found when he came to Interior Alaska in the summer of 1906. A member of the influential Boone & Crockett Club, he was cut from the same conservation cloth as Teddy Roosevelt. A hunter, yes, but more than that, a competent and caring naturalist who traveled widely throughout Denali by foot, snowshoe, and sled dog team.

Camped on a moraine above the Peters Glacier in January 1908, with the land and silence all to himself, Sheldon wrote, "When Denali Park shall be made easy of access with accommodations and facilities for travel . . . it is not difficult to anticipate the enjoyment and inspiration visitors will receive."

Many decades later, Sheldon's prediction has come true. Enjoyment and inspiration are commonplace among visitors to Denali. But will it remain that way?

In 1971, the year before the highway was completed between Anchorage and Fairbanks—connecting Denali to Alaska's two largest cities—annual park visitation was 30,000. Twenty years later 600,000 visitors came. A single dirt road, built in the 1920s and '30s, winds ninety miles across the park, cutting into mountainsides, crossing rivers, traversing open expanses of tundra and spruce forest. Dozens of buses travel that road every day of summer, each carrying about forty people who admire the scenery and watch for wildlife.

The bus system works on two premises: by reducing private vehicle traffic along the road it minimizes the risk of accidents, and maximizes the opportunities to view wildlife that otherwise might be displaced by more traffic.

But to those addicted to power and money, Denali is not being fully "utilized." Build another hotel, they say. Add more rooms. Add more buses, another road, a railroad, a monorail, a tramway. Anydamnthing. As for environmental impact, don't worry. Rangers scrutinize and scientists hypothesize, but MONEY TALKS!

Here, then, is a way of thinking that believes Denali National Park should be accessible to as many people as possible; that tourism, like cattle-ranching, is a volume-driven meat market; that scenery, more than anything else, is a commodity.

If the finest hotels can have "no vacancy," if the greatest concert halls can have limited seating, then why not our national parks? The theater is full; you are invited to the next performance. "It is the expansion of transport without a corresponding growth of perception that threatens us with qualitative bankruptcy of the recreational process," wrote Aldo Leopold in *A Sand Country Almanac*. "Recreational development is a job not of building roads into lovely country, but of building receptivity into the still unlovely human mind."

In a sweeping, grandiose state where the words "Last Frontier" carry the old, false assumptions of limitless resources and opportunities; where a political system embraces economic growth as though it were a religion; where the National Park Service must answer to that same political system—the best government money can buy, composed of men and women whose idea of a land ethic is as thin as a dollar bill; and where industrial tourism advances slowly and inexorably, like the tide; then if this is the way it is, and shall be, Denali is doomed. Not to a disaster, but to slow, insidious strangulation of its wilderness integrity.

Something has to change. Lines must be drawn and defended. For only then will Denali and other national parks remain pristine, and will landscapes beat to the rhythms of something more ancient than us all. Here, people will say, is a piece of the earth as it once was, and should forever remain: absolutely wild.

Permissions

1. "The Second Making of Man" by Julius Jetté was originally published in Vol. 38 of the *Journal of the Royal Anthropological Institute of Great Britain and Ireland,* in London, England. ©1908. Reprinted with permission of the Royal Anthropological Institute of Great Britain and Ireland.

2. "The Sage of Kantishna—Legends of Denali" by James Wickersham was originally published in *Old Yukon—Tales, Trails, and Trials,* in 1938 by the Washington Law Book Co., Washington, D.C. It is now in the public domain.

3. "Shq'uła Tsukdu: The 'Whistler' (Hoary Marmot) Story" by Shem Pete, as told to Jim Fall was originally published in *Upper Cook Inlet Dena'ina Oral Traditions: An Introduction to the Narrative Art of an Alaskan Athabaskan People,* by Jim Fall. This report, published by the Alaska Department of Fish and Game, Anchorage, was presented to the Alaska Humanities Forum in June 1990. ©1990 by Jim Fall. Reprinted with the author's permission.

4. "Discoveries in Alaska (1896)" by William A. Dickey was originally published in the January 24, 1897, edition of *The Sun,* in New York. It is now in the public domain.

5. "An Exploration to Mount McKinley, America's Highest Mountain" by Alfred H. Brooks was originally published in *The Journal of Geography* Vol. II in 1903. It is now in the public domain.

6. *The Shameless Diary of an Explorer* by Robert Dunn was originally published in 1907 by The Outing Publishing Co., New York. It is now in the public domain.

7. *The Wilderness of Denali* by Charles Sheldon was originally published in 1930 by Charles Scribner's Sons, New York. ©1930 by Charles Scribner's Sons; © renewed 1958 by Louisa G. Sheldon. Reprinted with the permission of Scribner, a Division of Simon & Schuster.

8. *To the Top of the Continent: Discovery, Exploration and Adventure in Sub-arctic Alaska. The First Ascent of Mt. McKinley, 1903–1906* by Dr. Frederick A. Cook was originally published in 1907 by Hodder & Stoddard, London, and in 1908 by Doubleday, Page, and Co., New York. It is now in the public domain.

9. *The Conquest of Mount McKinley* by Belmore Browne was originally published in 1913 by Putnam's, New York, and reprinted in 1956 by Houghton Mifflin, Boston. It is now in the public domain.

10. "Attack from the Northeast" and "Going to Extremes" in *Mount McKinley: The Conquest of Denali* by Bradford Washburn and David Roberts was originally published in 1991 by Harry N. Abrams, Inc., Publishers, New York. ©1991 by Bradford Washburn and David Roberts. Reprinted with the permission of Bradford Washburn.

11. *The Ascent of Denali: A Narrative of the First Complete Ascent of the Highest Peak in North America* by Hudson Stuck was originally published in 1914 by Charles Scribner's Sons, New York, and reprinted in 1989 by the University of Nebraska Press. It is now in the public domain.

12. *Minus 148°: The Winter Ascent of Mt. McKinley* by Art Davidson was originally published in 1969 by W.W. Norton Co., New York, and reprinted in 1986 by Cloudcap Press, Seattle, Washington. ©1969 by Art Davidson. Reprinted with permission of the author.

13. *Wager with the Wind: The Don Sheldon Story* by James Greiner was originally published in 1974 by Rand McNally & Company, New York. ©1974 by Rand McNally, later transferred to James Greiner and then his wife Ida Greiner. Reprinted with permission of Ida Greiner.

14. *A Naturalist in Alaska* by Adolph Murie was originally published in 1961 by the Devin-Adair Company, New York, and reprinted in 1996 by The University of Arizona Press, Tucson. © by Adolph Murie and later The Estate of Adolph Murie. Reprinted with the permission of Louise Murie-MacLoed.

15. *The Wolves of Denali* by L. David Mech et al. was originally published in 1998 by the University of Minnesota Press, Minneapolis. ©1998 by the Regents of the University of Minnesota. Reprinted with permission of the University of Minnesota Press.

16. *Grizzly Cub: Five Years in the Life of a Bear* by Rick McIntyre was originally published in 1990 by Alaska Northwest Books, Seattle, Washington. ©1990 Rick McIntyre. Reprinted with permission of Graphic Arts Center Publishing Co., Portland, Oregon.

17. "Strange Grace" by Sherry Simpson was originally published in 1998 in *The Way Winter Comes* by Sasquatch Books, Seattle, Washington. ©1998 by Sherry Simpson. Reprinted in slightly truncated form with permission of the author and Sasquatch Books.

18. *Denali Journal: A Thoughtful Look at Wildlife in Alaska's Majestic National Park* by Tom Walker was originally published in 1992 by Stackpole Books, Harrisburg, Pennsylvania. ©1992 by Tom Walker. Reprinted with permission of the author.

Bill Sherwonit in the Peters Hills, Denali State Park, with The High One rising through the clouds in the distance   (© Bill Sherwonit)

About the Author

Born in Bridgeport, Conn., Anchorage nature writer Bill Sherwonit first visited Alaska in 1974 while employed as a geologist. After switching from geology to journalism during the late 1970s, he returned to Alaska in 1982 as a sports writer for *The Anchorage Times*. Sherwonit worked at the newspaper ten years, the last seven as its outdoors writer/editor. In 1987, while a reporter for *The Times*, he ascended Denali's West Buttress with a guided expedition.

Now a full-time freelancer, Sherwonit has contributed stories and photos to a wide variety of newspapers, magazines, literary journals, anthologies, and guide books. He's the author of four previous books on Alaska: *To the Top of Denali: Climbing Adventures on North America's Highest Peak*; *Iditarod: The Great Race to Nome*; *Alaska's Accessible Wilderness: A Traveler's Guide to Alaska's State Parks*; and *Alaska's Bears*. He also compiled and edited the mountaineering anthology *Alaska Ascents*. Now interested in creative writing—especially the personal essay form—as well as journalism, he teaches a class in "wilderness writing" at the University of Alaska Anchorage.

Sherwonit lives in the foothills of the Chugach Mountains with his wife, Dulcy Boehle. On a clear day, from their upper deck, they can see The High One rising grandly above the landscape, 120 miles to the north. At least once a year, and usually more, Bill explores the wilderness backcountry of Denali State and National Parks. He's finishing up a field guide to the Denali region, to be published in 2001 by the Alaska Natural History Association.

THE MOUNTAINEERS, founded in 1906, is a nonprofit outdoor activity and conservation club, whose mission is "to explore, study, preserve, and enjoy the natural beauty of the outdoors. . . . " Based in Seattle, Washington, the club is now the third-largest such organization in the United States, with 15,000 members and five branches throughout Washington State.

The Mountaineers sponsors both classes and year-round outdoor activities in the Pacific Northwest, which include hiking, mountain climbing, ski-touring, snowshoeing, bicycling, camping, kayaking and canoeing, nature study, sailing, and adventure travel. The club's conservation division supports environmental causes through educational activities, sponsoring legislation, and presenting informational programs. All club activities are led by skilled, experienced volunteers, who are dedicated to promoting safe and responsible enjoyment and preservation of the outdoors.

If you would like to participate in these organized outdoor activities or the club's programs, consider a membership in The Mountaineers. For information and an application, write or call The Mountaineers, Club Headquarters, 300 Third Avenue West, Seattle, Washington 98119; 206-284-6310.

The Mountaineers Books, an active, nonprofit publishing program of the club, produces guidebooks, instructional texts, historical works, natural history guides, and works on environmental conservation. All books produced by The Mountaineers are aimed at fulfilling the club's mission.

Send or call for our catalog of more than 450 outdoor titles:

The Mountaineers Books
1001 SW Klickitat Way, Suite 201
Seattle, WA 98134
800-553-4453
mbooks@mountaineers.org
www.mountaineersbooks.org

Other titles you may enjoy from The Mountaineers Books:

HIGH ACHIEVER: The Life and Climbs of Chris Bonington, Jim Curran
This biography of one of the world's best-known climbers examines Bonington's deepest motives and reveals the joys and occasional despair of living a life as a high-profile climber. At 65 years old, this self-described "climbaholic's" passion and enthusiasm remain undiminished.

A LIFE ON THE EDGE: Memoirs of Everest and Beyond, Jim Whittaker
The autobiography of the first North American to summit Mount Everest. Whittaker's account highlights the major events in his career including the creation of REI, an intimate friendship with the Kennedys, expeditions on K2 and Everest, and personal stories of friends and family.

HEROIC CLIMBS: A Celebration of World Mountaineering, Chris Bonington, editor
Encompasses the rich, broad spectrum of adventure that is mountain climbing in remarkable accounts by 40 of the biggest names in modern mountaineering.

MIXED EMOTIONS, Greg Child
The famous climber writes about his mixed feelings about climbing—the loss of friends, the thrill of achievement, and the soul-shattering moments of risk and survival; but it is precisely these experiences that compel him to write and to continue climbing.

THE BEST OF ROCK & ICE: An Anthology, Dougald MacDonald, editor
For more than 20 years, *Rock & Ice* magazine has published excellent writing from the world's best climbers. Now, for the first time, *Rock & Ice* editor Dougald MacDonald has gathered together a collection of the magazine's best essays.

ERIC SHIPTON: EVEREST & BEYOND, Peter Steele
Drawing upon scores of personal interviews as well as Shipton's own correspondence, Steele draws a full-bodied portrait of the mountaineer. From Africa to Everest to South America and the Southern Patagonia ice cap, Eric Shipton's adventures continue to fascinate readers.